# Universal
# Preschool

SUNY series in Public Policy
Anne L. Scheider and Helen M. Ingram, editors

Brenda K. Bushouse

# Universal Preschool

Policy Change, Stability, and the
Pew Charitable Trusts

Published by
State University of New York Press, Albany

© 2009 State University of New York

For information, contact State University of New York Press, Albany, NY
www.sunypress.edu

Production by Ryan Morris
Marketing by Michael Campochiaro

**Library of Congress Cataloging-in-Publication Data**

Bushouse, Brenda K.
    Universal preschool : policy change, stability, and the Pew Chritable Trusts /
Brenda K. Bushouse.
        p. cm.    (SUNY series in public policy)
    Includes bibliographical references and index.
    ISBN 978–0–7914–9387–8 (hardcover : alk. paper)
    1. Education, Preschool—United States—States—Case studies. 2. Education
and state—United States—States—Case studies. 3. Government aid to education—United States—States—Case studies. 4. Pew Charitable Trusts. I. Title.

 LB1140.23.B87 2009
 372.973—dc22

                                                                2008018974


10  9  8  7  6  5  4  3  2  1

*To Sophia and Maxwell, who provided daily reminders of the importance of high quality early education for every child.*

# Contents

# Acknowledgments

WRITING A BOOK ABOUT the universal preschool movement at the same time my children were in preschool presented an opportunity to ground my research with practice on a daily basis. We were fortunate to be able to pay the steep tuition for high-quality preschool education but most parents in this country are not able to do that. Universal preschool provides the promise for all children to have the opportunity afforded my children. But without quality, universal preschool is an empty promise. I could have written an equally compelling book on the states that have created high-quality preschool programs, many of whom do so by limiting access to families with lower incomes. I chose to focus the book on the anomaly aspects of creating expensive, new universal public programs but I fully recognize that access and quality must go hand in hand.

A book with six case studies requires a tremendous amount of time and effort. I thank my husband, Charlie Schweik, for supporting me every step of the way even when my research took me far from home for weeks at a time. I also thank Joanne Schweik for her tireless editing of my chapters and my parents, Ron and Nancy Bushouse, for help with child care. Kathryn McDermott provided timely feedback on the introduction as well as support at key junctures in the writing process. John Hird provided me with flexibility in my teaching schedule that allowed me to undertake this ambitious research project without taking a leave. Without all of their support, my research would not have been possible. As is the case with all research projects, they require not only time but also participants and money. Without the generosity of the people interviewed in this book, I would not have been able to understand the intricacies of the policy process. I wholeheartedly thank all of the people interviewed for their willingness to talk with me, in some cases multiple times. The travel required for this study would not have been possible without two grants from the University of Massachusetts: a 2004 Faculty Research Grant from the College of Social and Behavioral Sciences and a 2006 Faculty

Research Grant from the Office of Research Affairs. Research assistance was provided by the Center for Public Policy and Administration. I give many thanks to research assistants Emily Hopta, Chris Sun, and Maura Geary for their time and hard work.

SUNY Press Public Policy Series editors Helen Ingram and Anne Schneider were particularly helpful throughout the research project. From an initial conversation with Anne in 2004 as I was designing the project to the useful suggestions for revisions from both Anne and Helen, I deeply appreciate their support and encouragement. I also thank the two anonymous reviewers at SUNY Press for their helpful suggestions for revisions and Michael Rinella, senior acquisitions editor, Amanda Lanne, acquisitions assistant and Ryan Morris, production editor, for shepherding the manuscript through to publication. With the assistance and support of all named above, any remaining shortcomings in the manuscript are entirely my responsibility.

# 1

# Introduction

IN 1971, PRESIDENT Nixon vetoed legislation that would have created federal funding for the care of children under five. His veto message stated, "for the Federal Government to plunge headlong financially into supporting child development would commit the vast moral authority of the National Government to the side of communal approaches to child rearing over against [*sic*] the family-centered approach" (Veto of the Economic Opportunity Amendments of 1971). With this veto, Nixon reaffirmed that, with the exception of poor children, the education and care of children is the responsibility of families, not government. But flash forward thirty years and state governments are going where the federal government dared not tread. Currently forty-one states and the District of Columbia provide some form of state-funded preschool. Nearly a quarter of those states have removed income limits on participation, thereby opening up the potential for publicly funded preschool for all. For fiscal year 2008, twenty-nine governors recommended funding increases for preschool programs and no governors recommended decreases in funding (Pre-K Now 2007). How did responsibility for early childhood education move from a private responsibility of families to a public responsibility? Why did states decide that early education, in particular the education of preschool-age children, is the state's responsibility?

At the heart of this shift from private to public responsibility is segmenting preschool-age children from younger children and reframing them as a separate target group. Historically, children are constructed as dependent, meaning that they are deserving of benefits but have weak political power, and their condition is seen as "natural" and better served by private sector alternatives (Schneider and Ingram 1997). President Nixon's veto reflects this view. Policies targeted toward dependent groups are typically paternalistic with eligibility rules to participate in programs, less outreach, more responsibility on the dependent to seek out the program, and greater

1

reliance on hortatory tools that do not cost money (Schneider and Ingram 1997). This accurately describes federal policies for the care and education of low-income children under five over the last forty years. Federal policies (described below) set strict eligibility standards for participation and parents must navigate complex bureaucratic systems to attain services for their children. The status quo in the United States is that poor families are eligible for publicly-funded child care and preschool services but families with incomes above eligibility limits either make informal arrangements or purchase care in the private market. In other words, child care and preschool[1] for families below the income limits is a "public problem" but child care and preschool for families above the income limits is a "private problem." Given this context, how has the education of preschool-age children (i.e., three and four year olds) been framed by policy entrepreneurs to make it advantageous for state actors to support state-funded programs open to all children regardless of family income?

To understand this process, one place to start is to analyze how states were able to successfully pass legislation to create universal preschool programs. Between 1995 and 2002, four states passed legislation to create universal preschool programs. Georgia was the first state in 1995, quickly followed by New York in 1997, Oklahoma in 1998, and West Virginia in 2002. What becomes evident in the analysis of the "pioneer" states in this book is that passing universal preschool legislation was an internal process; pioneering states passed their legislation largely independent of the influence of nonstate actors and with little media attention. There was cross fertilization of ideas through membership organizations, such as the National Governors Association, but the impetus for the change came from state actors who maneuvered through a state policy process devoid of national actors pressing for or against the issue.

The policy processes for more recent states has changed significantly. One catalyst for change in state policy-making occurred in December 2001, when the Pew Charitable Trusts announced a new giving program specifically aimed to create universal preschool for all three and four year olds. Over the next few years, Pew implemented a comprehensive, well-funded strategy for advancing universal preschool policy change, particularly at the state level. Rather than a traditional strategy of providing grants for research to universities or policy planning organizations (i.e., think tanks) (Dye 1990, 2001), Pew chose to fund a network of actors that would advocate for a specific policy alternative: universal preschool for all three and four year olds. What emerged was a complex network of Pew-funded actors attempting to frame the "problem" of school readiness so that the policy solution was investment in universal preschool. One of the striking aspects of Pew's decision-making process is the reliance on tools more often found in the business sector than foundations. Pew's staff identified a goal that had a clearly measurable outcome and put in place a comprehensive strategy for achieving it.

### Why Universal Preschool?

There are three commonly cited factors that contributed to the rise of universal preschool in pioneer states and Pew's decision to invest in universal preschool: (1) absence of federal policy action, (2) emerging research on the importance of early brain development, and (3) publicity surrounding longitudinal studies of preschool participation.

#### Federal Policy

Currently there are three main policies to provide federal funds for the education and care of young children: the Head Start Preschool program, child care subsidies for low-income families, and subsidies for special needs children. Head Start was established as one of several programs authorized by the Economic Opportunity Act of 1964, an initiative of President Johnson's War on Poverty. The goal of the program was to lift children out of poverty by providing them with the necessary physical, emotional, social, and academic skills to enter school ready to learn. The program targeted, and continues to target, children living below the federal poverty line. The program, administered through the Department of Health and Human Services, provides federal grants for preschool education and comprehensive intervention services to low-income and special needs children. However, like many of the federal programs at that time, it bypassed state governments and provided Head Start funds directly to a locally designated grantee, typically a nonprofit community action agency. Bypassing the white power structure of the state governments was a federal strategy in the 1960s to empower black communities to improve their economic conditions (Judd and Swanstrom 2006). While this was necessary at the time, it set in motion a separation between the state government and Head Start programs that would prove troublesome when state governments began their own preschool programs (to be discussed in chapter 3).

In the midst of the civil rights struggle and massive federal expansion, child advocates, notably Marian Wright Edelman, advocated for federal child care legislation. Between 1968 and May 1971, congressional support increased for a federal child care program. By 1971, broad bipartisan support led to passage of a bill to create a framework for a universally available, comprehensive child care program. The program would have been federally funded, with family contributions along a sliding-scale based on income. Despite its passage in the legislature, the controversial bill was opposed by conservatives who felt that it threatened the values of personal liberty and limited government, and by many state governors who opposed an administrative structure that bypassed the states and placed control over the program at the local level. Amid the controversy over both ideology and structure, Nixon vetoed the bill in 1971. Even though the bill failed, it marked the first time that the federal government had considered a child care program on its own merits (Cohen 2001).

Since President Nixon's veto in 1971, child care advocates made little headway in advancing their agenda at the federal level. Efforts toward federal funding of comprehensive, universal child care were blocked and replaced with federal support for targeted programs. Child care advocates attempted to create federal regulatory requirements for child care, the Federal Interagency Day Care Requirements, but national standards were eventually rejected because of the costs associated with both compliance and enforcement. The only advances in federal funding for child care were for programs tied to welfare. In 1974, President Ford signed Title XX of the Social Security Act, which provided federal funds to the states for social services to residents. The use of Title XX funds was left to the discretion of the states, but child care provision was explicitly established as an allowable use of funds. Under Title XX's income eligibility requirements, only low-income individuals and families could receive benefits.[2] After this, no major changes occurred for over a decade.

The 1990 Omnibus Budget Reconciliation Act contained allocations for the Child Care and Development Block Grant (CCDBG) and the At-Risk Child Care Program under Title IV-A of the Social Security Act. These programs were, and continue to be, targeted toward low-income families with working parents; the Child Care and Development Block Grant is limited to children in families with income below 75 percent of the state median income, and At-Risk Child Care is limited to families at-risk of becoming welfare-dependent.

Federal provision of child care rose on the national agenda again in 1996 during intense debates over welfare reform. Congress dramatically reformed the nation's welfare system with the Personal Responsibility and Work Opportunity Act of 1996 (PRWOA). This landmark legislation replaced the prior system of income-supports to enable mothers to stay at home with their children, with a system requiring parents to work. PRWOA forced states to require both parents in a two-parent family to work in order to be eligible for PRWOA funds, with the exception of disability, the presence of a child under the age of one, or lack of access to child care; however, states could allow mothers with children under six to work twenty hours per week (Cohen 2001). Because the federal government required parents to work, it then had to increase federal aid for child care. It is important to note that while federal policy interventions in the 1960s sought to lift children out of poverty, the purpose of federal grants after PRWOA was to support the welfare-to-work movement.

The only federal early childhood program without income eligibility rules targets a separate group: special needs children. The Individual with Disabilities Education Act requires public schools to provide preschool services for special needs children (United States Department of Education 2007). The federal government distributes a formula-based grant to school systems to arrange education for special needs preschool children. States can deliver the services themselves or contract with an education provider. In response to the federal mandate to provide special needs preschool, some states admit non–special needs children into their preschool programs. Public schools are allowed to charge tuition for non–special needs children while the parents of special needs children do not pay tuition. In fiscal year 2006, the federal government spent approximately $350 million on special needs preschool education (United States Department of Education 2007).

The Head Start preschool program, child care subsidies, and special needs preschool firmly limit federal funding to low-income and special needs target groups. Several attempts to expand federal policy beyond care for these target groups have been unsuccessful. In Sally Cohen's book, *Championing Child Care*, she analyzes three waves of federal legislative activity and concludes that there is little potential for federal policy expansion (2001). Longtime early childhood advocates agree and, while advocacy for federal change continues, there is widespread agreement to target state policy change (Zigler, Gilliam, and Jones 2006, 279).

*Early Brain Research*

The importance of the first three years of life was brought into sharp focus starting in the late 1980s, with the emergence of new studies in early brain development (Zigler, Gilliam, and Jones 2006). Improvements in technology and tools used to study the brain led to research with clear implications for early childhood education (Carnegie Corporation of New York 1994). Researchers discovered that stages of brain development occur more quickly early in life—the brain is 70 percent developed by age one, and by age three it has reached 90 percent of its total growth (Shore 1997). Some of this development happens during the prenatal period and the structure and wiring of the brain at birth are a function of genetics and biology. In the first months and years of life, the interplay between biology and experience, between nature and nurture, affects the course of brain development (Shonkoff and Phillips 2000). Since the activity level in the brain of a three year old is two and a half times greater than in that of an adult, stimulation during this period is critical. There are a greater number of synaptic connections in a young child's brain, and childhood experiences determine which of the neurons will create nerve networks that are the foundation for some sensory, language, and emotional development. Neurons that do not become part of the brain's wiring at this stage die (Shore 1997).

Different regions of the brain mature at different times and the coordination of stimulation with the developmental time-table is important. Missing the opportunity to establish neural connections can result in permanent deficiency (Lindsey 1998; Shore 1997). However, the concept of "critical periods" should not be overstated, since the plasticity that leaves the brain vulnerable to harm also allows the brain to progress at any age (Shonkoff and Phillips 2000). At all stages of growth, positive, nurturing relationships with caregivers are an essential component of brain development.

Public and private institutions and advocacy groups concerned with early childhood health, development, and education embraced these new scientific findings. In 1994, the Carnegie Task Force on Meeting the Needs of Young Children released *Starting Points*, a report that located the scientific research in the context of the changing lives of American parents. The report argued that the combination of developmental, social, and political factors led to a "quiet crisis" for children and families, as well as for the national economy (Carnegie Corporation of New York 1994).

The Carnegie Corporation presented five critical findings of the brain research, intended to guide strategies targeting young children:

1. The brain development that takes place in the prenatal period and first years of life is more rapid and extensive than previously realized.
2. Brain development is much more vulnerable to environmental influence than ever before suspected.
3. The influence of early environment on brain development is long lasting.

4. The environment affects not only the number of brain cells and the number of connections among them, but also the way these connections are wired.
5. There is new scientific evidence for the negative impact of early stress on brain function (Carnegie Corporation of New York 1994).

In 1997, the Institute of Medicine and the National Research Council of the National Academy of Sciences formed the Committee on Integrating the Science of Early Childhood Development. Chaired by Jack Shonkoff, this group of seventeen scientists analyzed research on the first five years of life in the neurobiological, behavioral, and social sciences. As a result, *From Neurons to Neighborhoods: The Science of Early Childhood Development* was published in 2000 investigating the impact of early childhood experiences on brain development as well as on social relationships (Shonkoff and Phillips 2000). While parents, educators, and even policy makers may have assumed the central role of the childhood environment, this research provided evidence that high-quality early education and care programs would result in improved developmental outcomes for children.

*Longitudinal Studies of Preschool Participation*

Part of the strategic choice to invest in preschool is due to the emergence of longitudinal studies indicating economic returns from investment in preschool education. Three separate studies concluded that both children and society gain when children participate in high-quality preschool. From 1962 to 1967 the Perry Preschool Program in Ypsilanti, Michigan provided preschool for 123 low-income African-American children. The children were randomly assigned to either a program group (n = 58) or a control group (n = 65). An assessment of the participants at age twenty-seven, and again at age forty, found that Perry Preschool participants had higher earnings, were more likely to hold a job, had committed fewer crimes, and were more likely to have graduated from high school (Barnett 1996; Schweinhart et al. 2005). A key finding of the Perry Preschool Program was that for every dollar invested into preschool, the public benefit equals up to $7.17. This became a frequently cited statistic by advocates for public investment in preschool.

The Abecedarian Project operated between 1972 and 1977 at the Frank Porter Graham Child Development Center at the University of North Carolina, Chapel Hill. The 111 participating children were also primarily African American and low-income. The children were enrolled in the study shortly after birth and were randomly assigned to either the Abecedarian program or to a control group. Evaluations were conducted at program completion and at ages eight, twelve, fifteen, and twenty-one, and findings show benefits to the treatment group in educational attainment, lower need for special education services, and higher employment rates (Ramey and Campbell 1984, 1991; Campbell and Ramey 1994, 1995).

The Chicago Child-Parent Centers were originally developed in 1967, using federal Title I funds available to public schools serving low-income students. The research began after the program was in operation, so random assignment was not possible. Instead, a representative sample of 989 children was selected and compared to a similar group of 550 children. Children who participated in the Child-Parent Centers fared better than those in the comparison group in the areas of educational attainment, need for special education, and crime rates (Reynolds and Temple 2006, 1995; Reynolds et al. 1993).

Reynolds and Temple (2006) reviewed the cost-benefit analyses conducted on these studies. While there are differences between the preschool programs, some of which had significant impact on program cost, the economic benefits in the areas of earnings capacity, crime savings, and special education savings have been consistent across the studies. The public benefit per dollar invested varied between a low of $2.69 for the Abecedarian project to a high of $7.16 for the Perry Preschool Project (Reynold and Temple 2006, 49). The data analysis provides strong evidence for the social returns of increased investments in high-quality preschool programs for low-income children.

The combined factors of no federal policy action, emergence of early brain research, and findings from longitudinal preschool studies created a policy milieu in which policy entrepreneurs were able to successfully build support for policy change. The objective of this study is to analyze the policy change process in states that have passed universal preschool legislation. But because passing legislation does not automatically translate into a successful program, I also analyze the success and failure to stabilize budgetary and political support for the new program. The creation of universal preschool programs provides a rich opportunity to assess the policy process literature for its ability to explain the change process.

## Policy Process Literature

Schneider and Ingram's (1997) method of categorizing target populations according to their political power (weaker, stronger) and their construction as deserving or undeserving accurately represents the federal policy environment for children. As discussed above, children have weak political power but are constructed as deserving. Because providing benefits to children is costly, policy tends to rely on rhetoric. Any burdensome policies for children tend to be by omission. In other words, policy does not exist and therefore is not noticed. One of the particularly amazing transitions addressed in this book, is the anomaly of the preschool-age children target group being awarded benefits, as opposed to rhetoric. As described above, there is a long history of funding programs for low-income children in the United States but the states studied in this book are committing to providing preschool for all children, regardless of family income. How did it become politically advantageous for elected officials to support preschool for all instead of preschool for some? The following section divides the literature into the main topics to be addressed in the analysis of state passage of universal preschool legislation and includes: Issue reconstruction, policy entrepreneurs, agenda setting and policy change, and policy stability.

*Issue Reconstruction*

Baumgartner and Jones state that *issue definition* is the "driving force in both stability and instability, primarily because issue definition has the potential for mobilizing the previously disinterested" (Baumgartner and Jones 1993, 16). Images are a combination of empirical information and emotive appeals that are evaluative and set the *tone*. In order to change the policy image, policy entrepreneurs must create a *causal story* (Stone 1997). The image of the issue must change from that of a private "misfortune to a public problem amenable to government solutions" (Baumgartner and Jones 1993, 28). But that still does not assure that the problem will be linked to a particular policy alternative. Policy entrepreneurs must ensure that their favored policy alternative is the one adopted once the "problem" emerges on the government agenda. Cobb and Elder state, "Those wishing to mobilize broad groups attempt to focus attention on highly emotional symbols of easily understood themes, while those with an interest in restricting the debate explain the same issues in other, more arcane and complicated ways" (Cited in Baumgartner and Jones 1993, 30). Similarly, Sabatier and Jenkins-Smith (1993) place importance on the role of *core policy beliefs*, to attract actors into a coalition for change. A key issue to be explored in the chapters that follow is the process of issue reframing that resulted in attracting previously disinterested actors and ultimately policy passage.

*Policy Entrepreneurs*

The role of policy entrepreneurs is central to understanding policy change. Kingdon (1995) portrays policy entrepreneurs as having a willingness to invest resources in the hope of a return and wanting to promote their interests, values, or getting a thrill of being integral to the policy process. The entrepreneurs play a critical role in the "softening up" of the political environment. But for a policy entrepreneur to be heard, he or she must have: (1) some expertise in the area, an ability to speak for others, or authoritative decision-making position; (2) political connections or skilled in negotiation; and (3) persistence. A policy entrepreneur must be able to recognize an opportunity to couple his or her policy idea to a problem in order to have a chance at affecting the decision agenda. Sabatier and Jenkins-Smith (1993) assume that actors are *instrumentally rational*, meaning that they seek to use information and other resources to achieve their goals, that goals are usually complex, and that an individuals' ability to perceive the world and to process that information is affected by cognitive biases and constraints. This means that on salient topics, actors' perceptions are strongly filtered by their preexisting normative and perceptual beliefs. Drawing on prospect theory, they assume that actors weigh losses more heavily than gains, and that this leads actors to view adversaries as more powerful than they are. To understand actors' goals, it is necessary to identify policy core beliefs, rather than assuming rational self-interest. This modeling of the individual is important for how coalitions behave. Because actors share policy core beliefs, there are decreased transactions costs in coordinating action. This is an important factor in overcoming collective action problems.

Mintrom (2000) develops a concept of the policy entrepreneur in which actors operate in a particular milieu that shapes the opportunities and actions open to policy entrepreneurs. To be successful, the entrepreneur must possess certain skills, such as social perceptiveness and the ability to move effectively across different social settings. But the key to his or her success is to be adept at framing the issue and choosing language that builds the support of others. An important aspect of the environment of the entrepreneur is that he or she is embedded within a milieu and at the same time has the skills to shape it; policy entrepreneurs must be able to understand the nature of the frames through which they and others view and come to recognize apparent policy problems. This ability provides the key to problem framing: the conscious effort to bring others to see problems in ways that are consistent with one's own positions and policy goals (Mintrom 2000, 324).

While these three perspectives are complementary, the emphasis on issue reframing makes Mintrom's conceptualization of the policy entrepreneur particularly compelling for understanding universal preschool policy change. Prior to the 1990s, a separate issue definition for preschool did not exist. With the exception of low-income children, the education of preschool-age children was part of "child care." In order for pioneer states and the Pew Charitable Trusts to advance universal preschool, policy entrepreneurs had to reframe the issue definition from child care to preschool education. To be successful, policy entrepreneurs also had to reframe the problem so that universal preschool could be the logical policy solution.

*Agenda Setting and Policy Change*

To understand the rise of preschool on state agendas, we can draw on the multiple streams framework (Kingdon 1995; Zahariadis 2003) and the punctuated equilibrium model (Baumgartner and Jones 1993, 2002). In the multiple streams (MS) framework, three streams (problem, policy, and political) come together to open a window of opportunity for policy change. In the problem stream, ideas come from anywhere, every idea has a history, and nobody leads anybody else. Adapting the garbage can model to agenda setting, the process is characterized by "organized anarchies" with problematic preferences (goals are not clearly defined), unclear technology (processes are not well understood), and fluid participation (actors drift in and out). In the policy stream, Kingdon (1995) identified policy communities made up of specialists both inside government (staffers, bureaucrats) and outside (academics, consultants, analysts for interest groups). They can be fragmented or focused but they operate in a different stream than the political stream. The policy community devises the short list of ideas but the criteria for the idea's survival are technical feasibility, value acceptability, and anticipation of future constraints (e.g., effect on the budget).

But even with the problem and policy streams joined, the key to opening a policy window is joining with the political[3] stream. When the three streams join together, the probability of an item rising on the decision agenda dramatically increases (Kingdon 1995, 178). The political stream is affected by the swings in the pendulum of national mood, organized political forces, turnover and turf battles in government, and consensus. Whereas in the policy stream consensus is reached through persuasion, in the political stream consensus is the result of bargaining and bandwagon effects.

Kingdon likens the opening of the policy window to riding a wave. When it opens the policy entrepreneurs have an opportunity to move their issue onto the decision agenda. In this conception policy entrepreneurs are much like tigers who lie in wait ready to pounce on their prey. They have their alternative ready to go and when a problem comes up they pounce to couple it to their policy alternative.

The joining of the three streams opens a policy window in which change is possible. Policy windows may open due to changes in the political stream (e.g., change in administration, shift in distribution of seats, national mood) or problem stream (e.g., focusing event). But windows also close because: (1) participants may feel that some action has been taken and the pressure is off; (2) participants may fail to get action; (3) the focusing event fades; (4) key personnel may change; or (5) no viable alternative is found. The occurrence of windows can be predictable such as the reauthorization of legislation, the result of a spillover effect from another policy area, or seemingly random. Kingdon states, "Government does not come to conclusions. It stumbles into paradoxical situations that force it to move one way or another" (1995, 189). However, as he clarifies in the second edition, there are structures and forces that place bounds on the process, which make it less random than it may appear.

One of the issues raised by the MS framework is the degree to which the streams are independent. In the original version published in 1984 the streams are described as developing independently. In the 1995 edition, Kingdon uses the term "loosely coupled" to describe joining of streams. Zahariadis (2003) contributes nuance to the process but maintains that the streams are separate, yet often interconnected. The political and policy streams may weave together at various times but in the MS framework the actors and the processes are "in the main" different. The MS framework was developed by Kingdon through a study of agenda setting at the federal level and Zahariadis's work focuses on Western European contexts, but preschool policy change is occurring at the state level. For preschool policy change, the relevant questions raised by the MS framework are (1) the identification of actors in each of the three streams, (2) the degree to which the streams are independent, and (3) whether the opening of the policy window was the result of three streams converging.

In some cases, universal preschool policy change at the state level is incremental but for others it moved quickly onto the decision agenda and was created with little opposition. To explain such different experiences for universal preschool policy change, Baumgartner and Jones's (1993, 2002) punctuated equilibrium model (PEM) is particularly useful. This model explains why there are periods of stability and also periods of dramatic change in policy making. Baumgartner and Jones hypothesize that if there is a general principle of policy action in place, policy making tends toward incrementalism. But if there is a new principle under consideration, then policy-making tends to be volatile. On the federal level, the volatile policy making process that culminated in Nixon's 1971 presidential veto was the result of the introduction of a new policy principle: federal funding of child care for all children. The root cause of volatility was the attempt to redefine child care from a private responsibility to a public one.

In the PEM, the timing of policy change is a function of an S-shaped curve. Similar to the policy diffusion logistic growth curve, negative feedback occurs at either end but in the middle positive feedback results in rapid change. When policy entrepreneurs invest resources into a process with negative feedback it results in smaller marginal effects; however, if they invest resources in a process with positive feedback it results in larger marginal effects. A key issue for policy entrepreneurs is to identify opportunities for positive feedback to increase their success in achieving policy change.

For federal policy, the policy window for expanding early childhood policies has remained closed for a decade. Any investment of resources would yield negative feedback. The status quo of targeted early childhood programs does not appear to have any opportunity for positive feedback leading to a policy window on the horizon. But policy windows at the state level have opened and policy change has occurred. A key issue to be explored in the policy change for preschool is what led to universal preschool rising on the S-curve so that positive feedback was possible.

*Policy Stability*

Baumgartner and Jones (1993) state that, when volatile change occurs, it can be achieved in the absence of counter mobilization. Contrary to pluralist models of countervailing forces, waves of enthusiasm sweep through the political system as political actors become convinced of the value of some new policy, often in the absence of serious opposing voices. But after the policy change occurs, it does not necessarily establish the political support to ensure its survival. In order for it to survive as the new status quo, it has to achieve stability.

Central to the PEM is the concept of a "policy monopoly." A policy monopoly has a definable institutional structure that is responsible for policy making supported by a powerful idea that is associated with the institutional structure. The structure serves to limit access from outsiders to the policy process through the formal or informal rules of access. This

is possible because the prevalent understandings of the policy are so positive that they evoke only support or indifference by those not involved
(thereby ensuring their continued noninvolvement). These policy ideas are
generally connected to core political values that can be communicated
directly and simply through image and rhetoric such as progress, fairness,
and economic growth—things no one taken seriously in the political
system can contest. If a group can convince others that their activities
serve such lofty goals, then it may be able to create a policy monopoly.

In the PEM, "stability is enforced through a complex system of mutually noninterfering policy monopolies buttressed by powerful support
images" (Baumgartner and Jones 1993, 15). Stability may be maintained
over long periods of time by the existing structure of political institutions
and the issue definition processed by those institutions. It is issue definition and institutional control combined that make possible the alternation
between stability and rapid change in political systems. For this reason,
policy monopolies try to maintain a single understanding of the issue definition in which there is support for the positive image and a rejection of
competing images.

But they also must prevent destabilization of the institutional structure. Baumgartner and Jones use the term "policy venue" to refer to "the
institutional locations where authoritative designs are made concerning a
given issue" (1993, 32). While the choice of venue impacts the way in
which a policy image is received, there are no immutable rules that spell
out which institutions in society must be charged with making decisions.
It could be assigned to a public agency, private market, federal or state
legislators, the courts, private individuals, or families, and so on. Policy
venues can change over time and, if they do, during these moments, dramatic policy changes often result.

Baumgartner and Jones emphasize the dynamic nature of policy
monopolies. They state, "The degree to which problems are tightly linked
to images is related to the degree to which a single arena of policymaking
exerts monopolistic control over a policy. Where images are in flux, one
may also expect changes in institutional jurisdictions. Conversely, where
venues change, the terms of the debate may be altered still further. Where
venues are tightly controlled, on the other hand, changes in image are less
likely; where changes in image are ruled out, the odds of effecting changes
in venue are correspondingly lower" (Baumgartner and Jones 1993, 38).
For universal preschool, the PEM leads us to examine the political struggle to create and maintain a positive policy image and to control the venue
in order to create a policy monopoly.

The PEM focuses on the conditions for achieving stability of the
policy monopoly but contributions from Sabatier, Jenkins-Smith and col-

leagues (particularly Sabatier, 1988 and 1999; Jenkins-Smith, and Sabatier, 1993) can be drawn upon to understand the network of actors supporting the policy monopoly. They develop the concept of "advocacy coalitions" consisting of actors who (1) share a particular belief system— that is, a set of basic values, causal assumptions, and problem perceptions and (2) show a nontrivial degree of coordinated activity over time (Sabatier 1999, 138). Shared policy core beliefs are not easily changed and include basic causes of the problem, method of financing programs, and desirability of participation by public versus experts versus elected officials. They are systemwide, salient policy preferences that are a source of ongoing cleavage (Sabatier 1999). In this framework, policy core beliefs are the glue that holds the advocacy coalition together. Actors will give up secondary aspects (beliefs not shared systemically) before acknowledging weaknesses in the core.

While the advocacy coalition literature tends to focus on mature advocacy coalitions that have been trying to influence policy for a decade or more, it can be used to understand the strong commitment to universal preschool across a wide array of actors. In mature coalitions, the participants regard themselves as a semiautonomous community who share a domain of expertise and there are specialized subunits within agencies at all relevant levels of government to deal with the topic. Externally there are interest groups that regard this as a major topic (Sabatier 1999). This is in contrast to nascent subsystems that may emerge because (1) a group of actors becomes dissatisfied with the subsystem's attention to a problem, or (2) a new issue or new conceptualization of a situation arises. On major controversies within a mature policy subsystem, when policy core beliefs are in dispute, the lineup of allies and opponents tends to be rather stable over periods of time. To change the policy core attributes requires significant changes in socioeconomic conditions, public opinion, systemwide governing coalitions, or policy outputs from other subsystems. But not all perturbations will result in policy change.

The main difference between advocacy coalitions and policy monopolies is the degree to which the commitment to a particular policy image or policy core belief is internalized. For policy monopolies, policy ideas are connected to core political values that can be communicated directly and simply through image and rhetoric. They are constructed to achieve policy change and then maintained in order to exert monopoly power over the policy. For advocacy coalitions, policy core beliefs are internalized by the actors involved. A mature advocacy coalition maintains core beliefs regardless of whether the image of those core beliefs leads to monopoly power over the policy process.

The policy process literature suggests that in order to understand the creation of universal preschool policy change, we need to consider framing, policy windows and policy change, and the process to achieve stability for universal preschool policies. Most of the policy process literature was developed through empirical research at the federal level. The MS framework was developed through Kingdon's study of federal transportation and health policy-making. Baumgartner and Jones's PEM was developed through analysis of longitudinal media data. Sabatier and colleagues's advocacy coalition framework, with a few exceptions, was developed through federal policy research. Only Mintrom's policy entrepreneur concept was the result of state research; he studied the creation of state school choice policies. Analyzing universal preschool policy change provides an opportunity to assess the explanatory power of these contributions at the state level.

## Book Overview

The main focus of this study is on explaining the anomaly of a dependent group, preschool-age children, being awarded costly benefits, a rarity in public policy. The study analyzes the change process in six states: Georgia, New York, Oklahoma, West Virginia, Tennessee, and Illinois. In chapter 2, I explore the policy change process of the four "pioneer states" to identify the role of policy entrepreneurs in reframing preschool from "babysitting" to early childhood education and the process leading up to the policy change.

All the states included in the study passed legislation that created the potential for universal access; however, few states have actually achieved that in practice. For this reason, chapter 3 is an analysis of the success and failure of the "pioneer" states of Georgia, New York, Oklahoma, and West Virginia, in attaining political and budgetary stability for their preschool programs. The experiences of these states vary tremendously and it sheds light on the explanatory power of PEM.

The more recent states of Illinois and Tennessee vary from the pioneer states in one important respect: investment by the Pew Charitable Trusts and Pew-funded actors in the policy change process. None of the literature discussed in the prior section addresses the role of foundations in the policy process. For that we have to turn to elite power theorists such as Dye (1979) and Domhoff (1998) who explain policy making as a function of the power of elites in society. Foundations are elite institutions; they exist because wealthy individuals and families created them. However, the role that Pew Charitable Trusts is playing in advancing state policy change is not adequately represented by elite power theorists. Chapter 4 explores the role of the Pew Charitable Trusts in achieving its stated goal of universal preschool for all three- and four-year-olds. After describing the history of Pew and its shift over time to advancing specific policy alternatives, the discussion shifts to an analysis of the creation of the universal preschool giving program. Pew's strategy for advancing policy change is comprehensive and brilliantly executed. It has established a strategic network of organizations who all share a core policy belief: public investment in universal preschool will yield public benefits. The external resources that Pew brings to states and the strategies with which it advances the universal preschool policy alternative sheds new light on the role of foundations in policy processes.

Chapter 5 analyzes the impacts of the Pew Charitable Trusts on state policy-making. Pew and Pew-funded actors invest in a great number of states with the goal of advancing policy change but Illinois and Tennessee are the two states that have successfully passed legislation.[4] The policy-making processes in these two states benefited from external resources that were unavailable to the pioneer states. Through an analysis of the strategic investment by Pew and Pew-funded actors, it provides the opportunity to assess the impact of external resources on state policy processes and compare it to state policy-making in the internally resourced pioneer states. Chapter 5 also includes a discussion of Pew and Pew-funded actors' investment in the pioneer state of New York, the only pioneer state that has received significant Pew investment after the policy change process. After New York passed its legislation in 1997, the funding for the preschool program was politically controversial. For nearly a decade, the preschool program did not achieve a stable policy monopoly. When Pew and Pew-funded actors began investing in New York, it provided the resources that culminated with an increase in funding for the program. Combined with the election of a new governor committed to the preschool program, New York made strides in making the program universally accessible.

The final chapter synthesizes findings and assesses their contributions for understanding policy processes. In addition to theoretical contributions, the chapter explores the meaning of the answers to the questions of who, what, where, and how universal preschool emerges in states. But it also raises additional questions about the role of foundations in a democracy, the potential for "tangled outcomes," and the future of universal preschool when Pew funding ends.


*Methodology*

The case selection was limited to states that passed legislation with universal access. I am expressly interested in explaining the anomaly of the universal preschool policy change process, which means that I included the states who were the first in the country to pass the legislation allowing for universal access. Many other states are leaders in early childhood because they have created high-quality, targeted preschool programs, such as North Carolina, but I was expressly interested in the decision to pass legislation allowing for universal access. To control for venue, I only included states that passed legislation. I omitted states such as Florida because the universal preschool program was created through the initiative process and New Jersey because the program was created through the courts (and is not state wide). As is the case with many natural experiments, there were no identified cases of failure; however, there is important variation in (1) the success and failure of pioneer states to achieve stability for their preschool programs and (2) the impact of the Pew Charitable Trusts in the policy change process.

Understanding the policy change process required a mixed methodology. I reviewed print sources including archival government documents, research reports, advocacy publications, newspaper coverage, and relevant Web sites; however, in some states there were few print sources available. For example, coverage of the policy change process by the newspaper for the capital region in Oklahoma was virtually nonexistent. Because of the scarcity of sources, the print source data were combined with interviews with a wide range of actors including elected officials and their staff, government agency personnel, journalists, child advocates, child care industry advocates, public school officials and advocates, and university researchers. These interviews were conducted in person or by phone from 2005 to 2007. To understand the role of the Pew Charitable Trusts, I relied on interviews with Pew staff and grantees, review of Internal Revenue Service 990 forms to identify grant history, and an exhaustive review of the interconnected Web sites of Pew grantees. Only through the combination of interviews with print sources was it possible to develop a reliable account of the sequence of events and the roles of various actors that eventually resulted in policy change for the six states and policy stability in the four pioneer states.

# Policy Change in the Pioneer States

W HEN ASKED TO name states that are national leaders in providing preschool, one might guess New York or California but few would guess Georgia, Oklahoma, and West Virginia. Traditionally Southern states have not been leaders in education or social programs. But since the 1980s, education has been on Southern states' agendas. In 1986, the Commission on the Future of the South issued a report calling for increasing the financial investment in education, upgrading preschool programs, stemming the dropout rate and reducing adult illiteracy. The report stated, "In the South's long, even commendable, journey of progress, too many are left behind with education and skills [that] better prepare them to function in Henry Grady's Atlanta of 1886 than in Andrew Young's of today" (Hansen 1987, 1). In 1988, The Southern Regional Education Board (SREB) announced its "Goals for Education: Challenge 2000." The SREB membership included three of the four states who would later pioneer universal preschool: Georgia, Oklahoma, and West Virginia. The report, developed over a nine-month period by a commission of seventeen Southeastern educators and politicians, named twelve educational goals to reach by 2000. The report called for providing free preschool and full-day kindergarten to all at-risk children and requiring readiness tests before children enter first grade (White 1988). Consensus was building across the region that reliance on luring industry with the inducements of cheap labor, no unions, and low taxes was insufficient for continued economic growth. The new thinking was that the path to improve the attractiveness of Southern locations for companies was to invest in building strong public school systems. This would achieve two objectives: (1) it would create a better-educated workforce and (2) strong public schools would attract professional workers to relocate to Southern states. With momentum for public education investments building, Georgia and Oklahoma passed legislation to create universal preschool programs in 1995 and

1998 respectively, followed by West Virginia in 2002. Independent of the moves by Southern states, New York was pursuing its own universal preschool program, passing legislation in 1997 with a five-year implementation schedule. As discussed in the prior chapter, many states have created targeted preschool programs, but the pioneer states were able to pass legislation removing income limits and opening access to publicly funded preschool for all four-year-olds (see table 2.1 below).

This chapter explores the policy change process resulting in the passage of universal preschool legislation in the four pioneer states. The case studies begin with the first state to enact universal preschool legislation, Georgia, followed in chronological order by New York, Oklahoma, and West Virginia. The chapter concludes with an analysis of the explanatory power of the policy process literature for explaining the policy change.

## Georgia

The key to understanding the creation of universal preschool in Georgia is to understand the role that it played in Zell Miller's gubernatorial campaign. In the early 1990s Georgia's economy was a major focus of media and political attention. Georgia's Speaker of the House Tom Murphy called 1991 the "toughest financial session" the legislature had ever faced (Walston 1991a, 1). The *Atlanta Journal Constitution*, Georgia's newspaper of record, described Georgia as having a "stagnant" economy and a "faltering" economy (Walston 1991a, 1). In the midst of the economic difficulties, Zell Miller made education a central part of his campaign, with preschool being a major component. The question inevitably arises: why in difficult economic times would Zell Miller make creation of preschool part of his campaign strategy? The answer lies in the creation of a "lottery for education." Candidate Miller knew that he would have to create a new revenue source in order to fund an ambitious new set of education programs.

However the question remains, why preschool? By all accounts the answer to this is because Governor Miller wanted it. Raised in the northern mountains of Georgia, his commitment to education was a fundamental part of his belief structure (Hyatt 1997). He was raised on the Young Harris College campus where both of his parents taught, and, prior to his political career, Zell Miller also taught at the college. He believed in the power of education to improve the lives of all Georgians (Hyatt 1997). Even as far back as his 1974 campaign for lieutenant governor, early education had been on his agenda; he called for universal kindergarten during that campaign, although it would take ten more years before it would be passed.

While Miller's support of education is fundamental, the question still remains why he would focus lottery revenues on the education of four year olds. The answer from multiple sources is that Miller was familiar with educational trends and research and Georgia's poor education performance in national comparisons. For the preschool program, Georgia State University Professor Gary Henry states Miller was aware of the brain research and literature touting the benefits of high-quality early childhood programs. Once Miller became an advocate of preschool programs he sought to raise awareness of the importance of early education. He organized a 3,000-person conference on the preschool studies and brain research (Henry, Gary, personal communication, Atlanta, June 27, 2005). Miller could have directed the lottery revenues to improving K-12 education but instead he decided to concentrate funds on the years before and after: the preschool program directed to four year olds and the Hope Scholarship, a merit-based program that paid tuition and fees for college students. Several sources indicate that Miller wanted the new spending to have an impact and feared it would not have as great an impact on educational outcomes if the lottery funding were combined with existing education funding.

While Miller was becoming aware of the importance of early brain development, there were "softening up" processes at work by other actors. A precursor to state-funded preschool occurred in 1985 when then Governor Joe Frank Harris proposed an education reform bill, the Quality Basic Education Act, that included making full-day kindergarten "mandatory" (Hansen 1985, 1). In Georgia at that time, kindergarten attendance was optional and the Governor's bill would have required schools to offer full-day kindergarten. Thus Georgia became the second state in the nation, following Alabama, to provide full-day kindergarten. The issue was controversial despite the fact that 158 of 187 school districts already offered full-day kindergarten (i.e., 4½ hours of classroom activity). The controversy was partly due to poor word choice. The governor used the word mandatory, which was interpreted as forcing parents to enroll their children in full-day kindergarten. But the bill only required that all children not attending kindergarten pass a test before entering first grade. The test was mandatory but enrollment was voluntary.

This controversy reflects the transition occurring as early education evolved from a private responsibility to a public one. The dominant view of early education in Georgia at the time was that care of young children should be decided by the family, not the state. When the government came out with a bill that was misunderstood as mandating attendance in full-day kindergarten, it conflicted with the dominant view. Not only was it seen to infringe on the rights of parents to choose how to educate and care for young children, it also was not broadly acceptable to many political leaders because they did not agree that investment in early childhood was important. Many viewed early childhood schooling as babysitting, rather than education. House Speaker Tom Murphy stated, "I've never been a great advocate of kindergarten" (Hansen 1985, 1). However, the Department of Education supported the bill and attempted to reframe the issue as an investment that would improve Georgia's dismal national education rankings. The bill eventually passed but the support for public investment in early childhood was not yet widely shared.

The process of reframing early childhood education from "babysitting" to "preschool as a wise public investment" is important for understanding how a service that had been viewed as a private responsibility shifted to a public responsibility. With the babysitting framing, the responsibility for early education rests in the private realm: parents and guardians are responsible for providing care or purchasing it in the private market. With the exception of child care subsidies for low-income families, the cost of early education was borne by individual families. But in the 1980s, the shift to acceptance that there was a public responsibility to provide funding for preschool began to take hold and publicly funded preschool emerged as the preferred policy alternative. Articles in the *Atlanta Journal-Constitution* (*AJC*) informed readers of the research on the importance of early brain development and the famous Abcedarian and Perry Preschool projects that claimed high returns on early childhood investments. About every three months the *AJC* published early childhood articles mainly focusing on the returns on investment for early education programs and publicizing approval of investment ranging from Georgia, Southern, national and international perspectives. An April 1988 article provided a national perspective on public preschool highlighting Georgia's Board of Education's plans to pilot preschool programs for at-risk four-year-olds (Laccetti 1988). In August 1988, another article in the *AJC* provided an international and national perspective on the expanded role public schools can play in delivering a wide range of child care services (Hansen 1988).

As the issue of public funding of preschool was being brought to the general public through media attention, one Georgia County decided in 1988 to start a pilot full-day preschool program. DeKalb County started a program targeting at-risk children funded with county taxes. Media coverage of the program heralded DeKalb as being on the cutting edge of public education (Dickerson 1988). A Republican DeKalb school board member spoke directly to the babysitting framing stating, "What are you doing out there, trying to spend money on a babysitting service: But that's not what we're talking about. We're talking about educating students from low socioeconomic backgrounds, giving them a jump over what they would get sitting in front of the boob tube" (White 1988, 1). Although it would be nearly a decade before public funding of early education as a wise future investment became the dominant view, the 1980s served as a softening up period for publicly funded preschool. But to understand the creation of publicly funded preschool in Georgia, first it is necessary to understand the controversy over establishing a lottery to fund it.

In his gubernatorial campaign then Lieutenant Governor Miller set himself apart from the other primary candidates by calling for a lottery that would fund education. Similar to publicly funded preschool, the lottery was not a new issue in Georgia. The lottery experienced its own softening-up period in the 1980s.[1] In 1985, the Macon City Council voted to lobby for a statewide lottery in response to the Reagan administration's elimination of General Revenue Sharing. Macon faced the prospect of losing $2.6 million in federal General Revenue Sharing in 1986. To recoup the lost federal funds, the city would have had to increase property taxes by 30 percent, which was politically infeasible (Hopkins 1985a, 29). A legislative committee charged with finding new revenue sources advised the creation of a lottery, pari-mutuel betting or a sales tax increase (Hopkins 1985b, 12). But creating a lottery was a controversial issue in Georgia at that time. As one person interviewed said, "Georgia is the buckle on the Bible belt." Not surprisingly, the creation of a lottery was opposed by a coalition of religious groups including the Southern Baptists, United Methodists, and the Christian Coalition. Additional opponents included education interests who feared the lottery would supplant, rather than augment, existing funding for education (White 1990).

In the controversy over creating a lottery, a series of bills had been introduced that proposed or opposed a lottery. In the mid-1980s Governor Harris opposed gambling in any form but then Lieutenant Governor Miller was willing to let the voters decide (Hopkins 1985c). Miller had the support of many local governments, Fulton County in particular, that saw gambling as the key to relieving their financial burdens (*Atlanta Journal-Constitution* 1986). However, in Georgia, the constitution would have to be amended to allow gambling and that would require a two-thirds majority vote. At the state level, there was an annual battle to legalize gambling (Palmer 1988, 4) but there was insufficient political support to allow gambling until the 1990 gubernatorial election.

When Miller decided to run for governor he "hopped on the lottery bandwagon," tied the lottery to education and made it the centerpiece of his campaign (Secrest and May 1989, 1). Religious leaders immediately reacted. Leadership of the state's Southern Baptists and United Methodists, represented by the Council on Moral and Civic Concerns, came to the Capitol and expressed their adamant opposition, vowing to work and rally against the lottery. The *AJC* reported that "conservative church groups stand ready to storm the Capitol, crowd the halls, buttonhole their elected representatives, testify before committees and generally wield all their power against the sins of gambling" (Secrest 1989, 9).

Miller also faced opposition from the media. The *AJC* opposed the lottery, deriding Miller for wasting attention on the lottery and calling it a "public policy Hula-Hoop" that was harmless entertainment. The newspaper criticized Miller for making it a central campaign issue and went as far as to tell him to "shut up, please, and talk about something that matters" (*Atlanta Journal-Constitution* 1990a, 14).

Despite opposition from interest groups and the media, *AJC* polls indicated 70 percent of the electorate favored the lottery (Secrest 1989, 9); Miller was championing an issue with populist appeal. Throughout the campaign, Miller continued to advocate for creation of the lottery for education but was vague about the educational programs that would be funded by lottery revenue. The entrance of preschool as a preferred policy alternative occurred in December 1989 when campaign manager James Carville issued a draft education platform that proposed voluntary preschool for four year olds and changes in teacher certification (Scrogging 1989). The teacher certification was eventually dropped and college scholarships added to the platform, but Miller's commitment to dedicating the revenue to education continued. He threatened to oppose any bill that did not allocate lottery funds to education. In the legislative session prior to the election, many bills were introduced in the House and Senate calling for lottery funds to be allocated in different ways. In one bill (HR 11) the lottery funds would have been appropriated for indigent hospital care as well as education. But Miller threatened to veto his own bill if the lottery revenues were not dedicated to education.

In the Democratic primary, Miller stood alone in his vocal support of the lottery for education. Senator Roy Barnes opposed the lottery, but former Atlanta Mayor Andrew Young's position was that the voters should decide. Representative Lauren "Bubba" McDonald Jr. voted in favor of the lottery in the House Industry Committee but refused to make it a campaign issue. The front-running Republican candidate, House Minority Leader Johnny Isakson also refused to make the lottery a campaign issue (Secrest and May 1989).

Miller's choice to champion the lottery, while his opponents ignored it, proved a winning strategy for media attention. As a well-seasoned politician who had served as lieutenant governor for sixteen years and a term as state senator, Miller used his long-time opposition to House Majority Leader Tom Murphy to his political advantage. Speaker Murphy opposed the lottery and supported gubernatorial candidate Lauren "Bubba" McDonald in the Democratic primary. When the Senate passed a bill for a lottery referendum, Zell Miller knew Murphy would oppose the bill when it was discussed in the House, which indeed occurred. Even though the lottery bill died in the House Industry Committee with an 11-6 vote, Murphy's opposition gave the lottery issue attention from the media, raising the profile of Miller's key campaign issue (Hyatt 1997; May 1990a). The *AJC* reported, "Mr. Miller has made the lottery a symbol of seeming modernity against Mr. Murphy's apparent antiquity, the wave of the future against the undertow of the past" (Teepen 1990, 15). Miller called the death of the lottery bill the latest casualty of the "Murphy Mausoleum" (Scrogging 1990, 3). In the primary Miller swept every region, defeating Young, who many had hoped would become Georgia's first black governor (May 1990b).

After winning the primary, Miller sought to make the general election a referendum on the lottery. In the general election, Republican candidate Johnny Isakson supported the lottery but "Miller put a face on it" (Henry, Gary, personal communication, Atlanta, June 27, 2005). By creating the image of a four year old going to preschool and a high school graduate going to college, Miller created an easily conveyed idea that would garner the support of Democratic women for preschool and Republican suburban voters for the Hope Scholarship program. But the state economy was at the forefront of lawmaker concerns. Georgia legislators told state agencies to prepare for four-percent cuts in an effort to pare $332 million from the $7.8 billion budget, and deeper cuts were expected for the next year (Blackmon 1990, 1). With a $456 million budget shortfall, proposals that would increase revenues were more likely to garner support. Miller won the election and the *AJC* and many others interpreted Miller's electoral success to be a public mandate for a lottery ( *Atlanta Journal-Constitution* 1991a, 3).

Now that Miller was elected as governor, he publicly made his election a mandate for a lottery, which required that he persuade the legislature to approve a referendum for it. But passage of the lottery would require a two-thirds majority in both houses to pass and majority passage of a referendum by the electorate. An *AJC* poll prior to the beginning of the session found that, while 68 percent of senators supported the lottery referendum, only 44 percent of House members supported it. Overall only 49 percent supported the lottery referendum, far short of the required 66 percent (Cummings 1991a, 1). Longtime political adversary House Speaker Tom Murphy vowed to remain silent, but the issue was how House members would interpret his silence. The opposition to the lottery was generational with half of the legislators over fifty-five opposing it.

Despite the opposition from religious interests, the *AJC* poll found that even though 62 percent of legislators were Southern Baptists or United Methodists, only one-third of them opposed the lottery (Cummings 1991a, 1). At this stage of debate, the emphasis was completely on the lottery and there is no debate over the education programs that would be funded by the lottery.

In his inaugural address, Miller borrowed a phrase from Franklin D. Roosevelt: "Try something. If it works, try more of it. If it doesn't, try something else. But for God's sake, try something" (Cummings 1991b, 1). What Miller wanted to try was the lottery. It was the only campaign promise mentioned in his speech and by introducing the legislation on the first day of the session, he made it front and center of his agenda. In typically theatric style, Governor Miller "tacked the lucky number seven onto two lottery proposals and rolled them [giant dice] into the opening session of the General Assembly" (Walston 1991a, 1). The biggest hurdle to the lottery was not the Senate, which had supported Miller's previous lottery bill, but in the House. Miller personally lobbied for the lottery bill, which was a departure from former governors (Cummings 1991c, 1). He brought back campaign manager James Carville to help him wage the battle. Miller wined and dined opposition members and refrained from public criticism of them. He targeted legislators who were undecided and did not try to persuade those who had a moral opposition to the lottery (Hyatt 1997).

One of the most contentious issues was who would control the lottery funds. Miller wanted to make sure that lottery funds did not supplant existing education funding (Cummings 1991). Opposition during the campaign from the Georgia School Boards Association, and the fast-growing Gwinnett County Parent Teacher Association, among others, led Miller to advocate for an independent lottery commission to administer the lottery and direct proceeds to specific educational programs (Pendered 1990, 5). With this arrangement, the governor would appoint the commissioners and circumvent the legislative budgetary process. However, to gain two-thirds majority support in the House, he abandoned that in HR 7. Not only was that change critical for House support but media support as well. The *AJC's* position was that the legislature should have full control over all funds the state collects (1990b, 14). The justification was that the appointed boards do not serve the best interests of the "consumers" but rather privilege some interests over others (Wooten 1991, 1). By removing the enabling language from the bill, the legislature could pass the lottery without having the struggles over power and money in the lottery until the following legislative session.

The first hurdle was to get HR7 passed in the House Industry Committee. In 1990 the Committee blocked the lottery measure 11-6 but the chairman, Roy "Sonny" Watson Jr. interpreted Miller's election victory as indicating public support for the lottery. He vowed to stay neutral, saying that he would vote in favor of it but would not try to persuade the Committee to vote one way or another (Walston 1991b). Former political foe House Speaker Tom Murphy pledged to call a vote quickly after the lottery passed the Committee. He gave an endorsement of sorts to the *AJC* prior to the committee meeting, stating "I am not predicting one way or the other. I think it will come out [of] committee quickly. I suspect it will pass the House" (Cook and Walston 1991, 1). As the Committee meeting date drew closer, Murphy increased his public expressions that the lottery would pass. Speaking to the Business Council of Georgia, Murphy predicted that the Committee would pass by a "two-to-one vote" (Cook and Walston 1991, 1).

State Democratic Representative Roger Byrd led the opposition to the lottery in the Committee. He opposed the lottery because he thought it preyed on the most vulnerable population and that it would not do anything for education in the long run (*Atlanta Journal-Constitution* 1991b). Despite that opposition, there was growing support for the lottery. Before the Committee met, the House Floor Leader reported to the *AJC* that the lottery bill was close to having the two-thirds majority required for the constitutional amendment (*Atlanta Journal-Constitution* 1991b). Some opposition was voiced by black legislators led by Representative Billy McKinney, who felt Miller preempted them on the lottery because HR7 went to the full Committee and their gambling proposals were assigned to a subcommittee (Baxter 1991, 2). McKinney wanted all gambling measures sponsored by black legislators considered by the full committee and assurances that blacks would be involved in the management of the lottery. To gain black legislators' support, Miller pledged that minority firms would get the chance to participate in lottery contracts but made no specific promises. He also announced that he would not oppose a Senate bill to allow horse racing but would not delete HR 7's ban on pari-mutuel gambling. Rep. McKinney tried to amend the bill in Committee to remove the ban on pari-mutuel betting but the amendment failed and he eventually voted in favor of the lottery (Walston 1991c).

The January 29, 1991, meeting of the House Industry Committee was held in the largest committee room in the Capitol with an overflow crowd watching from the hallways via closed-circuit monitors (Walston 1991c). The minutes indicate that public speakers alternated between pro and con but give no hint at the number of speakers or the content of their remarks (Georgia Industry Committee 1991). The main opposition was the Council on Civic and Moral Concerns, formerly the Georgia Temperance League, funded by the Southern Baptist and United Methodist churches.

The Concerned Black Clergy, while worried because of the impact on the black population, had not reached consensus on the lottery (Walston and White 1991). The National Day of Prayer chairman testified that no person who "prayed to the true and living God" would support a lottery; however this angered Chairman Watson and he ended up casting his yes vote, despite committee chairmen not being required to vote.

Proponents included big business hoping to financially benefit from the estimated $58 million in annual contracts and commissions (Walston 1991d). While the archival records do not list speakers in attendance, the *AJC* reported that the room was packed with high-powered lobbyists hoping to interject language favorable to their interests. For example, the Georgia Association of Convenience Stores was hoping to get more than the standard 5 percent of lottery sales revenue. Other businesses included ticket printers, computer systems and telecommunications firms, and advertising and marketing firms hoping for multi-million-dollar contracts. While some proponents did their own lobbying, others pooled their resources to create the Georgians for a Lottery Referendum. Formed in 1989, it combined, among others, ticket printers, and horse-racing proponents, who supported the lottery because they saw it as a "foot in the door" to legalizing pari-mutuel betting. The group hired three veteran lobbyists in 1990 and raised funds for the Miller campaign (Walston 1991d). At the end of the meeting, the committee voted 16-7 in favor of the bill (Georgia Industry Committee 1991).

With Chairman Watson voting in favor, along with the Rules Committee Chairman Bill Lee, House leadership sent a signal that they were behind the lottery (Walston 1991c). Once the unamended bill was approved by the committee, the House voted two days later on the bill. After four hours of intense debate, the bill passed 126 to 51 in its original form. The bill needed a two-thirds majority and passed with six more votes than required (*Atlanta Journal-Constitution* 1991c).

The *AJC* predicted that, unlike the protracted House debate, the Senate would pass the bill in less time than a "Woody Woodpecker cartoon" (Pomerantz 1991, 3). The Senate Finance and Public Utilities Committee held a public hearing on February 5, 1991, to discuss the lottery legislation (HR 7). No records exist of who attended the hearing or what was said, but committee notes indicate that several amendments were offered but failed. In the end, the committee passed the legislation without amendment (Georgia Finance and Public Utilities Committee 1991, 1–2). On February 8th, the full Senate passed the measure 47–9 without amendment (Walston 1991). Although the Governor was not legally required to sign the lottery bill, he chose to do so to gain media attention. With two-thirds majorities in both houses and the ceremonial signature of the governor, HR7 would now be on the November ballot for a yes or no vote by Georgian citizens.

Miller vowed to run television ads and make stump speeches support- ing the referendum (*Atlanta Journal-Constitution* 1991d). But before the referendum could pass, the sticky issue of enabling legislation for the lot- tery needed to be resolved. In November 1991, Miller unveiled his plan as part of a fifteen-city, two-week tour to maintain media interest (Sherman 1991). At a meeting of the Georgia Business Council, Miller proposed that three new educational programs would each receive 30 percent of lottery proceeds with the remaining 10 percent held in reserve. The programs were vaguely described as including a voluntary preschool program for at- risk four-year-olds, equipment for K–12, and a scholarship fund to assist high school students who attain a "certain grade point average...and whose family meets a certain income requirement" (Miller quoted in Sherman 1991, 1)

Even though attention to the preschool program was minimal, by 1991 the *AJC* supported the preschool program and cautioned against siphoning educational funds for other purposes (*Atlanta Journal- Constitution* 1991e). *AJC* editorials even went so far as to state, "No proposal is more important to the long-term educational prospects of Georgia than the governor's preschool program. And none offers as much promise" (*Atlanta Journal-Constitution* 1991f, 24). The media also praised Miller for his political acumen in generating support for the lot- tery referendum. The *AJC* ran photos and stories of Governor Miller playing with young children, with positive supporting statements such as, "How do you sell a state-operated lottery proposal to voters? Exactly the way Gov. Zell Miller is selling it" (Akerman 1992, 16). Opposition forces, including the Georgia Lottery Truth, conceded that "We don't have the prestige, the power or the finances the governor has" (Walston 1992, 1). In the end, voters approved the referendum by a 52 percent margin (Monastra 1992).[2]

The advocacy environment for and against the referendum was focused on the lottery; there was virtually no attention to preschool at that time. This is due in large part to the absence of policy advocates in the development of the preschool policy alternative. Preschool emanated from the Miller campaign and did not flow from an advocacy coalition or a cluster of hidden advocates pushing for a preschool program. Since the education of four year olds had not previously been separated from the education and care of children younger than four, there were no estab- lished advocacy groups for preschool. Education interests, while support- ive of a lottery-funded pilot program, wanted the preschool program incorporated into the public school funding formula (Sherman 1991).

With the establishment of the lottery, the funding for preschool was firmly created. The policy process had been volatile but it had nothing to do with support or opposition to preschool. Because preschool was nested in the lottery controversy, it emerged with very little scrutiny. The ease with which the preschool program was created stands in stark contrast to the struggles it faced to survive in the first three years. The struggle to build political support for preschool required the creation of a new institutional structure and expansion to universal access (discussed fully in chapter 3).

## New York

Unlike Georgia in the early 1990s, when Zell Miller had to create a lottery to fund his education programs, New York in the latter 1990s was experiencing economic prosperity. Tax revenues were exceeding expectations and politicians were feeling flush with cash. To enact universal preschool, policy entrepreneurs could draw on the rising revenue stream; however, the story of how universal preschool legislation was passed in 1997 is nested within a much bigger political battle. How universal preschool came to be in New York has little, if anything, to do with preschool but everything to do with competition between branches of government to wield political power. The political battle in New York was between first-term Republican Governor George Pataki and Democrat Speaker of the Assembly Sheldon Silver. Governor Pataki came to office in 1995 after having been elected on a platform of cutting social programs and taxes (Perez-Pena 1997). While the Senate had a Republican majority, the Assembly was controlled by the Democrats. Representative Sheldon Silver became Speaker of the Assembly in 1994, after having served in the Assembly since 1976 (New York State Assembly 2006). Speaker Silver had long been a champion of education and wanted to enact major new education spending programs during this time of fiscal prosperity. At the same time, Governor Pataki wanted to pass property tax cuts as promised during his campaign.

But the political battle over education revenue and spending is nested within a larger battle over which branch of government would control education. Unlike many other state departments of education in which commissioners are appointed by the governor or elected by the public, in New York the State Assembly appoints the Board of Regents and the Regents appoint the Commissioner of Education. Because of this institutional arrangement, the Commissioner answers to the Regents and by extension the Assembly, but not to the governor. New York State's budget process for education first starts with the Board of Regents, which develops the education budget and presents it to the Assembly. The governor develops his own budget and then the two branches of government negotiate until a compromise budget can be passed. In New York, budget battles between the governor and legislature are legendary and frequently the budget is not approved until long after the new fiscal year has begun. The delays in budget-bill passage are due in no small part to the battle for control over education spending. This was indeed the case in 1997, when the universal preschool program was created.

But before 1997, there was a long softening-up period for state-funded universal preschool in New York. Unlike Georgia in which publicly funded preschool had a modest softening-up process, New York has a long, illustrious history of state-funded preschool education. As early as 1946, public schools were allowed to establish nursery schools, although no state funds were provided (Mitchell 2004). Public funding of preschool began in 1958 when the legislature provided funding for experimental programs for disadvantaged children. By 1964, a number of districts had created programs for disadvantaged children under the age of five. These programs were studied by the U.S. Department of Health, Education, and Welfare (now divided into the Department of Health and Human Services and the Department of Education). The study concluded that participating children outperformed the control group on IQ and other cognitive tests (DiLorenzo 1969, cited in Mitchell 2004, 5). In 1965, when the federal Head Start program was launched, the federal government chose to bypass state departments of education and funnel program funding directly to Head Start grantees. Governor Nelson Rockefeller opposed this decision and in 1966 responded by creating a state-funded early childhood program for disadvantaged children called Early Pre-K (EPK). Unlike Head Start, the EPK programs were located in public schools and state funding paid for the program. Of the thirty-nine original participating districts, some cities blended federal funding and others opened their programs to all preschool-age children (Mitchell 2004). But due to lack of funding, EPK expanded slowly. In the 1970s, the program was level-funded for six years. It was not until the election of Governor Mario Cuomo in 1983 that funding increased again for EPK (Mitchell 2004). In 1977, nearly 10 percent of four year olds were served by the state's EPK program but during the Cuomo administration participation grew to over 25 percent. In the fall of 1997, prior to the implementation of the new preschool program, New York was already serving one-third of its four year olds (New York State Education Department 1999).

In addition to the state EPK program, under Mayor Koch's administration, New York City tried to implement its own universal preschool program. In 1985, Koch first announced his goal of providing early education services to all four year olds in New York City. His vision took the form of the Giant Step Program. Mayor Koch created the Commission on Early Childhood Education to plan and implement the initiative. Many heralded the program curriculum as providing a high-quality early education grounded in early childhood development principles (Gatenio 2002). The program implementation built on existing systems including Head Start, child care, and public preschool initiatives. However, after three years of operation, the Giant Step program had an enrollment of only 7,000 out of the estimated 40,000 children eligible for the program. The primary reason cited for the low enrollment was lack of capacity. The existing systems were already operating around capacity and there was a lack of suitable and affordable space to expand enrollment in the Giant Step program. The Giant Step program was eventually cut by the Dinkins administration for a complex set of reasons, including the fiscal trauma New York City faced in the wake of federal budget cutbacks during the Reagan administration. But the program was reinvented in the form of SuperStart, a targeted program, which survived until 1991 (Gatenio 2002). Some argue that the experience of New York City provided the blueprint for the development of the state's universal preschool program in 1997. Speaker Silver represents the 64th District in lower Manhattan and was familiar with the history of preschool in New York City.

With the long history of public sector involvement in early education, New York policy entrepreneurs did not have to convince legislators or the general public that public investment in early education was important. No one on record opposed investing in early education; rather, the issue was over who would be allowed to participate in publicly funded early education. In 1983, newly elected Democratic Governor Mario Cuomo proposed increases in EPK and established the Permanent Interagency Committee on Early Childhood Programs (PICECP) to streamline funding and coordinate programs for greater effectiveness. PICECP was comprised of directors and commissioners of the state agencies dealing with children and had a citizen advisory committee appointed by the governor (Mitchell 2004). In 1988, Governor Cuomo called for making preschool universal, but his focus, which was shared by early childhood advocates, was broader than preschool and included newborns to five year olds. However, the momentum for expanding state investments in early education abruptly ended with the election of Republican Governor George Pataki in 1994. After taking office in 1995, he dissolved PICECP and its Advisory Committee, changed the name of EPK to "Targeted Pre-K" and tried unsuccessfully to cut the program's budget (Mitchell 2004).

The reversal of support for early education investments were due to Governor Pataki's campaign promises to cut spending, cut income and business taxes, and impose new restrictions on welfare recipients. After the social spending expansions of the Cuomo administration, Pataki's push for cuts was an abrupt change. The 1995 budget negotiations between Governor Pataki and the Republican-controlled Senate and the Democrat-controlled State Assembly were heralded by the *New York Times* as "a drastic reversal of New York's fiscal traditions" (Sack 1995, 1). But beyond early education, Pataki wanted to take control of the entire education budget. He proposed a constitutional amendment to eliminate the Board of Regents and make the State Education Department more accountable to the governor. In response, Education Commissioner Thomas Sobol resigned (Richardson 1996) and ultimately the constitutional amendment was never passed.

Over the next two years, Democrats continued to clash with the Republican governor and Senate majority. The battles came to a head in the 1997 budget negotiations. At that time, Democratic Assembly Speaker Silver was advocating major education spending programs including a $2 billion bond proposal to build or repair public schools, $1 billion to make preschool universal, $60 million to create full-day kindergarten programs in all schools, and $445 million to reduce class size in K–3 to a maximum of twenty children (Dao 1997, B7). The *New York Times* reported that Pataki and Senate Republicans wanted to scale back that plan but they were open to part of it, particularly expanding preschool classrooms. But their support hinged on the willingness of Democrats to support the Republican proposal to cut $1.7 billion in school property taxes, the main tax revenue source for public school districts (Dao 1997, B7). In essence, the deal would require massive expansion in state education funding at the same time budget cuts would decrease the amount of property tax revenue being generated for education.

With the 1998 election drawing near, Governor Pataki wanted to soften his image and what better way than by supporting programs for children. But choosing to support preschool was extremely problematic for him politically because of his renegade lieutenant governor. In his first election, he had chosen Betsy McCaughey Ross, a political novice, to be his running mate as lieutenant governor. After the election, the governor asked her to research education reform. While Pataki was interested in abolishing the Regents to create more executive control over education, Ross's report focused on investing in early childhood. In September of 1996, Ross issued a report, "Preparing for Success: Expanding Prekindergarten and Educational Daycare" that called for expanding the targeted preschool program to universal access, among other early childhood program changes aimed to invest in future school success. To fund the program, she proposed a ten-cent-per-pack tax on cigarettes.

The politics of the situation for Governor Pataki were thorny to say the least. Ross had a very public feud with Pataki and eventually ran against him in the 1998 election as a Democrat (Nagourney 1998). In 1996, Pataki tried to ignore Ross's report but she made that increasingly difficult by pursuing support for her recommendations from the New York Board of Regents, the same body Pataki had tried to abolish (Karlin 1997). When addressing the Regents, Ross even went so far as to praise Pataki's nemesis Democratic Assembly Speaker Sheldon Silver for his support of preschool (Kolbert 1997). She also solicited endorsements from the New York State United Teachers, the New York State Federation of Prekindergarten Administrators Association, and the New York State School Boards Association (Yu 1996). Republican Senator Frank Padavan (R-Queens) sponsored her plan, Senate Bill 350, calling for doubling the number of children in preschool programs over four years (Karlin 1997). Although the bill was never passed, Ross kept up her crusade through public speaking and letters to media outlets (Ross 1997).

Early childhood advocates feared Ross's endorsement would be the "kiss of death" for preschool. But in the end it was not. New York State has a long history of early childhood activism that had already been called to arms in the wake of the 1996 federal welfare reform legislation (Kolben, Nancy, phone communication, July 12, 2007). In reaction to Silver's fall 1996 legislative activity, "a group of citizens, advocates and organizations concerned about early education met to strategize about how to advance early education in New York" (Mitchell 2004, 9). Advocates did not know exactly what Assemblyman Silver would propose for preschool and attempted to impact the policy alternative by building support for preschool. In February 1997, the group held a legislative breakfast in Albany attended by many distinguished early childhood experts. They presented evidence on the importance of early brain development, in particular the Carnegie Corporation report that had just been released, titled "Years of Promise" (Carnegie Corporation of New York 1996). They held one session for legislators and another for advocates but in both sessions they advocated for investments in early childhood. They also brought in a speaker from the Georgia Business Education Roundtable who had worked with Zell Miller to talk about the success of Georgia's universal preschool program (Mitchell 2004; Schimke, Karen, personal communication, Albany, October 11, 2006).[3]

After the legislative breakfast, several members of the planning group became actively engaged with Assembly staff in drafting the legislation. They tried to amend the legislation to require a diverse delivery system (i.e., collaboration between public schools and private providers) and were successful in winning a 10-percent base for collaboration. They also advocated for full-day preschool but were not successful (Schimke, personal communication, Albany, October 11, 2006). However, the real surprise was the speed with which the legislation went forward. Advocates had hoped to see policy change in two years but Assembly Speaker Silver was successful in getting legislation passed in August, just six short months after the advocates' legislative breakfast.

The unexpectedly speedy process for the preschool program occurred because both the Democrats and Republicans wanted to claim a victory prior to the 1998 election. Pataki had campaigned on cutting taxes and wanted to claim success, even if it meant supporting increased educational spending. This was politically possible because the changes in property taxes would begin to appear in tax bills before the November 1998 election, but the new spending programs for education would be phased in over several years. The phased-in spending meant that the real budgetary reckoning period would not occur until after the election but Pataki could claim success in effecting tax cuts prior to the election (Perez-Pena 1997).

In the end, both sides got what they wanted: New York's 1997 budget simultaneously enacted property tax cuts and increased education spending. The final education bill was a package of education reforms called Learning, Achieving, Developing by Directing Educational Resources (LADDER), which included funding for reduced class size in grades K–3, incentives for full-day kindergarten, and a five-year commitment to fund universal preschool for four year olds (amended Education Law § 3602). The universal preschool (UPK) program received $67 million for 1998–99 with priority given to districts based on need and number of eligible four-year-olds. By 2001–02, the UPK program was supposed to be universally available to all four-year-olds with annual funding of $500 million. One reason why such a deal could be struck was that the economy was strong. Revenues had exceeded expectations, which meant that Republicans and Democrats could both get what they wanted without having to face the budget consequences (Perez-Pena 1997).

According to advocates, there was no opposition to UPK. There was opposition to public spending in general but not for UPK specifically. Business interests, which have proven important in other states, were neutral on UPK. The Chamber Alliance of New York State declined to participate in this study but, according to advocates, even though it prefers a targeted program it did not oppose the UPK program. Child care providers "grumbled" about UPK but did not organize to oppose it.

Passage of UPK in New York was the result of a prosperous economic climate that allowed diametrically opposed policies to be passed simultaneously. While the state had a long history of public funding and a well-established early childhood advocacy community, none of the advocates expected UPK to emerge in 1997. The policy change was volatile and the result of a compromise with the governor to enact property tax cuts and a phased in implementation of UPK. Unfortunately for New York, the economic and political climate was about to experience a drastic change that would create a long-term struggle to fund universal preschool.

## Oklahoma

Unlike Georgia and New York, in which the development of universal preschool was linked to a high-profile election and received considerable media coverage, the development of universal preschool in Oklahoma evolved quietly through a series of incremental changes. The preschool program began in 1980 with a small pilot program funded by the state legislature. The program was started when Dr. Ramona Paul at the State Department of Education was asked by the elected State Superintendent what she would like to see for early education. She said a program for four year olds just like kindergarten (personal communication, Oklahoma City, September 16, 2005). She wanted high standards with a 1:10 teacher-student ratio and maximum group size of twenty. She wanted the preschool program to be taught by certified teachers who were employed by the public schools so that salaries and benefits would be comparable to K–12 teachers (thereby decreasing turnover, a significant problem in the low-wage child care industry and a main factor in program quality). It was also important to her that the pilot program be open to all children without income eligibility rules, because she felt strongly about the power of children learning from each other (Paul, Ramona, personal communication, Oklahoma City, September 16, 2005). The State Superintendent agreed and Paul moved forward to develop a pilot program together with representatives from Head Start and the Department of Human Services. But the creation of the pilot preschool program was not without opposition. According to Paul, some legislators opposed the program because "if we provide preschool women will go to work" (personal communication, Oklahoma City, September 16, 2005), despite the fact that over half of the women in Oklahoma were already in the labor force (United States Bureau of the Census 1981). However the opposition did not prevent the program from being funded as a line item by the legislature. Twenty-four sites, in urban and rural areas, were selected based on a competitive grant program open to public schools.

While there was no coverage of the pilot program in the newspaper for the capital region, the *Oklahoman*, a blip of coverage in 1984 revealed the struggle over the framing of public provision of preschool. This occurred when State Superintendent of Education Dr. John Folks, an elected official, advocated for education reform that included making kindergarten mandatory and creating school-centered early childhood education. Folks reported to the press, "We could eliminate many of our problems in schools if we could identify the educational needs of our students at an early age" (Killackey 1984, 1). This position had been held by the Oklahoma Department of Education (ODOE); however, it was a framing that would take twenty years to be fully constructed. Folks's recommendations had the support of the state school board, but as the *Oklahoman* reported, "the issue over whether children should be in a formal school setting prior to the age of 5 is one that is hotly debated among both educators and parents" (Killackey 1984, 1). The opposition was from those who believed young children would be better cared for at home than in organized settings, a continuation of the opposition Dr. Paul faced when starting the pilot program.

The pilot program continued to operate with annual appropriations until 1990. At that time Secretary of Education Dr. Sandy Garrett, a former first-grade teacher with a strong commitment to early childhood, together with House Education Committee Chairwoman Carolyn Thompson and Senate Education Committee Chairwoman Bernice Shedrick, worked to advance preschool. The three policy entrepreneurs' main goal was to stabilize funding for the preschool program by shifting it into the state school funding formula (Garrett, Sandy, telephone communication, September 7, 2006). The "policy window" for preschool opened in 1990 when Oklahoma undertook major education reform that resulted in passage of HB 1017, The Education Reform Act. Preschool policy entrepreneurs were able to, in Kingdon's phrase (1995), "ride the wave" of school reform.

Leading up to HB 1017, there were fairly distinct groups of policy entrepreneurs pushing for preschool and K–12 education reform. Republican Governor Henry Bellmon was the main advocate for K–12 education reform. He was aided in reform efforts by The Oklahoma Academy for State Goals, a nonpartisan, public policy membership organization. The Academy's 1989 conference on education resulted in eleven recommendations for education reform. While the primary focus of the conference was K–12, two of the recommendations involved preschool: (1) establishing new quality preschool programs and (2) improving the quality of existing programs (Oklahoma Academy for State Goals 2005). After the conference, a task force was created to "craft and promote HB

1017" (Oklahoma Academy for State Goals 2005, 14). The Academy deems this conference and subsequent task force report as a landmark event: "Academy research, public debate, and committed membership through and after the conference contributed immeasurably to the statewide awareness that education reform was vital for any hope of economic development and improvements in quality of life" (Oklahoma Academy for State Goals 2005, 14).

At the same time that the governor's task force gained momentum for education reform, support for preschool changes also gained support. The two streams of policy alternatives started to become entwined when, in the summer of 1989, a special legislative session was held. In August of 1989, House Speaker Steve Lewis proposed reducing class size, expanding preschool, and making full-day kindergarten mandatory (Greiner 1989, 12). The *Oklahoman* reported that Lewis's proposal generated some controversy; however, the controversy was not over public school provision of preschool but over whether there would be enough teachers to staff the classrooms (Casteel 1989, 1). Yet, opposition to public education of four year olds was still in force. Former Secretary of Education Sandy Garrett, who was elected as State Superintendent in 1990, explained and others confirmed that in 1990 the public education of four year olds was still controversial. Similar to the opposition Ramona Paul faced when starting the preschool pilot program, many in Oklahoma believed that "young children should be at home with their mothers." The stubbornness of the old framing resulted in policy entrepreneurs reaching a compromise in which the state would provide preschool free of charge only to Head Start–eligible families but would allow school districts to set sliding scale fees for families above Head Start income limits (Garrett, Sandy, telephone communication, September 7, 2006). Policy entrepreneurs could gain consensus that the state needed to provide early childhood education for poor children but there was insufficient support to open the program to all children. Therefore, they focused on achieving their primary goal: shifting the preschool program to the state school–funding formula. The policy entrepreneurs were successful and won a .5 reimbursement level for half-day preschool. And, as part of the changes, they were able to formalize standards for the preschool program (70 Oklahoma Statutes Annotated § 1–114 2004). With passage of this reform, Oklahoma created a statewide, targeted preschool program funded through the state school funding formula.

Despite the fact that the Education Reform Act was major legislation, coverage in the *Oklahoman* was again very limited. The entire bill received only a few paragraphs in the back of the paper when the Senate passed its version, SB 183, by a voice vote of 28-18 in February 1989, and of this, only one phrase was devoted to preschool (Greiner 1989, 12). The only other blip of coverage was in August of 1989 when House Speaker Lewis proposed reducing class size, expanding preschool, and making all-day kindergarten mandatory (Casteel 1989, 1; Greiner 1989, 12). The lack of media attention to preschool, which continued throughout the 1990s, ended up working to the advantage of those seeking to expand the preschool program because it allowed preschool supporters to stay beneath the radar of potential opponents who strongly held the "young children should be home with their mothers" view.[4]

The expansion of Oklahoma's targeted preschool program into a universal preschool program came from a series of incremental changes in the 1990s. A 1993 legislative change created an incentive system for the kindergarten program that would prove pivotal in framing the case for expanded preschool. In that year the legislature, under pressure from rural school districts with declining enrollments, passed an amendment that enabled school districts to be reimbursed for four year olds in kindergarten (70 Oklahoma Statutes Annotated § 1–114 2004). This change, which came to be known as the "4's in K" program, allowed rural areas with excess capacity in kindergarten classrooms to admit four year olds and receive the same reimbursement weight, 1.3, as for five year olds (70 Oklahoma Statute Annotated § 18–201.1 2004). In the 1990 school reform, half-day kindergarten was made mandatory but schools received the same reimbursement rate regardless of whether they offered a full- or half-day program. This meant that it was more cost effective for schools to offer half-day kindergarten because one teacher could teach a morning and an afternoon class of twenty children each. Because the reimbursement rate for preschool was only .5 for a half-day program while the reimbursement rate was 1.3 for half-day (or full-day) kindergarten, there was an incentive for schools to channel four year olds into the 4's in K program rather than the preschool program. The 1993 legislation created an incentive for school districts to expand the number of half-day kindergarten classrooms and, as one person interviewed put it, to "fill them up with four-year-olds."

Initially the expansion incentive was limited because the program was expensive; state reimbursements were based on the prior year's enrollment, which meant school districts that admitted four year olds into kindergarten had to cover the first year of the program before they would receive increased state aid. However, after a few years the legislature shifted the date for enrollment count to the current year, which then created a greater incentive for public schools to expand the number of kindergarten classrooms (70 Oklahoma Statute Annotated § 18–201.1 2004). While placing four year olds in kindergarten was individually rational for the school district, especially in the rural areas with declining enrollments, the kindergarten expansion was collectively irrational because adding more students without increasing the total amount of state aid diluted the amount of per-pupil-aid each school received (Eddins, Joe, telephone communication, July 5, 2006).

According to advocates, there was an expectation that the 4's in K program would grow in enrollment as school districts realized the potential to serve four year olds with a kindergarten reimbursement rate. Because of the potential impact of dilution, advocates were able to use 4's in K growth as a useful framing device for advancing changes to the preschool program. Preschool advocates framed the 4's in K program as a "bad" program that was developmentally inappropriate for children. They argued, instead, in favor of increasing the reimbursement rate for preschool in order to provide the incentive for public schools to expand the "good" (i.e., developmentally appropriate) preschool program. A strong proponent of this framing was Representative Joe Eddins (D-Vinita). Eddins was elected to the Oklahoma House of Representatives in 1995 and soon became an ardent supporter of preschool education. A cattle rancher without prior background in early education, Eddins was appointed to the House Education Committee. As a freshman legislator, Eddins turned to Bob Harbison for help to understand early childhood and the two "hit it off." Eddins states, "Everything I know about early education I learned from Bob" (telephone communication, July 5, 2006).

Representative Eddins looked to Bob Harbison because Harbison had become a strong advocate for early education in Oklahoma. Harbison's commitment to early education grew from volunteer research he undertook for the Tulsa Chamber of Commerce in the early 1990s. In the late 1980s, the Chamber conducted a study of educational issues in Tulsa and found that nearly 25 percent of first-grade children were not ready to learn and that Tulsa had over a 25 percent high school drop-out rate. The Chamber research linked drop-out rates to the potential for high future social costs growing from incarceration and enrollment in social programs. The Chamber study asked, "what can we do *now* to better prepare our children through education, to increase their opportunities for success after high school?" (Tulsa Chamber of Commerce 1990a, 1 emphasis in the original). In the spring of 1990, Tulsa Chamber of Commerce members went to Yale University to meet with Professor Edward Zigler and toured the School of the 21st Century.[5] Through a series of meetings, the Chamber gained an appreciation for Zigler's vision at the same time they were learning about the limited participation of children in early education programs in Tulsa. By the end of 1990, the Tulsa Chamber had committed itself to making "the City of Tulsa a world-class center for early childhood education" and had developed a comprehensive plan for services (Tulsa Chamber of Commerce 1990a, 5; Tulsa Chamber of Commerce 1990b). Bob Harbison, a retired corporate executive, was asked to evaluate the plan and recommend further action. Harbison did not have any background in early childhood issues but had served on many boards of nonprofit service organizations and was looking for a new challenge. In the summer of 1991, he agreed to undertake "a 90-day project to see what could be done for early education" (Harbison, Bob, telephone communication, July 10, 2006). It required ten months instead of three, but he took the materials the task force had collected and turned it into a strategy for early education. Thus began Harbison's role as a committed policy entrepreneur for early childhood.

For three consecutive years, Eddins tried to change the education of four year olds in Oklahoma through amendments to raise the reimbursement rate for full- and half-day preschool programs. His attempts failed in 1996 and 1997, but both Eddins and Harbison say that those failures were important in winning people over. Eddins reports that in the first two years the amendments were opposed by representatives of rural school districts that benefited from the 4's in K situation. Eddins attempted to persuade superintendents that placing four year olds in kindergarten was developmentally inappropriate, but he also told them about the negative impact of dilution when some of the bigger school districts started admitting 4's in K, which would have decreased the amount of per-pupil aid for all schools (Eddins, Joe, telephone communication, July 5, 2006). By 1998, Eddins's arguments had become increasingly persuasive.

At the beginning of the 1998 session, Eddins and Harbison were pushing for increasing the preschool reimbursement weight from .5 to .7, as they had done the prior two years. This time they were also advocating for an increase in the income eligibility to 185 percent of the federal poverty level, and for elimination of the 4's in K program. It is important to note that neither Eddins nor Harbison was advocating for universal preschool in 1998. As discussed below, universal access was a welcome surprise. At this point, they were trying to gain support for increased reimbursement weight, increase in income-eligibility level, and elimination of the 4's in K program. To gain support for the amendment, Eddins even went as far as talking to each of the 101 House legislators about the importance of replacing the "bad" 4's in K program with a "good" pre-K program (Eddins, Joe, telephone communication, July 5, 2006). He persuaded them that if they supported the amendment, public schools in their districts would get reimbursed for half- or full-day preschool programs, which would be attractive to the schools and allow them to end the practice of placing four year olds in kindergarten without incurring a loss in state aid. In the end, Eddins won a unanimous vote of 99-0 for the amendment.

When Eddins met with the Democratic-controlled Senate leadership to advocate for preschool he encountered some opposition. Leadership of the Senate was protective of their school districts with 4's in K. They wanted to be assured that their school districts would not be penalized financially by the legislative changes. Eddins reports that once school superintendents supported the bill, then Senators supported it. However there were still preschool opponents who believed four year olds should be at home with their mothers. Eddins found that there was a generational divide; while the older generation still thought children should be home with their mothers, the younger generation of educated professionals accepted the claim of a causal link between early education and educational success (Eddins, Joe, telephone communication, July 5, 2006). In the end, senators voted along party lines.

While Eddins worked to convince fellow legislators, State Superintendent Sandy Garrett was working with the Appropriation and Budget Committees in the Senate and House to calculate the expected cost if the income eligibility was removed. Apparently, the original source for removing the income eligibility was the House Appropriations Chairman Representative Jim Hamilton, but the interesting twist in the move to universal coverage is that it did not originate from the policy advocates themselves. At some point in committee deliberations Representative Hamilton said, "let's put the [financing] weight in for all children" (Garrett, Sandy, telephone communication, September 7, 2006). By that time, preschool enrollments had grown and had gained widespread acceptance; however, conservatives in the state still held on to the belief that children should be cared for by their mothers until school age. The framing of the change was important in its ultimate success: By using the simplified language of "putting the weight in for all children," the change appeared incremental. Superintendent Garrett is careful to point out that they never used the term "universal" because that would not have garnered the necessary political support (telephone communication, September 7, 2006). The committee passed a version that increased the financing weight for half-day preschool to .7 and full-day preschool to 1.3, the same weight as for a kindergarten classroom, and opened enrollment to all four-year-olds regardless of family income (70 Oklahoma Statute Annotated § 18–201.1 2004).

Several sources interviewed indicated that one of the reasons for the unanimous support of universal preschool in the Oklahoma House of Representatives was that very few legislators realized the impact of the changes. The changes were incremental and framed as correcting the 4's in

K "problem." In addition, the school code was complex and difficult to understand. For example, the section on child-reimbursement weights now reads, "Multiply the membership of each subparagraph of this paragraph by the weight assigned to such subparagraph of this paragraph and add the totals together to determine the weighted pupil grade level calculation for a school district" (70 Oklahoma Statute Annotated § 18–201.1 2004). Given the tortured syntax in the code and the complexity of the weighting schemes in the total aid calculation, it is not surprising that few legislators took the time to understand it.

In terms of interest groups, several sources indicated that there was only support for the expansion and no effective opposition. According to "the mother of preschool" Ramona Paul, the American Federation of Teachers in Oklahoma City and the National Education Association representing others in the state supported these changes (personal communication, September 16, 2005).

Head Start supported the changes to the preschool program, though Head Start Collaboration Director Eva Carter was initially suspicious (telephone communication, September 22, 2006; Eddins, Joe, telephone communication, July 5, 2006). Two major factors contributed to winning Carter's support. First, Representative Eddins convinced her that expansion of the preschool program would increase revenues to serve Head Start children. While on the surface this seems illogical, he persuaded her that public schools could continue to collaborate with Head Start to provide services for four year olds. At the time of these discussions, both Eddins and Harbison say the universal access issue had not yet been raised. With a targeted preschool program, both Harbison and Eddins envisioned the public school preschool program collaborating with Head Start to deliver a full-day preschool program for low-income children. Since Carter's intent was to arrange collaborations, Eddins was identifying a key linkage to gain the support of Head Start. Second, Carter, as well as many other advocates, wanted to end the practice of placing four year olds in kindergarten, and expansion of the preschool program was one way to achieve that goal. In the end, Carter and the Oklahoma Head Start Association supported the expansion of preschool, which was good news for Eddins because Head Start had seen the expansion of public preschool as a threat in the early 1990s. Head Start and the ODOE had been on opposite sides of issues such as credentialing of teachers, protection of existing Head Start programs in public schools, and public schools becoming Head Start designees (Carter, Eva, telephone communication, September 22, 2006). Head Start was successful in protecting itself in these areas and had the potential for mounting opposition for the 1998 expansion. However, once Carter and other members of the Oklahoma

Head Start Association were convinced of the benefits of the preschool program changes, they joined Eddins and other child advocates in educating legislators to ensure passage of the legislation (Carter, Eva, telephone communication, September 22, 2006).

Another potential source of opposition was the Oklahoma Department of Human Services (ODHS). Since ODHS licenses child care centers and administers child care subsidy programs, care of four year olds had been under ODHS jurisdiction until the public preschool program was created. According to Nancy vonBargen, former Director of the Division of Child Care (DCC) at ODHS, they were engaged in conversations prior to passage of legislation and their main concern was the impact of the preschool program on child care programs. DCC also wanted to see collaboration with child care mandated in the legislation but were not successful in that regard (vonBargen, Nancy, telephone communication, October 17, 2005). In Oklahoma, the public school preschool program is taught by a certified teacher employed by the public school but preschool instruction can also take place in private child care, Head Start, or in public school settings (Paul, Ramona, personal communication, September 16, 2006). Because collaboration is voluntary, public school districts decide whether to collaborate with Head Start, private providers, or both. Some districts, such as Tulsa, have extensive collaboration with Head Start. But others, such as in Norman, struggled to bridge organizational culture and regulatory divides (Allen, Stephanie, personal communication, Norman, September 16, 2005). In Oklahoma, the individual school district has the power to decide whether it collaborates and to determine how the preschool funds will be expended, which means that there is variation across the state in how preschool affects the private child care industry and Head Start. But even though the final version of the legislation did not alter the voluntary collaboration language, it did not trigger countermobilization. As vonBargen noted, while she wanted mandated collaboration, its absence was not enough for her to oppose the legislation. Her hope was that preschool expansion would free up child care subsidy funds so that ODHS could raise reimbursement rates for children ages zero to three. According to vonBargen, that is exactly what has happened and the changes stabilized funding for preschool (vonBargen, Nancy, telephone communication, October 17, 2005).

A likely source of opposition was the Oklahoma Child Care Association; however, there was no organized opposition in the form of lobbying or any public relations campaign in the media to oppose preschool program changes. Interviews with child care industry representatives yielded expressions of frustration and fears about losing business but also a degree of fatalism (Stemp, Leona; Dennis Wells; Beverly Wells;

Angie Davis, personal communication, Oklahoma City, September 16, 2005). Unlike in Georgia where the transition was abrupt, the preschool program growth up until 1998 had been gradual in Oklahoma, giving the child care industry the opportunity to adapt. In the early 1990s, public preschool was primarily part-day programs (2½ hours) for low-income children, which allowed the private child care providers to supply the wraparound care (i.e., before and after preschool). Providers could receive the full-day reimbursement rate from ODHS if they supplied at least four hours of care. But since the 1998 changes created a full- and half-day weight for all four year olds, it provided an incentive for public schools to expand to full-day (i.e., six hour) programs and attract subsidized children as well as children from families who could afford to pay market rates. Because of the potential loss of revenue, the child care industry had good reason to oppose the 1998 changes; however, this did not occur. Representative Eddins, who had met with them to discuss the program changes, stated that they realized that the bill was going to pass regardless of whether they chose to oppose it. Some interviewed indicated that much of the reason why they did not organize effectively to oppose preschool was a lack of knowledge of the policy environment (Stemp, Leona; Dennis Wells; Beverly Wells; Angie Davis, personal communication, Oklahoma City, September 16, 2005). Child care centers, with the exception of large chains like KinderCare, have limited administrative capacity. In other words, they are so busy running their centers that they do not take the time to engage in the legislative policy environment. This is common across the case studies in this book.

But in Oklahoma there were concurrent changes in the child care delivery system that may have helped smooth potential opposition from private child care to expansion of the preschool program. The Division of Child Care at the Oklahoma Department of Human Services was able to implement rule changes in 1998 that represented a paradigmatic shift in child care. The changes were aimed at improving service quality, expanding access to more families, helping parents evaluate the quality of care, and making child care more affordable (vonBargen, Nancy, telephone communication, October 10, 2006). Oklahoma has strong licensing standards for child care, but licensing in child care is focused primarily on health and safety. ODHS wanted to see gains in the level of quality in service delivery that could not be achieved through licensing standards alone. After the federal welfare reform of 1996, a work group on child care came up with the idea of a quality rating system in which higher-quality centers would receive higher reimbursement rates. ODHS developed the Star Rating System, one of the first in the country, in 1997 and launched it in 1998. Centers with the highest rating of three stars receive an enhanced reimbursement rate for meeting all of the state quality guidelines and being accredited with the National Association for the Education of Young Children. This provides an incentive for centers to raise quality by pursuing accreditation (Gormley 2002) but it also creates an incentive for high-quality centers to accept subsidized children. vonBargen noted that through the development of this system ODHS commissioners and advocates were educated about quality child care, which allowed them to achieve major change to accessibility and affordability. When welfare roles dramatically decreased after the 1996 federal welfare reform, states were allowed to use Temporary Assistance to Needy Families (TANF) reserve funds for family support services. At that point, Oklahoma shifted TANF reserve funds to expand child care subsidies. This allowed them to raise eligibility from 130 percent of the federal poverty level to 185 percent and to alter the copay schedule to make it more affordable. vonBargen noted that everybody was on board for these changes, and the emerging research that linked investment in child care as a successful means of keeping families off welfare helped legitimize the changes beyond the child care policy community (telephone communication, October 10, 2006).

According to Harbison and others, these changes in the child care system decreased potential opposition from private child care to preschool expansion. Even though private child care was "losing" four year olds to public schools, they were gaining child care enrollment (if they accepted subsidized children). Elite child care centers that did not accept subsidized children would likely experience declining enrollments if parents shifted their children to public preschool programs; however, with the Star Rating System, if a high-quality center accepted subsidized children, it would receive adequate reimbursement. Anecdotal reports indicate that many church-based, part-day preschool programs have closed and that only the elite preschools with strong reputations have survived, but there has not been a substantial effort to organize to oppose preschool expansion.

Another reason provided for the absence of child care industry opposition was that even though collaboration was not mandated in the legislation, there was the potential for it to develop. Assistant State Superintendent Ramona Paul noted that they preferred a voluntary approach in which ODOE encouraged superintendents to collaborate (personal communication, Oklahoma City, September 16, 2005). From ODHS's perspective, the expanded public funding for four year olds by ODOE would free up child care subsidy dollars that could then be used to expand funding available for children ages zero to three. In addition, full-day kindergarten would be implemented by the year 2011 in Oklahoma. Public schools that face physical space constraints due to increased preschool and kindergarten enrollment would have to collaborate with child care in order to serve the public demand for preschool services (vonBargen, Nancy, telephone communication, October 17, 2005). The end result was that the child care industry did not launch an effective opposition campaign against the preschool expansion.

By April of 1998, all of the groundwork had been laid and a policy window opened for preschool. There was agreement among legislators, school superintendents, and child advocates that 4's in K was a problem and that voluntary preschool for all four-year-olds was the answer. According to Eddins, Carter, and others, school superintendents' support of the preschool program had increased and they had informed their elected representatives who, in turn, shifted from opposition to support. Except for the few legislators who clung to the belief that young children should be at home with their mothers despite the high labor force participation of mothers in Oklahoma, the controversy among legislators was whether four year olds would be educated in kindergarten or preschool. Either way they were going to be in educational settings (Eddins, Joe, telephone communication, July 5, 2006). Once House Representatives realized it was a choice between the "bad" 4's in K and the "good" preschool program, they sided with the preschool program. In the Senate, the vote went along party lines, but the Democrats were in the majority so the bill passed. When the bill reached Governor Frank Keating's desk, he ended his prior opposition and signed the bill.

Passage of the preschool program changes in Oklahoma happened quickly in 1998 without advocacy opposition or substantial media coverage. Neither Harbison, Eddins, nor ODOE characterizes it as a stealth bill, as others have (Kirp 2007), but the reality is that once the bill came out of committee in April, it was voted on, passed in both houses, and sent to the governor who then signed it in May. There was no coverage of the bill in the *Oklahoman*. Without significant opposition from the child care industry, ODHS, the media, or interest groups, universal preschool in Oklahoma quietly emerged.

**West Virginia**

The "stealth" descriptor for passing universal preschool rightfully belongs to West Virginia. The 2002 passage of universal preschool legislation in West Virginia was abrupt and seemingly out of no where for all but a very small inner circle of legislators and political appointees. Preschool was inserted into Senate Bill 247 by Senator Lloyd Jackson, chairman of the Senate Education Committee. The bill included pay raises for teachers among other issues important to education interests (Tomblin and Sprouse

2002). The preschool section was only four pages of a fifty-one-page bill. As discussed more fully below, Senator Jackson wrote the legislation with three of his staff members, and lobbied key members of the Senate and House to ensure its passage at literally the 11th hour of the last day of the legislative session. The legislation was passed without the knowledge or involvement of early childhood advocates, civil servants responsible for implementing the program, and to the astonishment of the supporters of the Educare program, the preexisting early childhood program.

Senator Jackson worked with the top political appointees in both the West Virginia Department of Health and Human Resources (WVDHHR) and the West Virginia Department of Education (WVDOE) to persuade them to support preschool. In order to win their support, the legislation provides WVDHHR with the power of first review of all the county preschool plans.[6] If WVDHHR does not approve a plan, then the county will not receive preschool funds. Counties can appeal the decision through circuit court but this aspect of the legislation provides WVDHHR with a rather large stick to force public schools to collaborate with Head Start and private child care providers. Jackson secured support of key political appointees but still had to overcome political opposition in the House.

The main political opposition came from House Chair of Education Committee Representative Jerry Mezzatesta. His opposition was based on a concern that state funding would replace federal Head Start funding for preschool services. In West Virginia, the population has been declining since the 1960s, and some public schools had started providing preschool to boost enrollments. McDowell County, one of the poorest in the state, began offering preschool but did not coordinate with Head Start. The two programs ended up competing for children and Head Start enrollment declined, leading to a decrease in federal funding of several hundred thousand dollars (Huebner, Bill, personal communication, Charleston, August 10, 2005). This scenario occurred in other counties and Representative Mezzatesta wanted the state to maximize the use of federal dollars in preschool provision. In order for Jackson's preschool legislation to pass, Head Start agencies would have to be solidly involved with any expansion of publicly funded preschool. To address this concern, and those of Head Start, Jackson's bill required public schools to collaborate with county Head Start agencies. If the Head Start agency refused to sign the plan, it would prevent the public school district from receiving state preschool funding.

Senator Jackson persuaded House Speaker Robert Kiss to support preschool. To gain House support for preschool, Speaker Kiss moved from his chair to the floor of the assembly to address Representatives, an unusual act that emphasized his support of preschool and aided in its successful passage (Jackson, Lloyd, personal communication, Charleston, August 10, 2005). Senator Jackson framed the issue as an important investment to improve educational outcomes for West Virginia's children and since the preschool program did not require additional budget outlays at the time of passage, there was no opposition to preschool based on budgetary concerns. Similar to Oklahoma, West Virginia has declining K–12 enrollments, which meant that the new program was not expected to require new funding in its initial years. In addition to the declining K–12 enrollments, approximately 40–50 percent of four year olds were already in a private preschool program and the assumption was that some parents would choose not to send their children to public preschool (Jackson, Lloyd, personal communication, August 10, 2005).

The new program mandated universal access of preschool to all four-year-olds by 2012. When asked about the choice of a ten-year implementation framework, Jackson responded that West Virginia had made the mistake of rushing all-day kindergarten implementation in 1989. Counties were forced to expand to full-day kindergarten and it led to seventeen counties running a deficit. The rushed implementation also created ill will with private child care providers when the public schools began serving five year olds because it negatively impacted their enrollments. With a ten-year implementation framework, Jackson thought that it would provide sufficient time to develop the program, build political support for the program, and manage controversies among the diverse interests (personal communication, Charleston, August 10, 2005). Without immediate budgetary impact and 2012 seeming very far away, the legislation passed.

While the top political appointees were involved in the preschool program negotiations, none of the line staff or early childhood advocates was aware that a preschool program was being discussed, let alone that legislation had been drafted. Passage of the universal preschool program came as a total shock to the civil servants in the WVDOE and WVDHHR. As discussed more fully in the following chapter, civil servants had to scramble to implement the preschool program for the 2003–04 school year.

Passage of universal preschool also shocked those who supported the existing Educare program, which had been started in 1998 by the Governor's Cabinet on Children and Family. Educare aimed to provide "financial resources to coordinate existing program and funding streams to better serve children and families" (West Virginia Development Office 2006, 6). Referred to as "glue money" because it was used to bring people together, the Educare program funded the creation of consortia that identified critical early education and care needs. The funding was used for a variety of purposes, including equipment, bonuses for staff salaries, supplementing sliding scale fee structures, professional development, developing new programs or expanding existing programs (Gebhard, Barbara, personal communication, Cross Lanes, WV, August 10, 2005). Initially the West Virginia legislature appropriated $1 million for the program to create five sites. In 2001, $500,000 more was appropriated to fund an additional three sites (West Virginia Development Office 2006, 6). In 2002, the Governor's Cabinet on Children and Family was seeking to expand to thirteen sites and to pass statutory language to firmly establish the program. However, soon Educare supporters had dropped the statutory language legislation due to political opposition and were fighting to maintain funding for the existing eight sites. On the last day of the legislative session, the House version of the bill maintained existing funding for Educare and the Senate version had increased funding. Supporters expected the end result to be no worse than level funding; however, they awoke the next morning to find that the Educare budget was zeroed out and universal preschool had taken its place (Gebhard, Barbara, personal communication, Cross Lanes, WV, August 10, 2005; Pore, Renata, personal communication, Charleston, August 9, 2005).

The demise of Educare was precipitous and unexpected by the Governor's Cabinet on Children and Family. The reasons for Educare's demise according to those closely involved with the process are: (1) that the program would have been too expensive to expand statewide; and (2) Educare did not have broad enough political support. First, Educare was a comprehensive approach to birth to preschool programs, but with limited availability. When asked about Educare, Senator Jackson stated that the program was high quality but that the evaluation of the program indicated that the cost to expand the program statewide would be far beyond what a poor state could afford. In his mind, it was better to have a universal program targeting four year olds than a limited program for zero to four year olds (personal communication, Charleston, August 10, 2005). Another key factor in the decision was that eliminating Educare would not have serious political repercussions. When the program was initially funded, it did not have strong support in the legislature and was seen as a pet project of then Governor Cecil H. Underwood. Subsequent governors were not as committed; Governor Bob Wise tried unsuccessfully to move Educare out of the Governor's Cabinet on Children and Family and into WVDHHR and Governor Joe Manchin III, elected in 2004, cut the funding for staff positions to the Governor's Cabinet on Children and Family and moved all the remaining child programs to WVDHHR. In addition to lack of support from subsequent governors, because Educare was administered by the Governor's Cabinet, it did not include WVDOE or the WVDHHR, the two agencies involved with early childhood programs. Without building linkages with these two key agencies and deepening support in the legislature, the

Educare program was politically vulnerable. In the end the Educare program was too expensive and dispensable without serious political costs.[7]

Media coverage of preschool in the *Charlestown Gazette* was limited to a column by a child advocate who was decrying the end of the Educare program (Pratt 2002). No one immediately rallied to support preschool but no one actively opposed it either. Prior to the passage of preschool there had been media coverage of early childhood linking public investment in early education to economic development. For example, Governor Underwood made that connection explicit in 2000, when he stated "Investing in child care is an investment in economic development for today and for our future workforce" (Governor Underwood quoted in Smith 2000, 1C). This statement was made after the state raised the income limits for subsidized child care from 150 percent of the federal poverty level to 200 percent.

Several sources indicated that consensus was building for the state government to take action with respect to early education. But while a policy change in early childhood education was expected in West Virginia, the particular policy alternative selected was not expected. Multiple sources indicated that there was an assumption that there would be an expansion or an alternative version of Educare. According to all sources interviewed, advocacy for preschool as a separate policy alternative did not exist. The selection of the preschool policy alternative in 2002 appears to have come from Senator Jackson. In the past, the education of four year olds had surfaced on the agenda due to the Head Start funds versus state funds controversy discussed above. State funding for the education of four year olds was not a new idea but previously the decision to provide it was made by individual school districts.

According to Jackson, he chose to champion universal preschool because of his exposure to the scientific research on early brain development, personal history, and a desire to leave a legacy of improved educational outcomes for West Virginia's children (personal communication, Charleston, August 10, 2005). The research on brain development and the importance of the early years was brought to Senator Jackson's attention by the Southern Regional Education Board (SREB). The SREB publicized the research through publications and meetings (Denton 2001). Because of this exposure, Jackson came to the conclusion that in order to improve educational outcomes of West Virginia's children, they needed to invest in quality early education programs. If educational outcomes were going to improve for older children, then he was convinced that the state had to start educating them at younger ages.

But this view was not new in West Virginia. When the legislature created the PROMISE scholarship, championed by Jackson, in 2000 and the

Educare program in 1998, they were inspired in part by Georgia's "book-ends" approach to education in which the lottery was used to fund the Hope Scholarship and the preschool program (Pratt 2002). Similar to Georgia's Hope Scholarship, the PROMISE Scholarship provides college tuition and fees for qualifying students to attend the institution of their choice. When Educare was created, a state official from Georgia expressed regret that her own state's program did not start until children were four year olds (Pratt 2002). As one Educare supporter lamented, if Senator Jackson had wanted to lead rather than follow, he could have chosen to invest in Educare expansion.

Jackson's choice to push for universal education for four year olds rather than a comprehensive program with limited accessibility was influenced, according to him, by his personal history. When his children were young there was no preschool available in his town. His wife quit her job in order to drive the children forty-five minutes each way to a high-quality preschool. As a Democrat, he said that he felt strongly that everyone should have access to high-quality programs and not just those who can afford to live on one income and have the time for such a commute (personal communication, Charleston, August 10, 2005).

But Senator Jackson was planning to run for governor in 2004, and a political calculation must have also influenced the timing of the preschool policy change. Jackson was well aware of the successful campaign strategy of Zell Miller. By championing the creation of the PROMISE Scholarship in 2000 and the creation of universal preschool in 2002, Jackson tried to replicate Miller's gubernatorial campaign success. A *Charlestown Gazette* reporter noted that the timing of the preschool legislation was such that Senator Jackson was planning to "go out with a bang" that would take him to the governor's mansion. Unfortunately for Jackson, he was defeated in the primary which meant that the preschool program lost its primary policy entrepreneur two years after its creation.

**Analysis**

A commonality among the four state cases discussed above is that prior to the passage of the legislation, the preschool policy alternative was not being championed by policy advocates. There was no advocacy coalition, mature or nascent, working to attach the universal preschool policy solution to a newly elevated problem. In each case, the policy entrepreneurs were elected officials who were able to advance publicly funded preschool as their preferred policy alternative. Policy entrepreneurs pushed specifically for preschool programs but they did so in the absence of an advo-

Table 2.1
Pioneer State Program Requirements

## Quality Standards

| | Teacher Degree | Teacher Specialized Training | Maximum Class Size | Staff-child Ratio |
|---|---|---|---|---|
| Georgia | AA or Montessori diploma | Degree in ECE or meet Montessori requirements | 20 | 1:10 |
| New York | BA prior to 1978, MA after (public); AA or CDA (nonpublic) | Certification in Birth–Grade 2 (public), 9 credits toward CDA (nonpublic) | 20 | 1:9 |
| Oklahoma | BA | Early Childhood Certification | 20 | 1:10 |
| West Virginia | BA (pre-k), AA collaborative programs | See footnote* | 20 | 1:10 |

*Source*: National Institute for Early Education Research. 2008. The state of preschool: 2007. *The State of Preschool Yearbook*. Retrieved October 9, 2008, from http://nieer.org/yearbook/pdf/yearbook.pdf.

*Teachers in public school settings that are not collaboratives must be certified in birth–five, early childhood, preschool special needs, or elementary education (with a pre-K/K endorsement). Teachers in community collaborative settings must have a degree in child development/early childhood or in occupational development with an emphasis in child development/early childhood.

cacy coalition or policy subsystem. In some cases, the broader set of actors involved in early education and care might be construed as an issue network, but the fact remains that there was no coalition, subsystem, or network of actors pushing for publicly funded preschool in any of these states.

In Oklahoma, interviews indicate that the work of Eddins and Harbison did not have a foundation of advocates who were pushing for the preschool program changes. Both Eddins and Harbison worked hard to smooth relations with the child care interests (ODHS, Head Start, and private child care) but the impetus for change came from them, not from a broader coalition of actors. In West Virginia, the passage of universal preschool was a complete shock to the early childhood advocacy community, as well as to the civil servants who would be required to implement the program. The West Virginia early childhood community was supportive of Educare, the preexisting early childhood program, and focused on public policies that would address children from birth to age five, not a program focused specifically on four year olds. For the other two states, the policy entrepreneurs chose the preschool policy alternative as part of a larger change objective. In Georgia, because Zell Miller wanted to win the gubernatorial election, preschool only became part of his campaign strategy when he was pressed to elaborate on the programs that would be funded by his central campaign issue, the lottery for education. According to every published source and every person interviewed, the preschool policy alternative came from the Miller campaign and was not due to pressure from preschool advocates. In New York, Speaker of the Assembly Sheldon Silver included universal preschool as one of a combination of early education programs in the LADDER legislation. While early childhood advocates participated in drafting the legislation in New York, the emphasis of the advocates was on advancing the issues relating to children from birth-to-five years. Because Silver chose to focus on a program for four year olds, advocates rallied to support the program. But prior to that time, there was no separate advocacy activity focused on four year olds specifically.

The lack of advocates pushing for the preschool policy alternative does not fit with Kingdon's three streams model in which the problem, policy, and political streams converge to open a policy window. In his model, Kingdon made a distinction between the *visible cluster* (i.e., president and administration, Congress, media, political parties and campaigns) as more critical in setting the agenda versus the *hidden cluster* (academics and researchers, career bureaucrats, congressional staffers, and administrative appointees below the top level) as more critical in affecting the alternatives. But in the preschool policy change, the visible cluster achieved both. The policy and political streams were not merely entwined, they were the same. Rather than the advocates having a policy alternative and waiting to ride a wave, the wave came with a policy alternative attached to the political stream. The choice for early childhood advocates and child care providers was whether to ride the wave or get caught in the undertow. While this metaphor may be stretched to its limit, it is not unlike the metaphor used by the child care providers interviewed for this study who likened public preschool to a train that they had to get on or get left behind.

Just as there were no coalitions of advocates pushing for preschool policy change, there were also no opponents. No advocacy group took a stance opposing preschool in any of the pioneer states. Any opposition to preschool occurred in the political stream and was not due to the merits of preschool but was rather part of larger political battles or budgetary concerns. In Georgia, the opposition was to the lottery, not the establishment of a publicly funded preschool program. When the program was created in 1992, it was initially targeted for low-income children. No one organized to oppose a program that would benefit poor children, especially when Zell Miller was providing a new source of revenue to pay for it. In New York, the opposition from Governor Pataki was due to his stated policy goals of cutting property taxes and reducing spending on social programs. He did not oppose preschool in particular but rather opposed increased social spending in general. In Oklahoma, the opposition to expansion of the preschool program was due primarily to concerns about the revenue impact on school districts. Once Representative Eddins convinced lawmakers that preschool was preferable to the 4's in K program, they supported the expansion of the preschool program. In West Virginia, the only opposition was due to Representative Mezzatesta's concerns about maximizing the use of federal funding prior to expenditure of state resources. It is important to note that political opposition to public preschool was due to budgetary issues rather than philosophical opposition to the government providing education for four year olds.

The reason for the lack of opposition to public investment in preschool programs was the successful construction of a positive image. In each of the pioneer states, the preschool policy solution was linked to the problem of educational outcomes. Policy entrepreneurs created a causal story in which poor educational outcomes were the problem and the solution was public investment in early education. In the three Southern states, this construction had been advocated by the Southern Regional Education Board since the 1980s. In the rhetoric surrounding the preschool policy change, the framing of the issue was consistent with this construction: Invest in young children (in particular in a public preschool program) to improve the educational outcomes of our children.

It is no accident that Georgia, New York, and Oklahoma created (or expanded) their programs in the 1990s. As discussed in the introduction, the research on the importance of the early brain research and economic benefits of early childhood investments emerged during this time. These findings were hard to miss if you were involved in state government. In addition to the Southern Regional Education Board, the National Governors Association (NGA) had been championing early childhood investments since the late 1980s. Since 1995, NGA released twenty-three publications on early childhood education.[8] While there was little coverage of the issue nationally (McAdams et al. 2004), the topic was buzzing around various state-level associations.

The policy milieu, in Mintrom's terms (2000), was consistent in three of the pioneer states. The successful passage of preschool legislation was preceded by a softening-up period in which there was increased investment in both the education of four year olds and expansion to full-day kindergarten. In both Oklahoma and New York, preschool programs for low-income children had been in existence for decades. In New York, the targeted preschool program had been operating since the 1960s and there had been attempts to expand the program by Governor Cuomo in the 1980s as part of a broader early education agenda as well as by the Board of Regents in the 1990s. By the time Speaker Silver made universal preschool part of his LADDER programs, while no advocacy group had been pushing for it, expansion of preschool was a familiar policy issue. In Baumgartner and Jones's terminology, preschool was not a new principle in New York. This was also the case in Oklahoma. The preschool program in that state started in the 1980s. The incremental changes in the 1990s shifted the grant-funded pilot program into a statewide program with priority given to low-income children, and stabilized the program by incorporating it into the state school funding formula. When the 1998 changes made the program universal and increased the reimbursement rate, it was another incremental change. But in both Georgia and West Virginia, publicly funded preschool was a new principle. But even in those states, publicly funded preschool had already been implemented in some school districts.

In addition to softening-up for preschool, two states had recent legislative activity related to full-day kindergarten that provided lessons learned for policy entrepreneurs. In Georgia, previous experience with full-day kindergarten led policy entrepreneurs to stress that the preschool programs were voluntary. In the 1980s, when education reform made kindergarten full-day, it was controversial because, while it mandated that public schools provide full-day kindergarten, it remained optional for children to attend kindergarten. The controversy over full-day kindergarten marked the shift in construction from babysitting to early education. While the babysitting construction still existed in the early 1990s, by that time full-day kindergarten had been implemented for several years, and the public, as well as politicians, were adjusting to the idea of public provision of early education. In West Virginia, the rushed implementation of full-day kindergarten resulted in disgruntled school superintendents (and their elected leaders) because in high growth areas full-day kindergarten required local districts to fund school construction without any state support. The experience of full-day kindergarten led Senator Jackson to include a ten-year implementation period for universal preschool. The lengthy implementation timeframe was intended to provide time to build support for the preschool program before having to win increased budgetary support.

A major problem in analyzing the policy change process at the state level as opposed to the federal level is the lack of print sources. Baumgartner and Jones's (1993) methodology for analyzing policy change involves coding the frequency and tone of media coverage over a long period of time. While this strategy works well for research at the federal level, state media coverage of preschool was insufficient for meaningful analysis. Media coverage of the preschool policy change was not available in the newspapers of record for either West Virginia or Oklahoma. In West Virginia, the stealth legislation took everyone by surprise but even afterward the coverage of the preschool program was confined to a few editorials. In Oklahoma, with very few exceptions, passage of successive changes to the preschool program flew under the radar of the newspaper for the capital region. When the program was made universal in 1998 there was no mention of it in the *Oklahoman*. Even in Georgia and New York, where the news coverage of the policy process was extensive, there was little emphasis on preschool. In Georgia, the emphasis was on the gubernatorial election and the controversy over establishing a lottery. In New York, the coverage emphasized the ongoing budget battles between the Republican governor and the Democratic assembly. With some exceptions, in both Georgia and New York preschool was portrayed as a pawn in a larger battle rather than a topic for news coverage in its own right.

With the dearth of media coverage, defining the preschool policy image was left to the policy entrepreneurs themselves. Baumgartner and Jones state that policy entrepreneurs will attempt to create a powerful image that evokes only support or indifference by those not involved. The policy ideas are generally connected to core political values that can be communicated directly and simply through image and rhetoric. No where is this more evident than in Oklahoma when Representative Eddins personally persuaded House legislators to support the preschool program changes. He actively pushed the causal story that the 4's in K program was "bad" and that the preschool program was "good." After three attempts, it finally gained acceptance leading to the 1998 unanimous vote in the House. In Georgia, Zell Miller staked his gubernatorial candidacy on the success of the lottery for education. As part of this strategy, he constructed an image of a poor four-year-old being given the opportunity to learn in publicly funded preschool. There were some who wanted the lottery funding to go to other programmatic areas but Miller stood firm on his commitment to targeting lottery funds for education; however, Miller faced considerable challenges in successfully building a policy monopoly for the preschool program. In New York, Speaker Silver advocated for preschool along with reduced class size in K–3, and incentives for full-day kindergarten; however, he too had significant challenges in protecting the preschool program funding. In West Virginia, Senator Jackson successfully won support for preschool but then lost his gubernatorial bid, which imperiled support for the preschool program. The following chapter explores the implementation process for preschool. While all four pioneer states successfully passed legislation for preschool, only Oklahoma created a solid policy monopoly for preschool. The other states struggled and some have not yet achieved stability for their preschool programs.

# 3

# The Challenge of Establishing
# a Policy Monopoly

THE CREATION OF state funded preschool programs in the four pioneer states changed the status quo, but the question immediately arises whether each new preschool program was accepted as the new status quo or whether it was challenged. In three of the pioneer states, there were attempts to kill the programs after the legislation was passed. Oklahoma was the only state that did not experience challenges after passage of the preschool legislation. To understand why some states were successful and others were not, the concept of a policy monopoly as developed by Baumgartner and Jones (1993) provides a useful analytic approach.

In order to create a policy monopoly, the punctuated equilibrium model (PEM) requires (1) a definable institutional structure responsible for policy making that can effectively limit access to the policy process and (2) a powerful supporting idea associated with the institution generally connected to core political values, which can be communicated directly and simply through image and rhetoric (1993, 298). The first research question for this chapter is: Did the policy entrepreneurs establish a policy monopoly for preschool?

If policy entrepreneurs were successful in creating a policy monopoly, the question then becomes: Is the policy monopoly stable? According to Baumgartner and Jones (1993), policy monopoly stability is maintained by two conditions. The first is the degree to which the structure of institutions for preschool is stable. Change in institutional arrangements can destabilize the monopoly. The second factor is the definition of issues processed by those institutions. Change in issue definition can bring in new actors who can destabilize the policy monopoly. A stable issue definition is created when only one side of the argument is legitimate. In the case of preschool, there must be unified agreement that public investment in universal preschool is the right policy alternative.

The preschool programs in each of these states have survived to this day, but that does not mean that they have achieved a stable policy monopoly. Even though policy entrepreneurs successfully passed legislation, the preschool program could still be vulnerable to competing forces that could reverse the change or prevent the program from attaining stability. In Baumgartner and Jones's terminology, positive feedback allows political actors to achieve a larger marginal effect for their efforts. As they invest more and more political resources, they achieve greater gains. However, if there is negative feedback, they may move the system to a new status quo only to have competing forces lead to the return to the prior status quo. The four pioneer states' experiences vary considerably in their success at attaining stability for the new status quo.

A key issue in understanding policy monopolies is the role of policy entrepreneurs. In each of the cases, preschool legislation was championed by elected leadership: In Georgia, Governor Zell Miller; in Oklahoma, Representative Eddins; in West Virginia, Senator Jackson; and in New York, Assembly Speaker Sheldon Silver. While passage of legislation necessarily involves more than elected leaders, without their leadership the legislation could not have passed. However, there is a shift in the role of policy entrepreneurs once the legislation is passed and moves into the state bureaucracy for implementation. The legislature sets the institutional rules, but then the implementing agencies set the policies through administrative rulemaking and incremental day-to-day operations. Mintrom writes, "As decision-making moves from the most general levels to the most specific, we can expect two things to happen. First the number of actors attempting to influence policy will diminish. Second, policymaking will advance in an incremental fashion.... As these political institutions mature, the collection of actors paying ongoing attention to policymaking will decrease to a small, stable set" (Mintrom 2000, 55). The question for preschool is the extent to which the implementation process has decreased to a small, stable set of actors.

This chapter assesses the experience of each of the pioneer states after the passage of preschool legislation. While all four successfully passed legislation to create the program, they experienced considerable variation in establishing stable policy monopolies.

## Georgia

Universal preschool in Georgia has become the "third rail" of politics (Vollmer, Mike, telephone communication, June 30, 2005). Even with the 2002 election of the first Republican Governor in 135 years, support for the program has not decreased. This marks a change since the first few years of the program, which had a very rocky start and could easily have stagnated. While its inclusion in the constitution protected it from elimination, budget allocations could have been diverted to other education programs, such as the popular Hope Scholarship. The successful establishment of a policy monopoly for the preschool program required both institutional change and skillful reframing of the preschool program.

When the preschool program was created, its original target population was at-risk children. In the 1992–93 school year, the lottery had not yet been created and the initial pilot program was funded by the legislature at $3 million. It served 750 at-risk four-year-old children at twenty sites, mostly within local school systems (there was one Head Start provider, one private nonprofit provider, and one private college) (Office of School Readiness 2000). The lottery referendum passed that year by a slim 52 percent majority, and in 1993–94, lottery funds became available to fund an expansion of the program to an additional 167 new sites (12 sites continued from the previous year). This expansion into 100 of Georgia's 159 counties served approximately 8,700 at-risk four-year-olds (Office of School Readiness 2000). During the 1994–95 school year, the program expanded to serve 15,500 at-risk four-year-olds. However, despite the numerical expansion, political support for the program was weak due to institutional barriers and competing policy images of early childhood education.

In the 1990s, Georgia was becoming more conservative, contributing to a political environment in which a program targeting poor children would not survive. Preschool was being labeled a "welfare" program in an increasingly antiwelfare environment (Vollmer, Mike, telephone communication, June 30, 2005). After a close reelection in 1994, Governor Miller decided to remove the income limits on the preschool program and open it up to every four-year-old in the state. Because the lottery revenues were exceeding all expectations, funding was available to make the program universal without requesting additional funds from the legislature. This solved the problem of an increasingly conservative political climate, and was a critical factor in the survival of the program.

The move to universality also altered the local role in implementation of the program. In the pilot program years, the focus was on providing comprehensive, integrated services to the low-income families of participating children. Local coordinating councils were formed, consisting of agencies involved in providing or coordinating services to participating families. Each council had to include at least one parent of a child enrolled in the program, as well as representatives from the local Department of Family and Children Services, Health Department, and Board of

Education. The councils were responsible for: (1) developing the program application; (2) establishing collaborations to provide available services to the children and families; and (3) developing and evaluating the program on an ongoing basis. Each coordinating council had the authority to decide which types of providers could participate (such as family day care homes and/or child care centers). With the transition to universal preschool, the coordinating councils became less important since not all families would need coordinated services.

While the move to universality was successfully changing the image of preschool from a welfare program, it did not stop opposition from conservative Christian interests concerned about government infringement into the private realm. Family Concerns, Inc., a 501(c)3 nonprofit advocating a conservative Christian agenda (www.familyconcerns.net), created a controversy over antibias curriculum in the state preschool program. The National Association for the Education of Young Children (NAEYC) Anti-Bias Curriculum is designed to help staff and children confront, transcend, and eliminate barriers based on race, culture, gender, and ability (National Association for the Education of Young Children 2006, 1). That Georgia had never actually adopted the NAEYC Anti-Bias Curriculum, did not stop a public skirmish over the issue. Family Concerns issued an action alert advising parents to keep their children out of universal preschool because the state's curriculum would "destroy traditional social norms and education." They charged that the state preschool program was "drawing children away from private and church directed children's day care [and that it] will open the door to state raised children where parents are replaced and values and beliefs are altered." Family Concerns charged that state preschool would promote gender blurring with communal bathrooms, that all sexual behavior would be encouraged, and that it would alter gender behavior and teach women to enter the workforce and men to be nurturers of children (Family Concerns 1996).

Unfortunately for Governor Miller, the disinformation flow was not just from Family Concerns. Elected State Superintendent of Education Linda Schrenko led Miller to believe that the state had adopted the NAEYC Anti-Bias Curriculum, which in turn led Miller to order the Georgia Department of Education (GDOE) to remove the curriculum, even though it never was approved. The reality was that GDOE required that state preschool curricula be developmentally appropriate and based on principles established by NAEYC. In the first three years of the program, four well-known curriculum choices were approved: Montessori, Bank Street, Creative Curriculum, and High/Scope. Participating centers had to submit their curricula to the GDOE for approval, and NAEYC's Anti-Bias Curriculum was never approved for use in Georgia's preschool program (National Association for the Education of Young Children 2006, 1; White 1996, 1).

In addition to opposition from conservative Christians, the preschool program faced significant political opposition due to the relative autonomy of GDOE. In Georgia, the State Superintendent is an elected position and, unfortunately for Zell Miller, the person in that position in 1994 was Linda Schrenko, a Republican elected by conservative Christians whose main agenda was to reduce GDOE's budget. Schrenko had no interest in expanding the state's role in education, especially to include the education of four year olds. Intense political infighting ensued between Miller and Schrenko, which resulted in delayed release of preschool program guidelines and insufficient staff to administer the preschool program (Raden 1999).

When Governor Miller announced the elimination of income limits for preschool in January 1995, Schrenko publicly supported it, but told the press that it was the governor's idea (Loupe 1995, 2). Miller set a timetable for implementation to occur by September, which gave the GDOE very little time to build the capacity to handle the increase. Much conflict and turmoil resulted in the build up to September, and while enrollment increased, an estimated 5,000 to 10,000 children were shut out of preschool (Raden 1999). Such rapid expansion led to insufficient development of basic systems to deal with enrollment, registration, and reimbursement. Without adequate time to review applications and develop monitoring systems, some low-quality sites were approved and some fraud occurred, but GDOE was reluctant to revoke grants because of the political pressure to portray the program as successful. The *Atlanta Journal-Constitution* criticized Miller for rushing implementation and for not prioritizing at-risk children (Ezzard 1995, 10).

By late 1995, Zell Miller had had enough. Concerns over program administration and the hostile political environment—both within and outside of the Georgia Department of Education—"convinced the Governor that he would have to act boldly to save Pre-K" (Raden 1999, 41). As part of the Education Reform Act of 1996, Governor Miller proposed to create the Office for School Readiness (OSR) to solve the institutional barriers to preschool program success. The new agency would administer the preschool program, license the providers participating in preschool, administer the federal Child and Adult Care Food Program, the Standards of Care Initiative (a program recognizing quality centers), and the Georgia Head Start Collaboration Project (a federally funded grant to coordinate Head Start with the state program) (Office of School Readiness 2000, 10). By all accounts, the reason for the shift from GDOE to OSR had to do with the controversy between Governor Miller and

Superintendent Schrenko over the preschool program. Sources indicate that Schrenko's opposition to preschool disappeared after the program was moved out of GDOE.

While creation of OSR may have solved the problems with Schrenko, the Christian Coalition (now renamed the Georgia Christian Alliance) opposed the creation of OSR on the grounds that the state voters elected the State Superintendent to make decisions, not a director appointed by the governor. Christian Coalition State Chairman Jerry Keen stated, "The residents of this state elected Linda Schrenko to put our educational system into the hands of parents. The Superintendent of Schools needs the authority to do what we elected her to do" (Cribb 1996, 1). Keen's press release pits parents' rights to raise children against a perceived infringement of those rights through the creation of a new government agency focusing on school readiness of young children.

Despite opposition from conservative Christians, the proposal to create a new agency had the support of the *Atlanta Journal-Constitution*, which based its endorsement on the potential for the new agency to coordinate programs for young children, and went as far as to state, "There is no better use of public money" (*Atlanta Journal-Constitution* 1995, 16). The legislature agreed, and in 1996 OSR was created thereby allowing Miller to make a crucial institutional change necessary to stabilize the program.

Governor Miller also made a key appointment through his choice of Mike Vollmer as the first director of OSR. Vollmer, known as a fixer of problem agencies, immediately recognized that the survival of preschool was a political problem, not a programmatic problem. Vollmer states, "Pre-K was on its death bed" (telephone communication, June 30, 2005). To find the solution, Vollmer staffed the new agency with politically savvy experts, who had administrative, budgetary and technological skills, rather than with early childhood education experts. He then drove around the state talking to preschool providers. By April, he had a plan to reverse the negative perceptions of the preschool program. In 1996, OSR stressed two things. First, in order to replace the negative babysitting construction, academics became the focus, defining the problem as school readiness and framing preschool as the policy solution. The Office of School Readiness stated that "the purposes of the Prekindergarten Program are to provide children with quality preschool experiences necessary for future school success...." (Office of School Readiness 2000, 10). Second, OSR chose to frame the universal preschool program as the "largest school choice program in the country" (Vollmer, Mike, telephone communication, June 30, 2005), thus providing an effective tactic for expanding conservative support for the preschool program.

By making the program universal, creating OSR, and successfully reframing the program, a stable policy monopoly was created for the preschool program. Popular support for the program soared. A 1997 survey by the Council for School Performance indicated that 85 percent of respondents agreed with the statement, "I support the use of lottery funds for Pre-K" (Council for School Performance 1998). The media also provided full support for the program. In March, 1996, a columnist for the *Atlanta Journal-Constitution* wrote, "For generations, the South has followed the lead of Massachusetts and other states in innovative, forward-looking programs. With Pre-K, we're on top" (Dickerson 1996, 18A). And, indeed, they were. Georgia was the first state to open publicly funded preschool to all income groups, and other states took notice. Georgia received national recognition in 1997 when the preschool program received the Ford Foundation-funded Innovations in American Government Award from the Harvard John F. Kennedy School of Government (Government Innovators Network 2006). Celeste Osborn, the second director of OSR stated, "I think there is such academic support. There is support from the business community, from the parent community. It would be very difficult to come in and significantly change the program" (Cited in Raden 1999, 67). Recent Commissioner of the program Marsha Moore agrees. Support for the program is strong and they have been able to increase funding for the program each year, regardless of whether the governor is a Republican or a Democrat (Moore, Marsha, telephone communication, July 15, 2005).

The successful issue redefinition from babysitting to early education for future school success is a powerful supporting idea connected to core political values that has been communicated directly and simply through image and rhetoric. The image of a four year old learning was successfully communicated to the adult population, but Governor Miller also took the message directly to the target population. In 1996, Governor Miller asked Director of OSR Mike Vollmer, "Did your mother read to you?" That conversation led to the distribution of 65,000 copies of *The Little Engine that Could* to every preschool student in the program. Miller wanted to send the message that children should never be afraid to fail and should never quit. According to Vollmer, two weeks before the Atlanta Olympics, Miller canceled all his appointments, including those with dignitaries associated with the Olympics, in order to personally write the cover letter accompanying the books (telephone communication, June 30, 2005).

According to Baumgartner and Jones (1993), a policy monopoly can be destabilized if the institutional arrangements or the issue definition change. Although there has been institutional change, the institutional arrangements for the preschool program are unlikely to destabilize the policy monopoly. The Department of Early Care and Learning (DECAL) was created in 2004 to combine administration of all early childhood programs (Office of School Readiness 2004, 1). This change allows, among other things, the same agency to both license and contract with child care providers for the preschool program.

The institutional structure for the funding stream for preschool is also stable. Because Georgia's constitution limits lottery funding to preschool and other specific education programs, lottery revenues cannot be redirected without a constitutional amendment. Since it would require a two-thirds majority vote in the legislature, and majority vote by Georgia's electorate, there is a significant hurdle for anyone trying to change the revenue flows. The preschool program could receive less funding in the future if lottery revenues decrease, but the program is not at risk of being cut.

Preschool in Georgia has stability in institutional structure and it has also attained a unified policy image. The dominant view is that investment in preschool is a wise public investment that will achieve gains in educational outcomes, improved workforce, and, ultimately, economic development. This is a powerful image that has been communicated by the media, Zell Miller, OSR Director Mike Vollmer and his staff, and recent Commissioner of DECAL Marsha Moore. The biggest threat to the policy image would be if the preschool investment did not lead to improved education outcomes. And therein lies a potential sticky thicket. The lottery legislation required that the program be evaluated. The institutional actor charged with arranging for the evaluation was the Georgia Council for School Performance. The council was independent of government agencies, and its five members were appointed by the house speaker (1), the lieutenant governor (1) and the governor (3). Through a competitive bid process, the council contracted with the Andrew Young School of Policy Studies at Georgia State University (GSU) to conduct a longitudinal study of the preschool program.

The GSU study tracked the educational experiences of 3,639 randomly selected students enrolled in the preschool program through third grade; however, the research design did not include a control group of children who did not attend preschool, which limited the robustness of the research design. The five-year study used analyses of teachers' ratings of their students, surveys of teachers and parents, and standardized test scores, but did not include direct assessment of the children by researchers. The teachers' assessments indicated that children's academic, social, and communication skills peaked in the first grade and then declined through the second grade. However, the study's lead researcher noted that "It is not clear if this represents a lack of readiness on the part of some schools to build on the children's skills developed during pre-K, a decline in students' performance, or higher expectations on the part of teachers in higher grades" (Henry et al. 2002, 2). GSU conducted a second study starting in 2001, as the longitudinal preschool study was ending. OSR provided $1.4 million, which was supplemented by $200,000 from the Pew Charitable Trusts-funded National Institute for Early Education Research. The research team utilized a more robust research design that compared students in state-funded preschool to those participating in Head Start and private preschool programs (combined n = 630). In the fourth year of the study, they added a sample of kindergarten students who did not attend a formal, full-day preschool (n = 225). For this study, they also added four direct assessments of the children and classroom observation to their data collection strategy. The main goal of the study was to understand the effects of Georgia's preschool program on four year olds. Overall, the findings were good for preschool. They indicated that across the three types of programs children gained substantially when compared nationally to their peers on the assessments of language and cognitive skills; however, there were not statistically significant differences between state preschool, Head Start, and private child care programs.[1] But the data also indicate that gains in two language measures lagged by first grade (Henry et al. 2005, vii). The results of this study showed that there was a narrowing of the educational outcomes among socioeconomic levels, but that additional resources would be needed to improve the performance of poor children.

The independent evaluation of Georgia's preschool program ended with that study. In 2000, Georgia created the Governor's Office of Student Achievement and shifted the evaluation of the preschool program from an independent assessment of educational outcomes to an internal assessment of preschool inputs. The evaluation of Georgia's preschool program is currently limited to collecting data on access to preschool and monitoring the inputs to the program (teacher certification, child staff ratios, curriculum, equipment, etc.). While an independent evaluation of the preschool program creates the risk of negative findings that would harm support for the program, the decision to shift from evaluation of outcomes to evaluation of inputs removes the opportunity to reap the benefits of positive findings. As will be discussed below, positive findings from an independent evaluation of the preschool program in Tulsa, Oklahoma, solidified the positive image construction of preschool for that state.

In Georgia, any battles over the preschool program are, as Mintrom (2004) predicted, among a narrow set of actors, mainly within the child care industry. Head Start providers want to make sure that their programs are preserved, and for-profit providers want to make sure that they are not put out of business. The industry concerns stem from their exclusion when the preschool program began. Even though the state preschool program was focused on at-risk children, many local coordinating councils did not involve Head Start in program planning. This created tension and fear that the state was going to take over Head Start. The tensions had a racial element, since Head Start is seen in the South as serving mostly African-American children, and is a symbol of Civil Rights triumph (Raden, 1999). In response, the preschool program guidelines were altered so that coordinating councils are now advised to include Head Start representatives.

The controversy with proprietary child care providers has not been resolved as satisfactorily. In 1995, when the preschool program was made universal, Georgia had a capacity problem. It was not feasible to build new public school facilities because of the short time period in which Governor Miller wanted to ramp-up the program. The only available choice was to rely on the existing industry. Government officials interviewed regard the decision as being pragmatic (Shapiro, Pam, telephone communication, July 21, 2005), but representatives from the proprietary child care industry regard it as begrudging. While each side had their concerns, according to a former president of the Georgia Child Care Association, when the state approached them to participate, they told their membership that the "train was leaving the station and we'd better get on board."

The proprietary child care centers were not well organized in the 1990s; however, the Georgia Child Care Association (GCCA), a membership organization of proprietary child care centers, has become more focused on political activism in recent years. In a conservative state, the last thing an elected official wants is to have small business owners complaining that the state is putting them out of business, yet proprietary centers say this is exactly what is happening. According to GCCA, the economics of child care are such that the four year olds are the most profitable age group to serve. With a ratio of 1:18, and teachers only required to have a high school diploma, the four-year-old classrooms were used to subsidize the more costly infant (1:6 ratio) and toddler (1:8 ratio) classrooms. With the state offering free preschool, proprietary centers faced the stark reality of "losing" their most profitable segment of the child care market. If the center participates in the preschool program, it receives one-time startup funding, but then has to maintain a 1:10 ratio, hire teachers with a minimum of an associates degree, and limit group size to twenty (Bright from the Start Georgia Department of Early Care and Learning 2005). This means incurring the increased labor costs for a higher-qualified teacher, but only being able to add two more children. Whether participation in the program makes financial sense for a proprietary center depends on the reimbursement rate, and this is the focus of current controversy. But any changes to the preschool program at this point will be incremental. The private child care lobby may win increases in reimbursement rates or additional funds to purchase classroom supplies, but publicly funded universal preschool is the new, stable status quo.

### New York

After the LADDER legislation passed in New York in 1997, hopes were high for creating universal preschool in five years; however, those hopes were too optimistic. Despite the relative ease of policy passage, achieving stability for the preschool program was a decade-long struggle. Unlike Georgia, which created a lottery to fund preschool, the New York preschool program, until 2007, depended on annual appropriations of state funds. Funding for the Universal Pre-K program (UPK) has been an annual rollercoaster ride, but the opposition has not necessarily been due to objection to public investment in early education. According to one early childhood advocate, "Pre-K has never been about four-year-olds. It's about politics." Attempts to cut the UPK budget have stemmed from clashing political ideologies rather than the merits of the UPK program. The discussion that follows analyzes the struggle to establish stability for UPK.

The LADDER legislation created a grant-funded preschool program in which eligible school districts could apply for UPK funds through the State Education Department (New York State Law § 3602-e). Eligibility hinged on the number of unserved four-year-olds and a district's wealth ratio (New York State Education Department 2001). While UPK was intended to become universal, the initial implementation favored high-demand areas with children not already being served by the Targeted Pre-K program (the state program for low-income children) or by Head Start. The LADDER legislation required that the regulations for UPK include qualifications of staff, staff/child ratio, health and safety requirements, and some procedural requirements of the grant process. But the legislation left the details, including the criteria for application selection, to be determined in the rulemaking process within the broad statutory requirement that preference must be given to innovative methods that maximize the utilization of existing resources of the school and community. The New York State Education Department (NYSED) would write the rules, with final approval by the Board of Regents. However, the legislature did not provide any additional funds for developing the program, which created an opportunity for early childhood advocates to play a significant role in launching the UPK program.

The legislation requires school districts to form an advisory board to assess the district's needs prior to applying for UPK funds. Each advisory board is appointed by the district's superintendent and consists of school board members, teachers, parents, community leaders, child care and early education providers, and a superintendent's designee. The advisory boards were required to hold public hearings during the 1997–98 school year to determine whether to apply for the UPK funds. The boards also had to establish the projected number of eligible children, benefits of participation to children, needs of parents, ease of utilization and accessibility of the program to parents, availability of facilities, and how best to combine school and community resources (New York State Universal Prekindergarten 1997, 3602-e). If the advisory board decided to pursue UPK funds, it then developed a plan. The final application step was approval by the school board.

Unlike Georgia, which provided funds for the coordinating councils (with a local match), the state legislature did not appropriate any funds for the planning process. This provided an opportunity for early childhood advocates to play an important role. The Schuyler Center for Analysis and Advocacy (then titled the State Communities Aid Association), a statewide child advocacy organization, joined with Child Care Inc., a nonprofit child care advocacy group mainly focused on New York City, to publish the only guide book to assist school districts in applying for UPK funds. With support from philanthropic sources, they published two volumes. The first volume, distributed in January 1998, provided a step-by-step guide to the UPK application process (Schuster 1998a). In addition, the guide included information on the program options, a sample district plan, media communication examples, and appendices providing resources. Written in a user-friendly manner complete with flow charts and financial planning charts, the guide was the only publication to assist school districts in accessing the UPK grant funds. A second volume was distributed in November 1998, with steps for success and guidance for understanding how to blend funding sources (Schuster 1998b). Given the lack of state funding for planning, it is a remarkable accomplishment that over half of the eligible school districts were able to apply in 1998.

While no state funds were appropriated for state or local planning, the program funding looked promising. In his 1998 State of the State address, Governor Pataki listed his accomplishments and included mention of the UPK program (Perez-Pena 1998, 6; the *Times Union* 1998, 10). Although the media chided him for taking more credit than was his due, the Governor's budget included increases in education spending, including $50 million for the UPK program (O'Brien 1998, 7). The education spending pleased the Democratic-majority Assembly, which eventually was able to negotiate for nearly $20 million in additional funds for UPK beyond what was in the governor's budget (see table 3.1). However, the process of negotiation was lengthy, and the final budget was not passed until long after the end of the fiscal year in April. The late budget and fluctuating amounts of proposed state aid made it very difficult for public schools to plan for UPK programs.

### TABLE 3.1
### New York State
### Universal Prekindergarten Program
### 1998–99 to 2006–07

| | Number of Eligible Districts | Number of Districts Participating | Available Appropriation (in millions) | Actual Expenditures (in millions) | Number of Children Served |
|---|---|---|---|---|---|
| 1998–1999 | 125 | 62 | $67.4 | $56.3 | 18,200 36% in CBOs |
| 1999–2000 | 241 | 97 | $100 | $ 83.6 | 27,400 51% in CBOs |
| 2000–2000 | 419 | 162 | $225 | $158.6 | 48,100 65% in CBOs |
| 2001–2002 | 224 | 188 | $163.3 | $176.8 (includes reserve money from 00–01) | 54,800 65% in CBOs |
| 2002–2003 | 224 | 189 | $204.7 | $195.4 | 58,300 63% in CBOs |
| 2003–2004 | 224 | 190 | $204.7 | $199.6 | 58,456 61% in CBOs |
| 2004–2005 | 224 | 192 | $204.7 | $200.7 | 56,919 62% in CBOs |
| 2005–2006 | 224 | 196 | $204.7 | $201.2 | 58,080* |
| 2006–2007 | 284 | 220 | $254.7 | TBD | 70,779† |

Source: New York State Education Department 2007. Universal Prekindergarten Final Report data for 1998–2006 and Universal Prekindergarten Application projections for 2006–2007.

Notes: Includes NYC as one school district; CBO is a community-based organizatioin.
*Projected data reported in 2005–2006 UPK applications. Final data being confirmed.
†Projected data reported in 2006–2007 UPK applications.

The controversy over the UPK funding level was reflected in the annual report to the legislature from the NYSED. The UPK section of the report had two parts: successes and challenges. One success was that 65 of the 114 eligible districts participated in the UPK program serving a total of 18,389 children (90 percent of the eligible population). Participation was heaviest in New York City, accounting for nearly 75 percent of the children served (New York State Education Department 2000). Other good news was that the local UPK programs developed collaborations with community-based early childhood programs that surpassed the 10 percent minimum. Collaborations in the first year accounted for 35 percent of the total UPK funding. The report also listed NYSED implementation of the program as a success; however, the report did not describe the crucial role of advocates in that process.

In terms of challenges, the report listed the logistical problems that arose due to the delayed budget process. It also raised an issue that had not been reflected in media accounts: state transportation aid could not be expanded to serve four-year-olds, a situation that continues to be a problem. Districts offering UPK either had to absorb the transportation costs or not provide transportation for UPK students. If a district did not provide transportation, it was particularly difficult for working parents because 81 percent of UPK classrooms were half-day (2½ hours) (New York State Education Department 2000). Other challenges included making the required collaborations work in school districts unaccustomed to working with community-based providers.

Despite implementation struggles, all was well for UPK support until after the governor was elected to his second term in November 1998. Despite a budget surplus, Governor Pataki announced that his 1999–2000 budget would not increase spending beyond the inflation rate. This amounted to a spending cut because of the multiyear phase-in that was previously approved for the LADDER programs. The education programs alone would require state spending to increase by over $1 billion. The *New York Times* predicted that the Democratic majority in the Assembly would interpret an austerity budget as a declaration of war (Perez-Pena 1999a, 1). Part of the reason for the dire language in the media was a change in the budget process the previous year in which the legislature drafted its budget largely without the governor's involvement. Previously, leadership in the Assembly and Senate would negotiate with the governor throughout the budget drafting process. The budget battles in Pataki's first term were legendary, and the change in procedure was intended to open the budget process to rank-and-file legislators. This however, had the negative consequence of delaying negotiations with the governor, which then led the governor to utilize his veto power more heavily. After an agreement with the legislature on the 1998 budget, Governor Pataki used his veto power to eliminate $1.6 billion from the budget (Perez-Pena 1999b, 1).

But even without that procedural change, the LADDER legislation was destined to face budgetary challenges. The Democrats won passage of the LADDER legislation only because they agreed to the governor's property tax cuts. However, by 1999, Governor Pataki was poised to renege on education spending programs and push for additional tax cuts. Media accounts and his opponents linked his fiscally conservative State of the State speech to his future national political ambitions (Jakes 1999, A4; Perez-Pena 1999a, 1). While the speech may have played well nationally, his budget proposal did not set well with Democrats. Pataki proposed deep cuts in Medicaid and tuition assistance for low-income college students, decreased welfare spending, and allowed only a 1-percent increase in aid to schools (Perez-Pena 1999c, 1). Despite surpluses, Pataki's budget not only reneged on his promise to fund LADDER programs, including UPK, full-day kindergarten, and smaller class sizes in K–3 grades, but also called for shifting early education funds into an Educational Improvement Block Grant for school districts to allow greater flexibility in spending (Schuyler Center for Analysis and Advocacy 2004). With this plan, funds previously targeted for early education would no longer be restricted to early education (Perez-Pena 1999d, 17). According to The *New York Times*, the plan "drew venomous responses from Democrats, who declared it dead on arrival" (Perez-Pena 1999c, 1). The budget negotiations were deadlocked for three and a half months. Despite a law that withheld legislators' salaries as long as the budget was overdue, the budget was not approved until August 4, 1999, making it the second latest budget in the history of New York State (Odato 1999, 1). Resolution was only possible when the governor allowed the legislature to add $1.1 billion in spending, and promised not to veto the addition. The restored funding allowed Assembly Speaker Silver to protect the LADDER programs from elimination and replacement with the block grant, but the future of UPK was in possible jeopardy.

With all of the indecision over UPK funding, and with the budget overdue, public schools and community providers scaled back plans to open UPK classrooms (Perez-Pena 1999d, 17). Frustration abounded across the state from school districts that would not have adequate time to plan, even if the budget were passed tomorrow. As one Board of Education representative complained, "We don't throw pixie dust on a school, and magically there appear teachers, classrooms, books and equipment....It takes months of planning and effort" (Stephen K. Allinger quoted in Perez-Pena 1999d, 17). School districts were caught in a catch-22 in that if the money were ultimately approved and not spent, it might get cut the following year, but if they planned for the classrooms and then the money was not approved, they would be stuck with bills they could not pay. With a governor hostile to UPK, school districts that could not absorb costs if UPK funding was not approved did not expand their programs.

The protracted budget negotiations limited participation rates in UPK for the 1999–2000 school year because school districts did not learn the amount of their UPK grant allocations until mid-July (New York State Education Department 2001). To compound the problem, fluctuation in the statutory funding formula used to calculate a district's per-child grant amount resulted in several districts having their grant allocation revised midyear, even as late as April 30th (New York State Education Department 2001). An amendment was passed to prevent that from recurring in the 2000–2001 academic year, but the damage was done to the existing programs that suffered decreased grants late in the academic year. The amendment created a reserve fund that provided districts with the flexibility to reserve some or all of their grants to combine it with the following year's allocation (New York State Education Department 2002). While this protected eligible school districts from losing unexpended UPK funds, it also prevented the NYSED from reallocating UPK funds to other school districts to expand access.

But the news for UPK was not all bad. The attempt by the governor to eliminate the dedicated funding for the LADDER programs galvanized advocates. In response to the governor's budget, the Emergency Coalition to Save Universal Prekindergarten was formed (Schimke, Karen, personal communication, Albany, October 11, 2006). Since the governor had said that "pre-K works" in 1998, the coalition made that the centerpiece of their resistance. An editorial in the *Times Union*, the newspaper for the Albany capital region, urged lawmakers to support UPK investment (the *Times Union* 1999, 18). In the annual report on education, NYSED credited the advocates, who had been indispensable in helping it to implement UPK, with organizing the Emergency Coalition to Save Universal Pre-K. NYSED gave a clear signal that it was closely aligned with the advocates stating, "[t]his advocacy group has kept the Department abreast of its lobbying activities on behalf of UPK" (New York State Education Department 2001, 190). Through intensive lobbying from the Coalition and commitment from Speaker Silver, the programs were saved, and the UPK program received a $100 million appropriation (see table 3.1).

In 2000, the state was still running a surplus and the governor used his State of the State address to advocate for education initiatives, including one to attract more qualified teachers to New York. But Governor Pataki again did not make a commitment to UPK or to other programs included in the LADDER legislation (Odato 2000, 1). Once the governor announced his budget, the legislature negotiated to expand funding by $1.4 billion in order to fund UPK and a number of other programs. But the compromise was that they would have to agree to $1.2 billion in tax cuts to take effect in future years (Hernandez 2000, 1). With his eye on the reelection of President George W. Bush, Governor Pataki was eager to complete budget negotiations and hit the campaign trail. State legislators were also eager to finish the budget and focus on campaigning (Hernandez 2000, 1). Due in part to all of the election-year pressures, the 2000 budget ended up giving everyone what they wanted. Governor Pataki and supporting Republicans got their tax cuts, and Speaker Silver and supporting Democrats got their increases in education spending.

In the midst of the 2000 budget negotiations, there was an attempt by Democratic assemblymen to oust Representative Silver as Speaker of the Assembly. The disgruntled rank-and-file members wanted to deconcentrate the Speaker's power and to force him to account for his discretionary fund spending. This controversy was an extension of the struggle for control over the budget in the previous year. New York has a history of concentrated power in budget negotiations. The standard process has been that the speaker of the assembly, the senate majority leader, and the governor come to an agreement that is then presented to the Senate and Assembly. Decisions made only by the leadership leave little potential for the rank-and-file to affect the budget. While the closed-door vote in December 2000 returned Silver as Speaker of the Assembly, it forced him to appoint a committee to study procedural reforms and to promise to provide members with information on the "tens of millions of dollars in discretionary funds at his disposal" (Jochnowitz 2001).

Despite the attempted coup, the election year ended up being a banner year for UPK. The 2000-2001 appropriation for the program increased dramatically from $100 million to $225 million. The increase allowed the number of eligible school districts to jump from 241 to 419 (see table 3.1). Since New York has 704 school districts, the program was not yet universal, but the annual increases in funding were moving the program toward that goal. As a result of the increased funding, enrollment in UPK nearly doubled; however, only 162 eligible districts participated in the program, while the remaining 61 eligible school districts placed their allocations into the reserve fund. The NYSED annual report indicated that 72 percent of the districts that did not apply for UPK funding were designated as Average-Need or Low-Need Districts, but that 28 percent were designated as High-Need Districts (New York State Education Department 2002). While the report does not explain why these districts did not create UPK programs, other sources indicate that the annual struggles to win funding prevented eligible school districts from fully expending their resources. But for others, it was due to infrastructure constraints. For example, the Candor Central School district was allocated $50,000 for UPK and $40,000 for reduced class sizes, but the school district did not have the classroom space to implement the programs. School officials had to ask voters to approve a school budget with a tax increase in order to pay for the classroom construction (Gormley 2001, 10).

While creation of the reserve fund protected unspent UPK funds for eligible school districts to use in future years, it also prevented the NYSED from reallocating those funds to school districts that were interested in creating preschool programs. The gap between the appropriated amount and actual expenditures in the first three years of the UPK program increased from approximately $10 million, to $20 million to $75 million (see table 3.1). Media accounts of school districts unable to use their "increases" in state aid fueled Governor Pataki's push for reform of state school aid distribution, which in turn led to a very complicated budget battle in 2001.

In 2001, Governor Pataki's objective was, once again, to reduce restrictions on how state aid could be spent by school districts by combining targeted programs into a broader block grant. But for those who were concerned with funding early education, elimination of targeted funding programs threatened the investment in early education. To stabilize funding, advocates began to push to shift UPK into the state school funding formula (Schimke, Karen, personal communication, Albany, October 11, 2006). The final and most expensive year for funding the LADDER legislation was 2001. Silver wanted to protect LADDER program funding by keeping it a targeted, as opposed to block, grant program. But with the opposition from the Governor, Silver noted that, "it might be a battle to make it happen" (Jochnowitz 2001, 3).

In addition to having concerns about protecting targeted funding, Silver and others worried that the economy was starting to cool. The prior four years of surpluses had enabled the governor and legislature to approve large spending increases along with simultaneous tax cuts. But all were beginning to realize that such diametrically opposed policy choices could not be sustained. With the LADDER legislation viewed as Democrats' (in particular Speaker Silver's) pet policy, and with the governor's commitment to tax cuts, the stage was set for an epic budget battle. Governor Pataki and Speaker Silver locked horns on the overall spending amount, with education spending at the center (Gallagher 2001, 5). The budget battle lasted throughout the summer and into the fall. Schools were forced to start the school year without a budget agreement. To break the stalemate, the legislature agreed to pass Pataki's "bare bones" budget with the strategy of passing a supplemental budget later in the year. With this agreement, funding appropriated for UPK was reduced from $225 million to approximately $163 million (see table 3.1). The overall reduction in education spending levels caused schools to reduce UPK and after-school programs, to eliminate plans to reduce class sizes, and, in some districts, to raise taxes (Archibold 2001, 1). School superintendents complained bitterly about having to cancel programs. A superintendent from outside of Rochester lamented, "You're only 4 years old once. This literally denies children a fantastic start on the path for a great education" (Steven Walts quoted in Archibold 2001, 1).

While Democrats hoped to pass a supplemental budget later in the year, the terrorist attacks of September 11th threw New York into turmoil. All media coverage of UPK ended due to the intense focus on the attacks and their aftermath. The economic effect of the attacks on the World Trade Center in New York City led to skyrocketing state budget deficits. In the end, funding for UPK remained at the "bare bones" budget level, and the number of eligible school districts was reduced from 419 to 224. However, the reserve funds ended up allowing some school districts to increase the number of children served in the UPK program. For the first time since the program was started, actual expenditures exceeded the appropriation (see table 3.1).

In 2002, the governor was facing a reelection campaign and his budget originally flat-funded UPK. He proposed shifting some UPK costs from the general fund to the Temporary Assistance for Needy Families (the federal welfare program). But in the end, the budget for UPK remained in the general fund. The 2002–03 budget restored approximately $40 million to the UPK program, making the total appropriation a little over $200 million, which was still $25 million below the 2000–01 appropriation. The increased funding and continued draw-down of reserve funds allowed UPK enrollments to increase by 6 percent. The gap between appropriated and actual expenditures narrowed to less than $10 million (see table 3.1).

After winning his third term in 2002, Governor Pataki was poised to advance major cuts to New York's budget. In education, Governor Pataki proposed $1.4 billion in cuts and elimination of funding for UPK, full-day kindergarten and reduced class sizes (i.e., the LADDER programs), as well as spending cuts in K–12 and higher education (Odato 2002, 1). He again tried to combine targeted education funding into a more flexible block grant. The response was swift and vociferous. Leaders in the Assembly, in cities, and in education publicly rebuked the governor for cuts to education. Speaker Silver visited preschools across the state in order to bring media coverage to the governor's plan to cut UPK and other education programs. New York City's mayor and its school chancellor both publicly opposed the cuts and were joined by the state education commissioner and the regents chancellor (Herszenhorn 2003, 1). The National Education Association in Albany wrote an opinion editorial criticizing the governor's plan and advising that the school formula be changed instead to make education spending actually follow a formula instead of being used as a tool for incumbent legislators (Rapaport 2003, 12). School superintendents from forty-eight districts published a letter to Governor Pataki in the *Times Union* urging the governor to view education as an investment rather than as an expense (Dedrick and Brewer 2004).

The opposition from the top was replicated in every direction. Since approximately 63 percent of UPK programs were located in community-based organizations, the threat to cut UPK generated vocal opposition from private providers of UPK. Without the state UPK aid, providers would have had to raise tuition. At one Montessori school profiled by the *New York Times*, tuition would have had to double without state aid, and consequently enrollment was down by two-thirds in anticipation of the tuition increase (Hernandez 2000, 1). The parents of the approximately 60,000 four-year-old children scheduled to enroll in UPK programs in the fall echoed the vocal opposition from providers. Part of the furor over cutting UPK was due to the timing: The announcement of the governor's budget cuts came after the preschool admissions process. This meant that parents had either missed the deadlines for private preschools or were forced to put down nonrefundable deposits to ensure that their children would have some place to go to preschool in the fall. The *New York Times* provided sympathetic coverage of parents scrambling to find alternative preschool arrangements. The coverage included the plight of middle-class parents who relied on UPK and could not afford to pay the market rates for private preschool programs, which in Manhattan could reach $14,000 for a private nursery school (Hernandez 2000, 1). Because enrollment in UPK was open to all income levels, parents of UPK participants came from a wide range of socioeconomic levels. They signed petitions, picketed, and attended rallies to protect the UPK program. In the end, UPK funding was restored to approximately $200 million, where it remained for two more years (see table 3.1).

Karen Schimke, President and CEO of the Schuyler Center for Analysis and Advocacy, believes that the governorr's threat to cut education programs was, on balance, a good thing to happen to UPK. The threat to education programs unified disparate education interests and aligned them with early childhood advocates. According to Schimke, "Pre-K put a face on the battle" (personal communication, Albany, October 11, 2006). Advocates were well organized and well funded to be able to effectively mobilize to save UPK. The Coalition to Save Pre-K went on a media blitz, getting about 100 stories and articles published in newspapers across the state, along with eight op-ed pieces between January to May 2003 (Schuyler Center for Analysis and Advocacy 2004). In April, they organized a reception for UPK that was attended by Speaker Silver, Republican Senate Majority Leader Bruno, NYSED Commissioner Mills, as well as the chairmen of the Assembly, the Senate Education Committees and the Children's Committees. Soon afterward, a press conference was called to put the spotlight on the more than 225,000 petition signatures supporting UPK delivered to the governor by the Coalition to save Pre–K. By May, the Senate and Assembly passed budgets restoring UPK and other education programs. The day afterward a "March for Public Education" was held in Albany. Despite the groundswell of opposition, Governor Pataki vetoed the legislature's budget; however, the legislature overrode his veto (Schuyler Center for Analysis and Advocacy 2004). This was a turning point for UPK. Although the budget remained level for the next two budget cycles, the governor did not try to cut the program again.

After the galvanizing of support for UPK in 2003, the momentum continued for investing in UPK and for stabilizing funding of the program. Part of the reason the mobilization was successful was that Pew Charitable Trusts began to fund the Schuyler Center and Child Care, Inc. in 2002. This allowed for the development of marketing materials to support early education investment that resulted in the creation of the Winning Beginning New York campaign. The Schuyler Center and co-conveners Child Care Inc., the New York State Child Care Coordinating Council, and the New York State Association for the Education of Young Children, developed the Winning Beginning campaign in order to create a "brand" for a movement for birth-to-five, not just preschool (Schimke, Karen, personal communication, Albany, October 11, 2006). The 2003 fight to save UPK helped to align disparate interests, and in doing so helped to solidify coordination among advocates for young children (Kolben, Nancy, telephone communication, July 12, 2007). With Pew funding, advocates developed an array of Winning Beginning materials to support investments in early education, including reports, research briefs, and an annual magazine. One of the research briefs titled, "The Pre-K Payback," presented data favoring investments in pre-̈school as a strategy to reduce costs associated with remediation (Belfield 2004, 1–4). Another provided research support for expansion to full-day preschool (DeSiato 2003, 1–4). After several years of coordinated effort, an action plan was published in 2005 with a two-year strategy for improving the entire early education system in New York (Center for Early Care and Learning 2004).

After years of concerted advocacy, in 2006 there was finally an increase in funding for UPK. In its annual budget, the Regents requested a $99 million increase for the UPK program (Stevens 2006, 1). In the end, UPK received a $50 million dollar budget increase, but that was a major triumph for a program that had been through such turmoil (see table 3.1). The future for UPK in New York appeared bright, especially because Governor Pataki did not seek a fourth term. In November 2006, New Yorkers elected Democrat Eliot Spitzer as governor. In the election, Spitzer released a televised ad calling for increased investment in UPK (Spitzer 2006). During the campaign, Winning Beginning NY issued a call for action in the governor's first 100 days that included, among other steps, establishing an Early Learning Commission to coordinate early education programs, and budgeting for expanded investments (Winning Beginning NY 2006). Governor Spitzer established himself as a strong supporter of UPK by raising the UPK budget by 50 percent in 2007. UPK funding was also changed to a formula, rather than grant, that runs in parallel with the K–12 funding. Governor Spitzer resigned unexpectedly in March 2008. It remains to be seen if Governor Paterson will share Spitzer's enthusiasm for UPK. But as discussed more fully in chapter 5, after ten long years of struggle, New York finally appears to be on its way to a stable policy monopoly for UPK.

## Oklahoma

The challenges to achieve stability for preschool in Georgia and New York stand in stark contrast to the experience of Oklahoma. After the universal preschool legislation was passed in 1998, Harbison told Eddins, "Now we just sit back and watch enrollment grow" (telephone communication, July 10, 2006). And, indeed it did. By 2005 enrollment in the preschool program doubled; it grew from 16,787 children in 1998 to 33,405 in 2005. The number of school districts participating in 1998 was already at 65 percent, but by 2005, 96 percent of school districts offered preschool programs (Illgen, Paul, and Garrett 2006). But Representative Eddins was far from passive in the process. He traveled the state to meet with school superintendents to educate them about the benefits of creating preschool programs or expanding to full-day preschool programs. Because of the complexity of the state school funding formula, Eddins often found himself in the position of correcting misconceptions that the preschool program would be a drain on school funding by laying out the financial calculations to school officials (telephone communication, July 5, 2006).

When the preschool program was a targeted program serving low-income populations, some public schools began collaborating with Head Start. In the earlier era, preschool collaboration with Head Start made financial sense because the preschool program was not fully funded. However, the 1998 change in reimbursement rates made preschool financially attractive to public schools and they were not legally obligated to collaborate with Head Start or with child care providers. While the Oklahoma Department of Education (ODOE) had been supportive of collaboration, it was the individual school districts that made the decision. For most public schools, learning to look beyond the campus to collaborate with private child care and Head Start providers was a brave new world. Beyond the financial calculation, there was a regulatory labyrinth for a school to contract for preschool with Head Start or child care providers. This is due to the fact that there are three separate sets of overlapping, yet contradictory, regulations for early education: federal Head Start guidelines, state child care licensing regulations, and public school regulations. For any collaborative arrangement to work, the preschool program had to meet at least two sets of regulations. In the 2006–07 school-year, approximately 13 percent of preschool enrollment was in collaborative settings and 40 percent of school districts provided pre-K in collaborative settings (Illgen and Garrett, 2007).

With the financial and regulatory impediments to collaboration, Head Start and private child care providers started to feel the pinch as the public preschool program expanded. From Head Start's perspective, they had been focused on low-income children and offered additional health services and parenting education. When children entered the public preschool program, instead of the Head Start program, they lost out on the additional services Head Start provides (Floyd, Kay, telephone communication September 15, 2005). Private child care providers were faced with the prospect of losing their four-year-olds to the public schools for either 2½ hours or 6 hours each day. Because working parents need additional care, child care providers could provide the wraparound care, but private child care providers were losing their profitable four-year-old population (Stemp, Leona, Dennis Wells, Beverly Wells, and Angie Davis, personal communication, Oklahoma City, September 16, 2005). Along with the financial impact, the Oklahoma Child Care Association also voiced concerns about the physical structure of public school classrooms and playgrounds not being adapted to the needs of four year olds, as well as about transportation challenges (Stemp, Leona; Dennis Wells; Beverly Wells; and Angie Davis, personal communication, Oklahoma City, September 16, 2005). Under child care licensing standards, there are, for example, strict standards for playgrounds (e.g., requiring enclosed fences) and bathrooms (e.g., hot water in hand-washing sinks) that are not required under public school regulations. Moreover, transportation is a very frustrating issue for child care providers because child care licensing requires children to be transported in child safety seats and to be attended at all times. This means that when a child care center transports a child to a public school, two adults must be present so that one can escort the child and the other can remain in the van with the other children. However, if the children are transported by the public school, they can ride on buses without safety restraints and can be combined with K–12 students. Child care representatives interviewed insisted that they do not want child care licensing to change because they think they have strict, good standards; rather, they want public schools to have to meet those standards (Stemp, Leona; Dennis Wells; Beverly Wells; and Angie Davis, personal communication, Oklahoma City, September 16, 2005). ODOE counters that the education level of public school teachers allows them to have regulations that do not spell out every contingency. They rely on the professionalism of the teachers to guide decisions about what is appropriate for four year olds (Paul, Ramona, personal communication, September 16, 2005).

All sides frame this issue so that their positions are what they think is best for children, which leaves little room for compromise. ODOE is firmly committed to the view that a certified teacher in the classroom is the key to quality. Head Start wants low-income children and their families to receive their services. Child care wants public schools to be held to the same licensing standards. While some school districts have creatively found ways to make collaboration work, the regulatory and attitudinal differences make it challenging. Because collaboration is voluntary, there is no legislative stick serving as a catalyst for public schools to partner with either Head Start or private child care providers. ODOE is trying to informally encourage school superintendents to collaborate and providing guidance (Illgen and Garrett 2007), but the decision remains within the purview of the individual school districts (Paul, Ramona, telephone communication, Oklahoma City, September 16, 2005). If they choose not to collaborate, there is little that child care or Head Start can do about it.

Despite these implementation struggles at the local level, there was no effective opposition at the state level to public preschool in Oklahoma. This is due to several factors. First, since the preschool program had been funded through the state school funding formula since 1990, the 1998 changes could be seen as incremental rather than the introduction of a new policy principle. When the reimbursement weights and eligibility changed, there was no need to alter institutional arrangements and, importantly, there was no new spending attached to the changes. Also, the awareness of financial impacts of the increased weight changes was muted due to the complexity of the state school funding formula. Few people fully understood the potential financial impact of the preschool program (Eddins, Joe, telephone communication, July 5, 2006). In addition, the preschool program did not require additional legislation, which allowed it to stay out of the legislative spotlight. The only correction was a minor change regarding Head Start teacher qualifications. As one policy entrepreneur put it, "Pre-K was able to stay under the radar." Tying preschool funding to the state school funding formula, in all its murkiness, effectively placed the program in the very stable education policy monopoly and prevented it from being singled out for legislative review.

Second, policy entrepreneurs encouraged voluntary preschool expansion in a way that allowed the program to expand its political base of support. In the civil, genteel political culture of Oklahoma it was far more effective to keep the number of people involved in the policy process to a minimum and to construct the changes as incremental rather than as a radical change in policy making. Once the legislation had passed, policy entrepreneurs continued to work quietly but persistently to build participation, and therefore support, for the program. One of the reasons that this was possible was because neither Eddins nor Harbison were statewide figures. Eddins was in his second term as a legislator and Harbison was best known in the northeastern part of the state. These two dedicated early childhood advocates, who had worked hard to effect change without raising the hackles of conservative interests, continued to work quietly in persuading schools to participate in the program. The ODOE also actively advocated for preschool expansion. Assistant Superintendent Ramona Paul's strategy has been to use her office as a "bully pulpit" to educate the 540 districts about the importance of preschool and about the need to collaborate. She challenged superintendents to show leadership in preschool and they have responded (Paul, Ramona, personal communication, Oklahoma City, September 16, 2005). As the number of participating school districts increased, a solid base of political support for the preschool program emerged.

A possible third factor is that another early childhood initiative came under fire and drew any potential backlash against state investment in early childhood away from preschool. At the same time that Representative Eddins was trying to build support for the expanded preschool program, child advocates, including Harbison, were pushing for the development of local networks to identify early childhood needs in order to build a coordinated early childhood network. Efforts to develop the network began in 1996 when a foundation-funded conference brought people together to talk about the needs of the child care system. The process moved forward when, in 1998, the Bank of America, through the

United Way of America, solicited grant applications to fund the Success by Six Program. As a result, thirteen communities were awarded grants to build community networks and child advocates received a grant to build a statewide network (Harbison, Bob, telephone communication, July 10, 2006; vonBargen, Nancy, telephone communication, October 10, 2006). This created the network of child care advocates who then were able to take action when opportunities arose.

Such an opportunity did arise when Republican Governor Frank Keating addressed the Tulsa Press Club in February 2000. As Keating spoke about the importance of improving school performance, former Tulsa Republican Mayor Robert LaFortune challenged the Governor about his plans for early education. Keating responded that he would appoint a task force to consider it (Neal 2000). This became known as "La Fortune's question" because Keating's response signaled a shift in position. Prior to this time, Keating, with support of the *Oklahoman* and conservative business interests in the Oklahoma City area, was not convinced that investments in early childhood were key factors in improving school performance, and ultimately in improving economic development in Oklahoma. Tulsa had long adopted this position and there was considerable competition between the two major cities in the state. Keating's commitment to form a task force signaled a willingness to at least reconsider the issue.

But Keating's answer to La Fortune's question raised the hackles of the conservative opposition. When the task force released its report in December 2000, calling for a comprehensive early childhood system, it was met with strong opposition from the Oklahoma Council of Public Affairs (OCPA) and national conservative interests. In April 2001, the OCPA publicized "Blueprint for a Nanny State," which was written by Darcy Olsen of the conservative Cato Institute and now President of the Goldwater Institute. The article blasted the governor's task force for creating a scheme for "womb through age five" state-run child care, health care, and education (Olsen 2001, 9). The position paper challenged the policy of investing in early childhood to improve school success and suggested instead that Oklahoma should cut taxes and institute a school choice system (Olsen 2001, 9). The following month the OCPA published an opinion piece in the *Oklahoman* criticizing the task force for having biased membership (Dutcher 2001). The author, Brandon Dutcher, was the Research Director of OCPA and was also on the *Oklahoman*'s Opinion Board of Contributors. National criticism came from Phyllis Schlafley's Eagle Forum, which joined in on the opposition by criticizing the task force in its newsletter (*Education Reporter* 2002, 6).

The opposition led Keating to veto the bill written by his own task force. However, the task force continued to push for the bill, despite being formally disbanded. After three years of attempts, The Oklahoma Partnership for School Readiness Act was finally signed into law in 2003, but not by Keating. It became law only after Democrat Governor Brad Henry was elected to office. The legislation created a public-private partnership to pursue collaborations and strategies aimed at improving school readiness opportunities for young children and their families (Office of Governor Brad Henry 2003).

The preschool program was able to stay under the radar of conservative critiques throughout all of this controversy and was not included in newspaper coverage of early childhood issues. But in 2003, the *Oklahoman* raised the profile of the preschool program. This was due, at least in part, to the release of reports about the preschool program that showed that Oklahoma had become the national leader for providing universal preschool. In 2003, the Southern Regional Education Board published a study that concluded that Oklahoma led the twelve southern states in the number of children served by the state and by Head Start (Southern Regional Education Board 2003). In response, the *Oklahoman* ran an editorial that was complimentary in terms of the ranking and that urged schools to prioritize poor children (*Oklahoman* 2003, 6). But the spotlight really shone on Oklahoma starting in 2004, when the Pew Charitable Trust-funded National Institute for Early Education Research ranked Oklahoma as number one in the country for access to preschool (Barnett et al. 2004). This report was publicized nationally and was available for download on the Internet. All of a sudden, Oklahoma had displaced Georgia as the national leader in preschool. The *Oklahoman* published an article describing the ranking with even-handed coverage, noting the high-ranking for access, but lower marks on some of the other benchmarks for quality (Bratcher 2004, 6). But the newspaper's decision to start covering early childhood signaled a change in the relative importance of the issue in Oklahoma. Preschool was now something to be proud of, and those who had previously questioned public investment in universally accessible preschool were now warming to the idea.

The warming was accelerated when Oklahoma received national attention once again in 2005. Publication of an external evaluation of the Tulsa Preschool program demonstrated significant cognitive gains for students who participated in the program. Using a nationally normed test (Woodcock Johnson), the evaluation showed a 52 percent gain in letter-word identification test scores (prereading skills), a 27 percent gain in spelling test scores (prewriting skills) and a 21 percent gain in applied problems test scores (premath skills) (Gormley, Phillips, and Dawson 2005, 13). While all children benefit from participation, the gains were especially high for Hispanic children who experienced a 79 percent gain in letter-word identification, 39 percent gain in spelling, and a 54 percent gain in applied problems, above and beyond the gains that occur as the child ages one year (Gormley et al. 2004). The study had a rigorous research design that was able to control for selection bias, a problem with many previous evaluations of preschool programs. Not only was Oklahoma in the news for being number one in the nation for access to public preschool, it had a program that delivered improved educational outcomes. In response, the *Oklahoman* gave the study front-page coverage (Bratcher 2004, 2), and all of a sudden Oklahoma was the preschool program to reference when making the case for public investments in early education.

Coverage by the *Oklahoman* not only increased in frequency, but also shifted from covering controversy over public funding for early childhood programs to advocating for the preschool program. The paper began publishing articles adopting the argument that preschool investment better prepares children for kindergarten, which then improves future school success (McDonnell 2004, 23). The turnaround in support for early education is a major shift, and has been interpreted by some to represent a fundamental shift in the conservative business community toward acceptance that investment in early education will improve educational outcomes. At this time, Oklahoma has a stable institutional structure and a cohesive policy image. It has attained a policy monopoly with no challengers on the horizon.

## West Virginia

After a volatile policy process to pass universal preschool legislation, the challenge facing Senator Lloyd Jackson was to stabilize political support for his program. To do this, he had to address political opposition from Representative Jerry Mezzatesta, chair of the House Education Committee. In both 2003 and 2004, there were attempts to kill the preschool program primarily due to Representative Mezzatesta's concern about maximizing federal dollars prior to state spending on preschool. One strategy Mezzatesta tried was to separate preschool program funds from the K–12 budget in order to make it vulnerable to future budget cuts. Senator Jackson fought successfully to keep preschool included in the K–12 budget, thereby stabilizing budgetary challenges to the program. But while the senator was successful in keeping preschool in the K–12 education budget, he did not have sufficient control over the policy image of the program. In West Virginia, the construction of the preschool policy image as a wise public investment for successful educational outcomes had not become dominant. The position voiced across the spectrum of people interviewed can be summed up by an opinion editorial in the *Charlestown Gazette*, "No one I know opposes public schools offering voluntary kindergarten to 4 year olds. But no one sees it as 'the answer' to early care and education either" (Pratt 2002, 5A).

Even though they had been left out of the policy process, Head Start and advocacy groups such as West Virginia Education Association, West Virginia's Kids Count, and West Virginia Child Care United organized to save the program in 2003 and 2004. However, while the advocates were willing to fight to save preschool, it did not mean that they were united in their view of the preschool policy image. The West Virginia Education Association (WVEA), an advocacy group primarily for teachers, was involved with advocating passage of Senate Bill 247 because of its provisions for teacher pay raises. WVEA representatives stated that deliberation over preschool would have been preferred to stealth passage, but, once it was passed, they encouraged members to become involved in preschool (Bryant, Perry, personal communication, Charleston, August 12, 2005). West Virginia's Kids Count and former Educare supporters still strongly supported a birth-to-five focus for early childhood, and did not want to split the four year olds into a separate target group (Hale, Margie, personal communication, Charleston, August 11, 2005). After the preschool legislation passed, West Virginia Child Care United president, Helen Post-Brown envisioned, "[T]he school bus coming to take *my* children." (telephone communication, August 11, 2005) However, since that time she says that the preschool program has "worked out okay for child care," but she fears for the "mom and pop" child care centers if they do not get involved with a preschool collaboration. She added, "If schools come in and open pre-K programs for free, the small child care operations may not stay open, especially in rural areas." However, even though WVCCU's membership was afraid of the impacts of preschool on their businesses, Post-Brown notes that they supported it because they viewed it as good for the children and because the legislation requires collaboration. If the collaboration was not included, then they would have opposed it. But the organization is sufficiently concerned about the impacts of preschool on their businesses that it continues to employ a lobbyist (West Virginia Child Care United 2007, 1).

The political battle over the preschool program came to an abrupt stop in 2005 due to the removal of both push and pull factors. Preschool policy entrepreneur Senator Jackson relinquished his Senate seat to make an unsuccessful bid for the Democratic gubernatorial primary. This loss of preschool's policy entrepreneur was moderated by the departure of its primary antagonist: Representative Mezzatesta was not re-elected to the

House. With neither candidate returning to the legislature, the preschool program entered a new phase. One interviewee stated, "the best thing pre-K can do is to stay under the radar." This view was based on the fact that the preschool program at that time was expanding without causing any new budget outlays. As long as declining enrollments in K–12 provided funds for prescshool, the political battle over increasing the budget allocation for the program could be postponed.

While the political controversy over preschool ended in 2005, the program faced significant institutional challenges in its implementation, when two previously separate agencies had to work together. Prior to the preschool program, the West Virginia Department of Health and Human Resources (WVDHHR) had jurisdiction over child care (care of children before entrance into kindergarten, as well as before and after school programs for school-age children) and the West Virginia Department of Education (WVDOE) had jurisdiction over K–12. The new preschool program required WVDHHR to collaborate with the WVDOE to write the rules that would guide implementation of the program. It also provided WVDHHR with the power of first review of school district preschool plans. Initially, the collaborative process went well. The top political appointees had been involved in drafting the legislation and had supported the preschool program. Soon after the legislation was passed, a meeting was convened with the State Superintendent of Schools, the Commissioner and Secretary of the WVDHHR, representatives from the National Child Care Information Center (a national child care resource and referral agency that provides technical assistance), the Executive Director of the Community Action Program (grantee for Head Start), Governor's Cabinet on Children and Families, and implementing staff from participating agencies. This meeting set a positive tone for collaboration that carried the preschool program through its initial implementation phase.

While support from the top was important for establishing the spirit of collaboration, the civil servants charged with spearheading development of the new program were well respected in the early childhood community, had experience, and, very importantly, were able to function effectively as a team. Cathy Jones, Coordinator of Early Childhood/Even Start, was hired by WVDOE in December 2001, because of her extensive experience in early childhood education as a child care center director and advocate, among other capacities. Kay Tilton, Director of the Division of Early Care and Education, administers the federal Child Care and Development Block grant and licensing of child care centers and family day care homes. She brought thirty-four years of experience as a WVDHHR civil servant and extensive knowledge of the child care industry, regulatory environment, and institutional knowledge that only a career civil servant possesses. Bill Huebner was hired as the Director of the West Virginia Head Start Collaboration Office. He was formerly on the Governor's Cabinet on Family and Children and worked in the Educare program, the predecessor to the universal preschool program. He had knowledge of both Head Start regulatory requirements and prior collaborations between Head Start, child care, and public schools. In addition, WVDOE's Ginger Huffman, Preschool Special Education Coordinator, brought attention to the importance of inclusion of preschool children with special needs and WVDHHR's Ann Nutt, Director of Early Childhood Quality Initiatives, contributed knowledge of programmatic quality and curricula issues.

The spirit of collaboration established at that meeting generated a "can do" attitude among the civil servants responsible for implementing the preschool program. That was important because the legislation required participating school districts to submit preschool plans by July 2003. With the legislation being passed in March 2002, the implementing agencies needed to have the rules to guide school district applications for preschool funds made available in the fall so that school districts would have sufficient time to develop preschool plans. The civil servants' commitment and ability to work well together was all the more important because staffing for the task was very limited. Only WVDHHR provided four additional staff positions to implement preschool. WVDOE allocated Cathy Jones, but it did not reduce her responsibility for other programs or provide her with additional staff. Despite limited staff resources and no additional funds for starting up the program, Jones stated that a key to their success was the strength of the team at the state level (personal communication, Charleston, August 8, 2005). Having multiple agencies involved, staffed by people who work well together, enabled them to move forward and traverse the challenges of differing agency terrains.

To help design the program, representatives from state agencies in New York and Georgia were brought in to discuss their preschool programs. New York advised them to set the requirement for collaborative classrooms high (those with two or more funding streams). This led West Virginia to set the requirement at 50 percent. Georgia advised them to set the minimum requirements for teachers high at the beginning because of the difficulty in raising standards after the program was already established. West Virginia set high standards for public schools but reduced standards for child care providers. Whereas public school preschool classes are required to have certified teachers with early education certification, child care providers (nonprofit or for-profit providers in the community) are only required to have an associate degree or be working toward certification. For both public schools and child care providers, the teachers "are permitted" to teach in preschool classrooms if they are working toward certification.

To facilitate the rule-making process, WVDOE and WVDHHR established the Partners Implementing the Early Care and Education System (PIECES) Advisory Council. Efforts were made to include representatives from public and private early childhood agencies, higher education, legislature, business, early childhood advocates, parents, and community advocates. The team identified representatives from these groups, and submitted the names for appointment to the Secretary of WVDHHR and to the WVDOE Superintendent for approval.

The team adopted a three-pronged approach to rulemaking that successfully created an inclusive and transparent process. First, from May to November 2002 the PIECES Council met monthly to review drafts. They went through seven rounds of circulating draft rules for comment to a wide group of early care and education professionals, parents, and community representatives. Second, ad hoc committees comprised of both PIECES members and other stakeholders met to address key issues such as curriculum, health/safety, and transportation. Third, the team met with groups of interested people around the state to present the concept of universal preschool and to promote collaboration at the local level. They also made use of information technology to facilitate information flows by creating a web portal to disseminate information across the state and to answer questions posed by stakeholders in the field. After the initial rulemaking process, the Web portal was replaced by posting PIECES minutes to the WVDHHR Web site, thus continuing a transparent and inclusive decision-making process.

The culmination of all the team's efforts came in November 2002, when the rules were presented to the West Virginia Board of Education for approval. The monumental task of creating a new program had been successfully completed in eight short months and, in the process, important collaborative relationships had been forged that would be needed to sustain the program in the years to come. Jones, Tilton, and Huebner all describe the experience as exhausting but satisfying. The working group and the regional offices established relationships that built bridges and created the social capital necessary to create a foundation of trust.

The collaborative process for writing the program rules was successful on all fronts, and set the stage for the collaboration required at the local level by the preschool legislation. Similar to New York, each school district must submit an annual plan to participate in preschool. The plan requires representation from all stakeholders and, if the program is to be collaborative, Head Start and child care must sign off on it. This requirement gives Head Start and private child care bargaining power in the design of local preschool programs. Once the plan is approved by local stakeholders, it is sent to WVDHHR for review. If WVDHHR rejects the plan, the school district is ineligible for preschool funds; however, school districts have the right to appeal rejection of their plans in circuit court. Because a formal rule gives WVDHHR the power of first review, this agency remains involved in the implementation process. WVDOE has final approval power, but the school district plan only reaches WVDOE if it has been approved by WVDHHR. WVDOE's Cathy Jones and WVDHHR's Kay Tilton both state that collaboration is key and that "the triad" makes it work: Child care brings the capacity, public schools bring the certified teachers, and Head Start brings the services (personal communications, Charleston, August 8 and August 11, 2005, respectively).

The trust established during the rulemaking process in 2002 was severely strained with the revision of the preschool rules in 2004–05. In the first writing of the rules, Head Start and WVDHHR had an equal place at the table with WVDOE. But in the revision, WVDOE unilaterally revised the rules prior to involving either Head Start or WVDHHR. This essentially relegated WVDHHR and Head Start to "minor player" status. The reasons for WVDOE's unilateral move are both procedural and substantive. In West Virginia, the State Board of Education reviews and approves all rules related to public education. The Board consists of twelve appointed members with nine appointments by the governor and three ex officio members. The members serve overlapping nine-year terms, and no more than five members may belong to the same party (West Virginia Department of Education 2007). Because preschool rules involve public education, the State Board of Education has the power to approve rule changes, whereas the legislature has the power only to review, not change, public education rules. In contrast, all rule changes for WVDHHR must be reviewed and approved by the state legislature.

Representatives of the West Virginia Education Association stated that the revisions of preschool rules (colloquially referred to as 2525) went through the same process as all other rules under the jurisdiction of the State Board of Education (Bryant, Perry, personal communication, Charleston, August 12, 2005), namely, that revised rule changes are made within the education bureaucracy under the direction of the State Board of Education and then distributed to stakeholders for comment. What is apparent in talking to the various stakeholder groups is that the institutional rules governing the education rulemaking process clashed with the collaborative norm established by Kay Tilton, Cathy Jones, and Bill Huebner. While WVDHHR still has a seat at the table because it is the first to review school district plans, WVDOE's procedural practice of changing the rules to reflect the public education constituency and only afterward providing them to WVDHHR and Head Start replaced a level playing field with hierarchy.

Much of the rancor over the rule revision was due to process, but there were also significant substantive disagreements. Contentious issues that arose included square footage requirements for each child, fences around preschool playgrounds, transportation of preschool students, and licensing. The first three issues were resolved to some extent, but the disagreement over licensing remains. In the original version, the public school programs would have been held to WVDHHR's licensing standards for child care. With the revised rules, WVDHHR no longer has the authority to monitor public school preschool programs. Rather, WVDOE developed its own process and procedures manual for monitoring. This means that preschool programs in the public schools have different licensing standards than preschool programs in Head Start and private child care centers. This change frustrated many who thought West Virginia would have learned from Georgia's experience of having two sets of requirements. *Charleston Gazette* columnist Dawn Miller urged the two agencies to work together for the good of children (Miller 2005a, 2005b). But the tilt in favor of WVDOE's power to control the preschool program created a rift, and it remains to be seen if it can be repaired.

The rule revision controversy reverberated into the early education advocacy community. When the legislature reviewed the rules (it can review but may not alter), Margie Hale of West Virginia's Kids Count circulated data on how the rule changes would harm children. She was particularly concerned about the public schools not being held to WVDHHR licensing standards (personal communication, Charleston, August 11, 2005). Others voiced concern about whether WVDOE would effectively monitor preschool quality.[2] But the discontent for many advocates is part of a larger concern about the future of early education and care for birth to three year olds. Prior to the universal preschool legislation for four year olds, the Educare pilot programs focused on the full range of early childhood years. When the Educare program was cut, there was little immediate political backlash; however, those who were committed to Educare have regrouped and are actively pushing to reframe early childhood policy to include children younger than four. In October 2005, First Lady Gayle Manchin and A Vision Shared (a coalition formed by the West Virginia Council for Community and Economic Development) led a two-day policy forum addressing the importance of state investment in early education for economic development. The conference was held to highlight the results of a study by Marshall University, funded by the Benedum Foundation, on the economic benefits of early childhood education. Former director of the Governor's Cabinet on Children and Families Renata Pore, who was involved in organizing the conference, stated that the goal of the conference was to bring together nationally recognized leaders in early childhood with the business community in order to persuade them that early childhood is an important issue (personal communication, Charleston, August 9, 2005). This conference is part of a larger attempt to shift the focus from the education of four year olds to birth to five.

Media coverage in the *Charleston Gazette* was extensive. The conference was featured in an editorial, a column, and two articles. The editorial, titled "Preschool Good for Business," praised West Virginia's business leaders for recognizing "the value of early childhood education" (Charleston Gazette 2005, 2). Dawn Miller began her column with a quote from the Marshall University study's main author that stated, "The payoff for early childhood development is probably higher than any other economic development expenditure," and proceeded to argue in favor of replacing business subsidies with early childhood investments to generate "adaptable workers who know how to think" (2005b, 4A). Both articles touted the benefits of early childhood investment; one highlighted the Marshall study findings of a $5.20 return for every dollar invested in early childhood (Ginsberg 2005), and another highlighted the forum's focus on the importance of public investment in early childhood as a strategy for economic development (Finn 2005, 3). Former Senator Jackson, cochair of A Vision Shared's Early Child Development Focus Area Team and board member of the Benedum Foundation, was cited in the article for his support for reviving Educare or a similar program to focus attention on the earliest years. While this may appear to be a role reversal, Jackson stated that he never opposed Educare, but rather thought it was too expensive to expand statewide (personal communication, Charleston, August 10, 2005).

The deadline for universality is 2012, and it is unclear whether support for preschool will be sufficient to reach that goal. The legislative definition of universality is that every four-year-old must have access to a program that meets the procedural rules for the program. The program must be run by a public school or a program contracted through the public schools for twelve hours per week or more. The cost is free for Head Start and public schools, but child care programs are allowed to charge for wraparound services. Many who are closely involved with the program are concerned that the political commitment will not exist to reach universality. This is primarily because expanding to cover every four-year-old in the state who wants to participate will require new funding and capital construction in growth counties. According to Bill

Huebner, "Communities are coming to the wall" because there are more kids to serve and funding streams have been fully tapped (personal communication, Charleston, August 10, 2005). One of the challenges is that schools will need money up front to build new capacity. Perry Bryant of the West Virginia Teachers Association states that the School Building Authority will have to issue bonds, and that additional state funds will need to be allocated (personal communication, Charleston, August 12, 2005). To achieve universality, the legislature will have to increase the budget to an estimated $60 million from the current $37 million (Jackson, Lloyd, personal communication, Charleston, August 10, 2005). One rule change that has helped the growth counties is that the school funding formula is now based on current enrollment rather than on the previous year's enrollment. Prior to this change, growth districts did not see increased per pupil funding until the following year because the state school formula relied on the previous year's enrollment figures. This change applies only to the growth counties; the formula for counties with declining enrollments remains unchanged. This translates into funding schools with growing enrollments at higher levels when they need it to serve additional children, and shielding schools with declining enrollments from cuts for a year.

At the time of this research, the preschool program has not achieved political stability, nor has it been able to achieve a uniform policy image. While there does appear to be broad support for public investment in early education, it has not coalesced around the preschool program. Unlike New York, in which child care advocates joined with preschool advocates to champion increased investment in the preschool program, the advocates in West Virginia are primarily focused on returning to a policy image for early childhood that includes birth-to-five. While advocates may not oppose increased investment in preschool, they may not rally to pressure the legislature to appropriate the necessary funds to expand the program either.

The preschool program also faces the institutional challenges of straddling two government agencies. With the 2005 revision of the rules, WVDOE exerted its control over rule making for the program and made a decision to create a new set of regulations for preschool in public schools. This decision muddied the regulatory process and led to valid concerns by early childhood advocates about the quality-monitoring process. There was a tone of resignation in advocates' voices about the preschool program. The sentiment was that the WVDOE had won the preschool battle, and now it was time to focus on winning investment for the earliest years. The challenge for West Virginia preschool will be to prevent further retreat of agencies into their respective "silos." This challenge will become even more difficult now that the cast of players is changing. Media accounts indicate Governor Manchin and his political appointees to WVDOE and WVDHHR are supportive of preschool (Miller 2005a). But the challenge remains to find ways for two autonomous state agencies, with different approaches to the education of young children, to find sufficient common ground. In both WVDHHR and WVDOE, preschool is a small program within very large bureaucracies, and it remains to be seen how the leadership's commitment to preschool will translate to decisions on the ground. If the revision of the preschool rules is any indication, it will be a bumpy process. An additional challenge is that the triad of committed civil servants changed. Head Start Collaboration Director Bill Huebner and WVDOE's Cathy Jones resigned to take out-of-state positions and WVDHHR's Kay Tilton retired.

It remains to be seen if the institutional, budgetary, and political support for preschool will stabilize. But there is some good news for West Virginia in the form of its policy entrepreneurs, national recognition, and media support. Senator Robert Plymale, chairman of the Senate Education Committee, has emerged as a strong advocate for preschool. In 2006, West Virginia received national attention from the National Institute for Early Education Research. Its 2005 annual state report ranked West Virginia fifth in the nation for preschool access for four year olds and tenth in resources for preschool (National Institute for Early Education Research 2006). The *Charlestown Gazette* published an editorial praising the rankings and urging additional funding (2006a). A second editorial appeared later in the year that again urged support for greater investment in early education (2006b). With political leadership in the Senate, national publicity, and media support, West Virginia may be heading in the direction of greater stability for preschool.

## Analysis

According to Baumgartner and Jones, policy monopolies can be dislodged either by a dynamic process of jostling from challengers with different issue constructions or by a destabilized institutional structure. In the four pioneer cases, universal preschool was the new status quo, but there were varying levels of success in achieving stability.

For both Oklahoma and West Virginia, policy entrepreneurs inserted preschool programs into the education policy monopoly. In Oklahoma, the 1990 shift of the targeted preschool program from a line item into the state school funding formula stabilized budget support for the program. When the program expanded to universal access in 1998, political support for the program was never challenged, in large part because there was little need to amend the program and it stayed out of the limelight. But it was also skillful actions by policy entrepreneurs that led to increased school district participation in the program. Preschool was never the subject of a political battle, but it had a broad base of supporters that could have been drawn upon if needed. It was as if the program expansion happened while only a small group of insiders, and nobody else, was paying attention. With the arrival of media attention in the last few years, the stability of the preschool program is now assured.

The pursuit of stability for preschool in West Virginia had a very different outcome. The challenges for preschool are both institutional and policy image-related. With the loss of Senator Jackson, there was no elected official to champion the program. The preschool program has been able to stay under the radar since 2005 because it has not required additional budget outlays; however, to achieve universality by 2012, the budget negotiations will require that it be in the spotlight. Senator Plymale has emerged as a policy entrepreneur for preschool, but it remains to be seen if he can build the political support for the increased budget required to attain universality by 2012. The key question will be whether early childhood advocates will unite to fight for the program. At this time, advocates for early childhood investment have not coalesced around preschool for four year olds, and prefer to expand the policy image to include investments for younger children. They are actively working to reframe the policy image to include the full range of early childhood ages. To achieve success, they are expanding the range of early childhood advocates to include the business community by linking early childhood investments to economic development. The early childhood issue network may successfully dislodge preschool and seek to create a more inclusive policy image as the new status quo.

In addition to the political instability and diverging policy image, the institutional challenges of straddling two government agencies create another source of instability. Preschool is a small program in two very large bureaucracies. It is not clear whether the preschool program will be able to firmly attach itself to the education policy monopoly, despite being in the state funding formula. Governor Manchin's political appointees in WVDOE and WVDHHR have professed their commitment in media accounts, but it remains to be seen how hard anyone is going to fight to win additional resources for the program. The degree to which WVDHHR and Head Start will rally for preschool is an open question.

In New York, universal preschool continues to enjoy strong support from the speaker of the Assembly and a well-organized and well-funded network of advocates. The Board of Regents supports the program and the

Democratic Governor Spitzer showed his support by increasing funding for the program. The preschool program funding was not only increased in 2007, but it also was funded on a formula basis, rather than a grant program. Advocates indicate that this stabilizes funding for the program. However, with the March 2008 resignation of Governor Spitzer, New York lost its champion. But with committed political leadership in the legislature, and well-organized and funded advocates, if Governor Paterson supports UPK then New York may finally achieve a stable policy monopoly.

Georgia's preschool program required the engineering of new institutional arrangements to save the program. Because of the success of the lottery and the constitutional requirement to direct lottery revenues to preschool (and Hope Scholarship and other educational programs), the preschool program has been able to expand access. However, political support was far from certain when the program was first created. The governor created a new agency to rescue preschool from a hostile State Superintendent and expanded preschool from a targeted program to a universal one to generate broader political support. There are currently a stable image construction and a stable base of political support, and these are unlikely to be challenged in the near future. The only challenge to preschool is from the private child care industry, and the associated changes are likely to be incremental rather than an attempt to establish a new status quo.

Constructing a stable policy image for preschool is challenging because the program falls between two agencies. The state departments of education (DOEs) have jurisdiction over K–12, while the state departments of human services (DHSs) have jurisdiction over child care regulations and welfare programs that include child care subsidies. The creation of preschool in all four pioneer states forced these agencies to adapt. In Georgia, New York, and Oklahoma, the preschool program was placed in DOE. But only Oklahoma was able to create a stable institutional environment immediately after passage of universal preschool legislation. Even though both Oklahoma and Georgia had elected state superintendents, they had contrasting implementation experiences. In Oklahoma, State Superintendent Garrett was a longtime supporter of the preschool program and had been a key policy entrepreneur in 1990, when she was the Secretary of Education, in shifting the preschool program into the state school funding formula. She completely supported the expansion of the preschool program to universal access. In contrast, Georgia Governor Zell Miller's public feud with State Superintendent Schrenko forced him to create a separate agency for the preschool program.

Independence of the State Education Department from the governor proved problematic in New York, but for a different reason than in

Georgia. In New York, the legislature, not the governor, has oversight and appointment power over the New York Board of Regents. Governor Pataki tried to move education from legislative to executive control but was unsuccessful. The annual battle over education spending represented a philosophical difference between the executive and legislative branches of government, but it was also due to an institutional constraint on the governor's power to control education spending.

In West Virginia, the governor has the power to appoint State Department of Education officials but the State Board of Education has overlapping terms and limits the number of seats that can be occupied by one party. The State Board of Education approves rules for education and the legislature has only the power of review, not the power to alter. A key institutional issue for West Virginia is that preschool must have the support of governor's appointees in both WVDOE and WVDHHR, the state legislature, and the State Board of Education. Senator Jackson was able to build a coalition for the passage of preschool legislation but it remains to be seen if budget support for universality will happen by 2012.

The four pioneer states passed universal preschool without participation by national actors. Only in the struggle to attain stability for the preschool programs has support from national actors come into the state processes. Recognition from the National Institute for Early Education Research figured prominently in solidifying broad political support for universal preschool in Oklahoma (see table 3.2 for summary of NIEER ranking for pioneer states). Support from Pre-K Now, a national advocacy organization for universal preschool, provided funding to New York that was critical in building a cohesive state advocacy coalition. Both Pre-K Now and the National Institute for Early Education Research have a common source of funding: The Pew Charitable Trusts. In 2001 Pew emerged as a well-funded, national actor that could build a nationwide advocacy coalition for state policy change. The process for creating that coalition is the subject of the next chapter.

## Table 3.2
## Pioneer State Universal Preschool Program Rankings

## Access and Resources

| | Access Ranking | Resource Ranking | Total state program enrollment | School districts that offer state program | Income requirement | Hours of operation | Total state Pre-K spending (Millions) | State spending per child enrolled | Percent of state population enrolled |
|---|---|---|---|---|---|---|---|---|---|
| Georgia | 3 | 15 | 75,299 | 100% (counties | None | 6.5 hours/day, 5 days/week | $310 | $4,114 | 53% |
| New York | 9 | 20 | 84,660 | 32% | None | Determined locally* | $292 | $3,454 | 35% |
| Oklahoma | 1 | 21 | 34,375 | 97% | None | Determined locally† | $118 | $3,433 | 68% |
| West Virginia | 4 | 11 | 10,659 | 100% | None | Determined locally‡ | $47 | $4,441 | 46% |

*Source:* National Institute for Early Education Research. 2008. *The State of Preschool: 2007 State Preschool Yearbook.* Retrieved October 13, 2008, from http://nieer.org/yearbook/pdf/yearbook.pdf.

---

* Programs operate for either a half-day (2.5 hours) or full day (5 hours), five days per week.
† Half-day programs operate for 2.5 hours, while full-day programs operate for six hours. Many districts offer both full- and half-day programs. All programs operate five days per week.
‡ Programs typically operate two full days per week, or four full days per week with Friday reserved for activities such as home visits and planning. Some counties offer a full-day, full-week program.

# 4

# The Pew Charitable Trusts
# and Universal Preschool

THE DEVELOPMENT OF universal preschool in the four pioneer states was largely an internal state policy process. The policy entrepreneurs and advocates were all state actors. But national actors have arrived in the form of foundation funding from the Pew Charitable Trusts.[1] In late 2001, Pew decided to make universal preschool a new giving program. While there have been many foundations seeking to improve the lives of children, Pew's goal was "to fundamentally change the way this country invests in education for its three- and four-year-olds" (Pew Charitable Trusts 2007, 27). With total assets over $5 billion, Pew is a major player in the foundation world and has the power to bring considerable resources to inform policy change (Pew Charitable Trusts 2007). There are two aspects of the Pew giving program that are particularly interesting. First, Pew chose to invest its resources in a particular policy alternative, universal preschool for all three- and four-year-olds. This means that Pew decided what the right course of action was for the education of young children and then invested its resources to create a movement toward policy change. Second, the strategy Pew developed in concert with its grantees was to effect policy change primarily at the state level. As discussed below, there is a federal policy dimension to the Pew giving program, but the emphasis is on informing state policy change. Studying Pew's role in state policy change affords the opportunity to assess the impacts of the arrival of national actors (through Pew funding) on state policy-making processes. This chapter begins with a discussion of the role of foundations in public policy, provides a brief history of the Pew Charitable Trusts, and Pew's strategy for informing universal preschool policy change. Chapter 5 analyzes the state policy-making processes in specific states.

## Foundations in the Policy Process

There have been many important books published on the history of foundations and their relation to public policy that help place the Pew universal preschool giving program into historical context. There are rich case studies of the Carnegie Corporation (Lagemann 1989) and the Rockefeller Foundation (Brown 1979). There are several studies during particular eras such as Sealander's (1997) history of foundations and public policymaking from the Progressive Era to the New Deal and Weaver's (1969) history of American foundations through the mid-1960s. There are studies critical of the role of foundations in society, most notably Waldemar Nielsen's *The Big Foundations* (1972) and *The Golden Donors* (1985). More recently journalist Mark Dowie coined the term "philanthrocacy" to describe what he characterizes as the exercise of "great power in American life, power far beyond their wealth, and influence that extends beyond their founders' imaginations (2001, xxi). A less polemical analysis by Joel Fleishman focuses on the strategies utilized by foundations to achieve their missions. He asks, "Why would Amercia's wealthiest citizens give to support organizations that could be seen as undermining the bulwarks of privilege on which their own power was built?" (Fleishman 2007, 43). He presents a Marxist critique (foundations defend the interests of the rich) with a conservative one (foundations use their power irresponsibly to promote a liberal agenda) and rejects both. Rather, through analysis of twelve case studies, he argues that foundations have been overwhelmingly beneficial for society. But he also criticizes foundations for their lack of accountability and transparency and laments the lack of scholarly work, noting that foundations rarely allow scholars access to the records that would lead to published studies.

All of the works cited above are dealing with power, whether indirectly or directly. None of these contributions attempts to provide a theory of foundations' role in public policy but each has an implicit and sometimes explicit discussion of the power of foundations. For example, in a study of foundation influence on several social welfare policy areas[2] during the Progressive Era to the New Deal, Sealander, while not utilizing Kingdon's three streams model, comes to a distinctly Kingdonian conclusion: foundations were able to elevate issues on the agenda but they were less successful in determining the policy alternative. She found that even when the foundation's alternative was selected it had little control over the implementation process. The pattern that emerged was one in which private money invested to influence public policy often resulted in tangled outcomes (Sealander 1997). The Center on Philanthropy and Public Policy at the University of Southern California is trying to improve outcomes by bringing philanthropic, nonprofit, and policy communities together around research findings and policy issues (see, for example, Ferris 2003 and Ferris et al. 2006). Its mission is "to promote more effective philanthropy and strengthen the nonprofit sector through research that informs philanthropic decision making and public policy to advance public problem solving" (2007). While there is important scholarship on improving the practice of philanthropy (such as Ferris 2003 and Frumkin 2006), theory on the role of foundations in public policy remains an underdeveloped area of research.

The policy process literature cited in the prior three chapters does not mention foundations, but for decades sociologists and political scientists debated the role of elites in society and foundations were included in their models of policy making. The work of C. Wright Mill, G. William Domhoff and Thomas Dye from the elite power theory perspective clashed with the pluralist perspective of Robert Dahl, among others.[3] The elite power theorists gave foundations a privileged role in the policy process. In Domhoff's version of elite power theory, foundations play a role in both policy formation and the "ideology" process (i.e., the formation, dissemination, and enforcement of attitudes and assumptions that permit the continued existence of policies and politicians favorable to the wealth, income, status and privileges of members of the ruling class (Domhoff 1998). In Thomas Dye's schematic of the policy process, foundations receive their money from wealthy individuals and corporations that then provide grants to major universities and policy think tanks and provide research personnel to government commissions and councils, who then provide experts for the national news media and affect all branches of the government through their policy reports and recommendations and generation of media attention.[4]

But the universal preschool giving program at Pew diverges from Dye's schematic. Pew is engaged in the ways in which Dye describes but it is also engaged more directly. Pew chose a particular policy alternative and has supported the creation of a network of actors, beyond funding university and policy planning group research to achieve its goal. Pew's strategic plan for achieving universal preschool is brilliantly comprehensive. The section below begins with a brief history of the Pew Charitable Trusts followed by a discussion of the universal preschool giving strategy and its implementation.

### The Pew Charitable Trusts

The Pew Charitable Trusts was originally created through the combination of seven separate trusts all started by the heirs of the Sun Oil

Company fortune. Four adult children of Joseph Newton and Mary Anderson Pew founded the Pew Memorial Foundation joined by three other members of the extended family. The founders capitalized the foundation with 880,000 shares of Sun Oil Company stock, which returned an annual dividend of $1 per share. The foundation focused on four general areas of giving: scientific, charitable, religious, and educational. Two more trusts were created in 1957, the Mary Anderson Pew Trust and the JHP Freedom Trust. These three trusts increased with the death of J. N. Pew Jr. in 1963, after his will created a trust in his name. In 1965 a fifth trust was established by J. Howard Pew, as a further tribute to his brother. After the death of Mabel Pew Myrin in 1972, the sixth trust was established in her name. The seventh and final trust was established in 1979 with the death of Mary Ethel Pew (Gardner and Rardin 2001).

In its early decades, Pew was not well known. The founders preferred to give in anonymity and while there had been a federal administrative requirement that foundations file a report with the Internal Revenue Service since 1942 and a statutory requirement since 1953, it was not enforced. Pew allowed the first public mention of a gift with the opening of a building on Stanford University's campus in 1967 (Gardner and Rardin 2001). But while secretive, Pew was not immune to larger political forces. With the rising fear of communism, Congress authorized investigations into the role of foundations in 1952 and in 1954. While earlier in the century foundations were feared as agents of "creeping capitalism," in the 1950s they were under scrutiny for possible connections to communism. Especially after the perjury conviction of Alger Hiss, president of the Carnegie Endowment for International Peace, in a case involving communist espionage, foundations were a lightning rod for investigations for attempting to infiltrate the government and affect its policies (Commission on Foundations and Private Philanthropy 1970, 66; Nielsen 1972).[5] Despite incendiary charges at the beginnings of the investigations, no legislation was passed as a result (Commission on Foundations and Private Philanthropy 1970).

However, the federal scrutiny of foundations in the 1950s led to structural changes at Pew. In 1956, The Pew Memorial Foundation was restructured to create the Pew Memorial Trust and The Glenmede Trust Company. The primary purpose of Glenmede was to administer the newly formed trust and two additional trusts established in 1957. The structure allowed the Pew Memorial Trust to claim the privacy of bank-company relationship (Nielsen 1972); however, Pew historian Joel R. Gardner provides a more benign justification, "[it] enabled the Pews to establish individual trusts with specific missions and to participate jointly in the grantmaking process for all these trusts" (2001, 19). With a twelve-member board, nine of whom were major shareholders, Glenmede had the primary responsibility for grantmaking through its Committee on Grants. The nine major stockholders entered into a "stock succession agreement," which restricted sale of most shares to individuals approved by a two-thirds majority of the group of nine. This created an institutional mechanism for preserving the Pew family's traditions and legacy. Giving areas remained the same and grants continued to be made under conditions of anonymity. According to Gardner, large grants were given for building college campuses, in particular historically black colleges, and hospitals but there were also a large number of small grants for operating expenses for a range of religious and educational organizations. Between 1957 and 1969 the Trusts awarded 2,565 grants totaling $64.6 million with an average yearly allocation of $5 million, which according to Gardner was a fourfold increase over the average grant-making between 1948 and 1956 (2001, 20).

While no legislative changes resulted from the 1950s investigations, monumental changes came about in the 1960s. In 1964, IRS rules were changed in favor of publicly supported nonprofits rather than foundations. The Act extended an additional 10 percent deduction for gifts to charitable organizations which "receive a substantial part of their support from ... direct or indirect contributions from the general public" (Nielsen 1972). Because foundations do not receive contributions from the general public they were excluded from benefiting from this tax policy change. But it was in 1969 that foundations experienced, in Nielsen's words, "ejection from Eden" (1972). Nearly one-third of the changes to the tax code in that year were directed at foundations. Among the many changes, private foundations were split off from other 501(c)3 organizations to create a foundation category divided into three groups: private, publicly supported (receive donations from wide public), and operating (use funds to support their own programs). Tax incentives for donating to publicly supported and operating nonprofit organizations were increased to 50 percent but contributions to private foundations were left at 20 percent of the donor's taxable income. Private foundations were also taxed on their net investment income (set at 4 percent), whereas before that time their entire investment income was tax exempt. The changes also put the IRS in the position of censoring the substance of a broad range of foundation activity due to the establishment of a doctrine of "expenditure responsibility." Basically that meant that foundations were required to ensure that their grants were used only for the intended purpose.[6] Finally, for foundations that did not qualify as publicly supported, the act changed the prohibition against "political and propaganda" activity from "no substantial part" to a flat prohibition against it with language stating "otherwise attempting to influence legislation, including attempting to affect public opinion or communicating with persons participating in the legislative process" (Nielsen 1972, 375).

In 1972, philanthropy scholar Waldemar Nielsen's analysis titled *Big Foundations* placed Pew in the "underachievers and delinquents" category calling it "a furtive creature with antisocial psychosis" (Nielsen 1972, 119). The tone of Nielsen's book is critical, bordering on sarcastic, but at the time, foundations were secretive and the federal government had only just begun to force them to open up. Nielsen describes foundations as having an "obsession for privacy" that only compulsory reporting mandated by the federal government could force them to change. He continues, "Foundations have long been aware of their political vulnerability. But with the characteristic insensitivity of aristocratic institutions to new social trends, they have consistently misconceived its basis. They have tended to attribute it to 'public misunderstanding' of their good works or their 'lack of a constituency,' ignoring the fact that they are highly visible examples of special privilege accorded to the very rich by an inequitable tax system that is increasingly resented by the general public" (Nielsen 1972, 395).

Nielsen's assessment of Pew and the other large foundations was representative of the time, but the 1969 federal tax reform did force changes. Pew historian Joel R. Gardner states that the effect of the tax changes on The Pew Charitable Trusts was "profound." In order to meet the new federal distribution requirement, Glenmede had to sell some of the Trusts' non-Sun Oil holdings in order to raise additional funds. This was necessary because the Trusts had large holdings in the Sun Oil Company, whose dividends were paid partially in stock (Gardner and Rardin 2001, 23). But the shift in holdings translated into greater giving by Pew; by 1974 Pew gave $22 million compared to $9.4 million in 1970 (Gardner and Rardin 200, 124). Pew continued its commitment to a philosophy of individual freedom and free markets, giving to the conservative Hoover Institution and American Enterprise Institute. While the largest grants continued to be for education and hospital buildings, Pew also expanded to new giving areas such as the environment.

The increased giving, which reached $49.6 million in 1978, required Pew to hire professional staff. In the 1970s, Glenmede's staff grew to over fifty employees and, with the death in 1979 of the last of the original four founders, shifted into a new phase of organizational development. While Pew reaffirmed the philanthropic aims and goals of the founders, this was a new era for Pew. In 1979 the board decided to become more proactive in addressing the needs of a changing and complex society. The board decided to start initiating projects and programs and then find agencies capable of implementing them. A public signal of the change came in 1980 when Pew issued its first public annual report. As Pew continued to professionalize its administration, the Committee on Grants started to separate grants into categories and employed professional consultants to assist in the development of the direction for giving in each of the grant-making areas. As a result, Pew shifted from bricks and mortar to funding Trusts-initiated projects (TIPs). For each program area, TIPs provided staff and board support for making "sustained and focused investments to address significant issues or problems" (Gardner and Rardin 2001, 30).

During this time of rapid growth and professionalization, the identities of the Glenmede Trust Company and the Pew Charitable Trusts were redefined. The Trusts developed their own professional staff and administrative structures and, by 1984, were issuing five separate annual reports. In 1986 a single annual report was issued but the distinction between The Pew Charitable Trusts and Glenmede continued to develop. In 1987, a reorganization of Glenmede delineated its two functions—the Trusts' philanthropy and its growing investment-management business. Glenmede Trust Company became the largest of four subsidiaries of the Glenmede Corporation. Glenmede Trust Company had several business divisions and the Pew Charitable Trusts. The Committee on Grants at Glenmede became the board of The Pew Charitable Trusts. By 1988, the Pew Charitable Trusts had become the nation's second-largest private foundation in terms of giving.

Looking toward the 1990s, the board adopted four operating principles to guide its future, including a new focus on accountability and interdisciplinary programming. An evaluation unit was created to measure the results of the grantees' projects and attaining the Trusts' strategies. While not unique to Pew, this widely shared approach to grant-making adopts tools from the business world to measure results that in turn translate into achieving strategic goals. The Venture Fund was created to fund possibly high-risk but high-potential interdisciplinary efforts. The Trust continued its programs of culture, education, environment, health and human services, public policy, and religion. Part of the pro-active changes at Pew led the Trusts to expand its efforts at increasing public awareness of its giving. This led to the creation of the Public Affairs Department.

In the 1990s, under the board leadership of J. Howard Pew II and President Rebecca W. Rimel, Pew adopted a strategy focused on depth rather than breadth. They decided to focus on a few key issues and devote considerable funds to achieving their goals. The Trusts decided to take an advocacy stance on some issues but a neutral broker stance on others. Major areas included decreasing emissions contributing to global warming, campaign finance reform, and improving the practice of journalism, among others. The results-oriented philanthropy means that the Trusts select giving areas in which they think they can make a measurable difference. The goals are ambitious but feasible and the timing must be right. One common strategy is to play the role of a broker for informed dialogue among actors who are critical to effecting change. Gardner states, "when these parties interact effectively, their varied points of view enrich the dialogue; the public gains access to the information it needs for informed opinions, and policymakers are provided with credible research and analysis upon which to act" (2001, 40). This reflects one of the roles depicted in Dye's schematic. Pew's giving is intended to leverage its investments through increased interest from the public, the media and policy makers, and allied organizations.

On January 1, 2004, the Pew Charitable Trusts changed its legal status from a private foundation to a public charity. It was able to do this because there were seven separate trusts providing funding to Pew, which, as the Internal Revenue Service (IRS) agreed, thus passed the public-support test for public charities. By changing its legal tax status to a public charity, Pew now benefits from avoidance of the excise tax on its endowment as well as the inapplicability of the 5-percent-payout rule;[7] it also receives an exemption from state sales tax. It is no longer subject to the private foundation rules on "self dealing" and it will no longer be subject to private foundation restrictions on excess business holdings or to private foundation limits on grants to individuals and government officials. It must also raise funds from the public and has been successful in doing so. But as a public charity, the real benefit to Pew is that it significantly increases its ability to advocate for its policy agenda.

A vocal critic of this change, Pablo Eisenberg, Senior Fellow at the Georgetown Public Policy Institute and executive committee member of the National Committee for Responsive Philanthropy, criticized the IRS and Pew for the failure to recognize that the board of a public charity should not be governed by the wealthy family who donates the funds. The current Pew board is evenly split between family members and outside members. Eisenberg characterized Pew as a "bully" that tries to impose its priorities on other organizations and lamented that with its change in tax status Pew would be able to wield even more power and influence (2003, 38–38). But others, such as New York University Professor Harvey Dale, Director of the National Center on Philanthropy and the Law, viewed the change as more benign. Because Pew is now a public charity, donors to it are entitled a greater federal income tax deduction for their gifts. As discussed below, leveraging funds from multiple sources has been a strategy for effecting universal preschool policy change. Furthermore, Pew can engage in lobbying to some extent (Dale, Harvey, e-mail communication, December 18, 2007).

## The Preschool Strategy

The shift to funding universal preschool came about as part of a change in strategy in the Education Division. Dr. Susan Urahn became the Director of the Education Program at Pew in 2000. When she reviewed the portfolio of education investments, she concluded that she should recommend to the board that they shift from the K–12 investments and scattered higher education investments of the prior decade to a focus on preschool. According to Urahn (telephone communication, November 9, 2005), there were a variety of factors that led to the preschool focus. First, there was consensus building through a body of research on the importance of early brain development and public awareness of that research combined with longitudinal studies on the social benefits of high-quality preschool. This could be used to make the case that school could start at an age earlier than five. Second, data indicated that up to 80 percent of four year olds were already in an out-of-home placement, some in questionable quality settings. Third, polls indicated that the public was comfortable with four year olds in out-of-home care, which would allow them to avoid the "children should be home with their mothers" opposition. The polling data also indicated that the comfort level existed for three year olds but not for two year olds or infants. At the same time the preschool issue was gaining momentum, Pew's K–12 giving program had reached a point in which a shift in course was due. Pew had been funding the movement toward greater accountability in K–12. As the No Child Left Behind legislation wound its way through the federal policy process (eventually to be signed into law in January 2002), states were realizing that they would need to make changes in order to improve scores on achievement tests. Pew was at a crossroads: it could continue to invest in the accountability movement or it could shift to preschool.

A factor in the decision to pursue preschool was that it did not have the entrenched, polarized advocacy and bureaucratic environment that K–12 had. It was thought that policy changes for preschool would not face the resistance that would be incurred at the K–12 level. At the time Pew was deciding to invest in preschool, there were no foundations funding an opposing view; however, there were other foundations funding early education. When asked about the impact of Pew's program on other foundations' early childhood giving programs, an insider to the process at Pew stated that both Carnegie and Ford had already shifted away from early childhood programs and the Packard Foundation's stock market losses in 2002–2003 temporarily limited its ability to take on a larger role. However, the decrease in Packard funding to early education was temporary; a few years later, Packard was once again heavily involved, particularly in California. Smaller foundations, most notably the Foundation for Child Development, had giving programs but not with the singular purpose of Pew's universal preschool giving program. Once Pew began its giving program, it coordinated with other funders as part of the Early Childhood Funders' Collaborative, a group that meets regularly to discuss giving strategies.

But while the external environment looked promising for advancing universal preschool, in order to move the preschool proposal forward, it needed to go through Pew's "internal strategy cycle" (Planning and Evaluation Department 2001). First, universal preschool had to pass the "strategy development" phase. Education Program staff had to research and design a strategy and write a strategy paper. The Pew Planning and Evaluation staff convened and chaired a peer review process and made recommendations to management. Only after passing the internal review process, was the strategy paper presented to the board. What emerged was a well-developed, comprehensive strategy for informing policy change. When Dr. Urahn presented the strategy to the board it was well received (Urahn, Susan, telephone communication, November 9, 2005). With the support of the board, by December 2001 Pew made its first grant with a projected investment of $10 million per year over a ten-year period.

*Strategic Core: Research*

The strategy called for separating research from advocacy, which led Pew to fund two new projects: the National Institute for Early Education Research and the Trust for Early Education. According to those involved in the process, a firm decision was made that evidence should drive the process. To conduct research, Pew funded the National Institute for Early Education Research (NIEER) at Rutgers University (formerly the Center for Early Education Reesearch) with a $5.3 million grant in December 2001, and more than $20 million by 2006 (Kirp 2007, 160), NIEER was charged to "(a) develop a targeted policy-research agenda; (b) sponsor, conduct and communicate timely and rigorous research that addresses key policy questions; (c) provide clear, jargon-free translations of existing and emerging research to key public constituencies, policymakers and the media; (d) use the research to make policy recommendations and support technical assistance to states selected to participate in the initiative; and (e) provide a forum for convening and educating others about the policy issues in early education" (Pew Charitable Trusts 2001). The Director of NIEER, Dr. W. Steven Barnett, had been involved with creating the new initiative at Pew (telephone communication, September 6, 2006). Dr.

Barnett, Professor of Education Economics and Public Policy at Rutgers University, brings an illustrious career as an early childhood researcher to the enterprise. Among many important contributions, he published the cost-benefit study, *Lives in the Balance*, which found that every dollar invested in quality preschool generated over seven dollars in savings (Barnett 1996, 118). With funding from Pew, Barnett was able to expand his research organization at Rutgers, previously called the Center for Early Education Research (CEER), to have a national research focus. Prior to Pew funding, CEER was funded through foundation grants and a consortium of school districts with a primary focus on preschool and early intervention issues in New Jersey. CEER had become deeply involved with the preschool program for low-income children that resulted from the *Abbott v. Burke* New Jersey court cases.[8] After the transition to NIEER, Pew funds provided approximately 60 percent of its budget with the remaining 40 percent from other foundations and state contracts (Barnett, Steve, telephone communication, September 6, 2006). With the Pew funding, NIEER was, in the words of Barnett, "able to take on early childhood research that the federal government does not favor," such as quality improvements including teacher qualifications, extended day and school years, and curricula that emphasize broad goals for learning and development (Barnett, Steve, e-mail communication, November 20, 2007). The federal government is not a proponent of universal preschool but, with funding from Pew and others, NIEER is able to conduct the research that provides the information necessary to reduce policy makers' uncertainty about investing in quality preschool.

The structure of NIEER consists of a scientific advisory board made up of highly respected experts in early childhood research, staff researchers and administrative support, a research fellows program, and researchers available on a contract basis for specific projects. To date, NIEER has produced an array of publications targeting many different audiences. Each of NIEER's research projects is available in a variety of forms; the full reports are available for download, policy briefs for each report are published as a separate issue of *Policy Matters*, and one-page summaries are published as *Policy Facts*. There are also links to working papers and NIEER produced videos. For a broader audience, NIEER publishes *Preschool Matters*, a print magazine, containing brief articles related to preschool. Topics may include research but the scope is broader and addresses events, speakers, and so on. NIEER also maintains an online newsletter for disseminating media reports.

But by far the most prominent publication NIEER produces is its Annual State Report. This report ranks each state for its quality, access, and funding for preschool. First published in 2003, this annual report, available for download as a PDF file, provides easy access for a wide array of data on state provision of preschool. The report provides an easily disseminated tool for assessing individual states, relative performance, and trend data. High-performing states can utilize their rankings to showcase their preschool programs, as was the case when Oklahoma's preschool program achieved first-place ranking in access and benefited from the resulting press coverage. But the report also is an effective method for publicizing those states that do not have publicly funded preschool programs. A textbox titled "States with No Program 2004–2005" appears prominently on the first page of the 2005 Executive Summary, complete with a bright red title and vibrant blue background (Barnett et al. 2006, 4). The twelve states appear throughout the report with descriptive language such as, "the 12 states that have *perennially* had no program" (Barnett et al. 2006, 11, emphasis added).[9] The cumulative reference more than effectively conveys their laggard status.

In addition to the national research, NIEER has been instrumental in evaluations of state preschool programs. According to Barnett, "States underestimate the cost of evaluation. With the Pew funding, NIEER is able to contribute funds to help states evaluate their programs" (telephone communication, September 6, 2006). In 2005, NIEER published the results of a five-state evaluation of preschool programs in Michigan, New Jersey, South Carolina, Oklahoma, and West Virginia (Barnett, Lamy, and Jung 2005).[10] More recently NIEER published the first report on a longitudinal study of Arkansas's preschool program (Hustedt et al. 2007). NIEER also provides funding for others to undertake state research such as a study of the supply of teachers for the Illinois preschool program (Presley, Klosterman, and White 2006) and the evaluation of Oklahoma's preschool program in Tulsa (Gormley, Phillips, and Dawson 2005).[11] All of these reports are available for download from NIEER's Web site. In addition to research, NIEER maintains extensive links on its Web site to sources related to early childhood research including, but not limited to, Pew-funded organizations advancing universal preschool.

*Strategic Core: Advocacy*

With NIEER responsible for research, Pew set up the advocacy dimension of the initiative. In 2002, Pew funded the Trust for Early Education (TEE) as a project of the Education Trust (a separate 501(c)3 nonprofit organization), to educate the public and policy makers on the benefits of and need for universal education for three- and four-year-olds. Pew provided TEE with a $3.9 million grant in March 2002 to "help these state-based organizations and policymakers in their effort" to create universal pre-school. It provided an additional $4.4 million grant in May 2003 to continue to inform public debate on preschool at the federal level and in several states, work with media to increase coverage on early education, and build broader support for universal preschool "to demonstrate a wider scope of public endorsement" (Pew Charitable Trusts 2003). TEE also received funds from the Joyce and Kellogg Foundations. In its first year, TEE made four initial grants to organizations in Illinois, Massachusetts, New York, and New Jersey and awarded four planning grants to organizations in Arkansas, Oklahoma, Wisconsin, and North Carolina (Trust for Early Education 2007a). In all cases, the funding went to advocacy groups who were explicitly advocating for universal preschool. TEE's national strategy focused on attempts to build a "broad, bipartisan consensus for federal policies that support and adequately fund high quality pre-K programs for these children" (Trust for Early Education 2007b). The federal government, through the Child Care and Development Fund, Head Start and the welfare reform program (TANF), provides funding and sets guidelines for the care and education of millions of three and four year olds. These programs have different rules, different enabling legislation, and are administered by different agencies. A challenge for all early childhood advocates is to streamline the federal funding process. However, that is a daunting task. TEE's stated goal was far more modest, "to develop a federal QPK [quality pre-K] agenda with our state and federal partners" (Trust for Early Education 2007b).

The first major federal-level activity focused on by TEE was teacher qualifications for the federal Head Start program. Executive Director, Amy Wilkins, entered into a politically divisive battle over the reauthorization of Head Start and the Higher Education Act. In Congressional testimony, press releases, and other documents posted to its Web site, TEE advocated for requiring bachelor degrees for preschool educators and for greater collaboration of Head Start with state preschool programs. After receiving a written invitation to speak, she testified on June 3, 2003, before the House Subcommittee on Education Reform to discuss H.R. 2210, "The School Readiness Act of 2003" (i.e., reauthorization of the Higher Education Act). She advocated for higher educational requirements for Head Start teachers and pointed out that state-funded preschool programs serve more children than Head Start stating, "The significance of state funded programs serving a similar universe of children is a reality that Head Start policy must recognize" (Trust for Early Education 2007c). She received a second invitation to give testimony before the Senate Committee on Education to discuss Head Start reauthorization on July 22, 2003. She again called for higher educational levels for Head Start teachers, among other things (Trust for Early Education 2007d). The debate on reauthorization of Head Start ultimately comes down to an intergovernmental question: Should the federal government continue to provide a program targeting low-income children or should states provide preschool programs? The debate was not resolved until 2007, when Head Start was reauthorized. But rather than continue its focus on federal policy change, leadership and organizational changes placed the emphasis on advancing universal preschool at the state level.

In May 2004, Dr. Libby Doggett was promoted from state policy director to the executive director of TEE. In addition to leadership changes, organizational structure changes were afoot. Eight months after Dr. Doggett became the executive director, Pre-K Now was created to replace TEE. Whereas TEE was a project of the Education Trust, Pre-K Now is a project of the Institute for Educational Leadership (IEL). Pre-K Now receives approximately 90 percent of its funds from Pew (Doggett, Libby, personal communication, Washington, DC, June 20, 2006), which totaled $20 million by 2007 (Kirp 2007, 162). In addition, other foundations supporting Pre-K Now include: David and Lucile Packard Foundation, the RGK Foundation, Schumann Fund for New Jersey, the Foundation for Child Development, the McCormick Tribune Foundation, and CityBridge Foundation (Pre-K Now 2005a; Rubin, Stephanie, e-mail communication, November 14, 2007).

The stated mission of Pre-K Now is to support state-based campaigns for high-quality pre-K for all three- and four-year-olds, to build coalitions to achieve quality implementation, to impact state and federal legislation, and to raise public awareness about the need for universal pre-K. The choice of Pre-K Now for the organizational title is intended to associate the education of three and four year olds more closely with K–12 and distance pre-K from child care. Pre-K Now's strategy is to focus on high population states in order to reach the greatest number of children and to build momentum (Doggett, Libby, personal communication, Washington, DC, June 20, 2006).[12] But Pre-K Now invests in a range of states, not just high population states. The main criterion for Pre-K Now investment is the presence of leadership. This could be through the advocacy community or elected officials but there has to be leadership. Pre-K Now is not investing to create advocacy actors where none exist but rather to provide financial and technical assistance support to strengthen existing advocacy networks. This fits well with Pew's strategy of investing where the opportunity for change is most likely to be successful.

With the creation of Pre-K Now, the preschool strategy entered into a new phase of activism. Pre-K Now is run like an issue campaign with intensely focused staff who are working to effect policy change within the next five or so years. With a potentially short life span and a very clear mission, the organization has developed an intensive strategy for effecting policy change, with primary emphasis at the state-level. To advance change at the state-level, Pre-K Now funds coalition-building and works to publicize state preschool programs to other states. The assistance comes in an array of forms from convening meetings to funding sophisticated e-communications packages.[13] Mirroring Pre-K Now's national e-advocacy, advocacy organizations in funded states send out email notices to subscribers keeping them abreast of preschool legislative alerts, notices of news and publications, and maintaining well developed, informative Web sites. Pre-K Now also funds "earned" media, which are unpaid media attention through education of journalists (see discussion of Hechinger Institute below), writing opinion editorials and letters to the editor, meeting with editorial boards, suggesting story ideas to reporters, and organizing press conferences to release new policy research. Executive Director Libby Doggett, State Policy Director Stephanie Rubin, and Deputy State Director Danielle Gonzales keep abreast of all fifty states through regular contact with state preschool leaders. They arrange bimonthly phone calls with all of the grantees, networking meetings to promote cross state dialogue, host a national call series (In Focus) that features conversations with high-profile actors on topics relevant to the cause, and arrange satellite conferences (Doggett, Libby, personal communication, Washington, DC, June 20, 2006; Rubin, Stephanie, telephone communication, June 28, 2006).

In addition to state-specific investments, Pre-K Now started a campaign targeted for Latinos. In a 2006 report, Doggett states, "Latinos are the largest minority group and the most rapidly growing segment of the U.S. population. The future productivity of the nation's workforce depends, in large part, on their success" (in Garcia and Gonzales 2006, 1). The report presents comparative data for whites and Latinos on risk factors for academic failure and then highlights the finding of the Tulsa, OK study in which Latinos gained more than any other group in all three testing areas (Gormley, Phillips, and Dawson 2005). The report presents national data on lagging reading and math test scores as compared to their white counterparts and then makes the case for preschool investment to improve outcomes.

Pre-K Now's goal is to create awareness in policy makers, rather than targeting the general public. To achieve this, they work closely with NIEER and other research organizations to distribute nonpartisan analysis and research to policy makers. State Policy Director Stephanie Rubin states, "The evaluation research conducted by NIEER is critical for building momentum" (telephone communication, June 28, 2006). Pre-K Now also publishes results of nonpartisan research it commissions as a Research Series. The series provides concise, descriptive research reports on particular topics that can be easily understood by those unfamiliar with early childhood research. Pew, NIEER, and Pre-K Now work closely to "stay on message" and address the changing needs of the preschool policy environment. If a research need is identified by Pre-K Now, it will convey that to NIEER. If NIEER decides to undertake a new research project, it will coordinate with Pew and Pre-K Now to maximize its impact. While Pew and Pre-K Now do not influence or weigh in on NIEER's research findings, the tight interlocking relationships between Pew, NIEER, and Pre-K Now form the core of the universal preschool strategy.

Radiating from the core are "strategic partnerships" designed to create leverage. In Baumgartner and Jones's (1993) terms, Pew is expanding the range of actors in an attempt to destabilize the status quo and advance the preschool policy alternative. In the words of Susan K. Urahn, Managing Director of the Pew Preschool giving program, "We framed the issue of preschool as an integral part of children's educational experience, with the power to help reduce the achievement gap and enable more children to reach critical early learning goals and meet their potential. This framing fit into the emerging national concern over children's educational achievement and made it possible for us to bring in an array of diverse constituencies who had not previously been part of the policy debate on early education" (Urahn and Watson 2007, 5). In Schneider and Ingram's terms, through its grantees, Pew is helping to create an environment in which there are political benefits for supporting funding for preschool. With universal preschool, young children are receiving real benefits, not just empty rhetoric (Schneider and Ingram 1997). Pew successfully expanded the range of actors advocating for universal preschool to include a broad array of constituent groups including business, educators, law enforcement, elected officials, media, and child advocacy groups, each of which is discussed below.

*Strategic Partner: Business Community*

A key strategic move was to gain support of the business community. As early as the mid-1980s the Committee for Economic Development (CED) began advocating for investing in children as an economic development strategy. In 2002, CED issued a statement that was a "call for action" to create universal, free access to preschool (Research and Policy Committee, Committee for Economic Development 2002). Advisers to the process included W. Steven Barnett, Director of the Center for Early Education, who would later receive funding from Pew to create the National Institute for Early Education Research. In 2006, CED issued a Pew-funded report championing the economic promise of preschool programs (Committee for Economic Development 2006). On its Web site, CED states, "throughout its 65-year history, the Committee for Economic Development has addressed national priorities that promote sustained economic growth and development to benefit all Americans. These activities have quite literally helped shape the future on issues ranging from the Marshall Plan in the late 1940s, to education reform in the past two decades, and campaign finance reform since 2000" (Committee for Economic Development 2007, 1). With this strategic alliance, Pew successfully expanded the set of actors promoting Preschool to include at least part of the business sector. In his research on think tanks, Andrew Rich labels CED a "maverick" think tank with a reputation in the business community for supporting policies out of line with the mainstream (Rich 2004, 44). Thomas Dye portrayed CED as a "central organization for developing consensus among business and financial leaders on public policy, and communicating their views to government officials" (Dye 1979, 130). However, according to Dye, CED's influence began to wane after the Reagan years (Dye 2001) (CED did not receive any mention in his 1986 and 1990 editions of his classic book (Dye 1986, 283; 1990, 291)). More recently, however, CED has played a central role in several important policy issues such as campaign finance reform, federal budget deficit reduction, lobbying reform, and most recently health care reform, as well as universal preschool (Hanson, Janet, personal communication 2007). CED's decision to champion universal preschool was definitely in line with CED's "maverick" reputation of the past.

*Strategic Partner: Media*

Pew provides funding to two media organizations: Hechinger Institute and Education Writers Association. The Hechinger Institute on Education and the Media at Teachers College, Columbia University, receives Pew funding to educate journalists on early education. While it receives funding from a variety of sources, the prominence of preschool on its website indicates that prekindergarten funding from Pew is a primary focus. On the main page of Hechinger's Web site, the top bar of links includes: About Us, Seminars, Fellowships, Resources, Education Journalism Today, and Pre-Kindergarten (Hechinger Institute on Education and the Media 2007, 1). There is no link for K–12 or higher education, only pre-K.

Funding Hechinger serves an important role in the campaign to inform policy change: getting the media to pay attention to the education of young children. With Pew funding, the Hechinger Institute hosts a seminar for journalists on issues related to preschool and early childhood education thereby educating journalists on the importance of early childhood and the universal preschool policy alternative in particular. The seminars include a range of perspectives on early education, including voices in favor of universal preschool and also critical. Among the latter was University of California Berkeley Professor Bruce Fuller, who published *Standardized Childhood* in 2007, criticizing universal preschool, and who was heavily involved in the defeat of California's universal preschool ballot initiative. To assess preschool media coverage, Pew funded Hechinger to commission an analysis of U.S. newspaper coverage of early childhood education (McAdams et al. 2004). This allowed Pew to evaluate the impact of its giving program to increase media coverage of early childhood. Another strategy for increasing media coverage of early education is to make Hechinger the go-to source for early education media information. The Director of the Hechinger Institute, Richard Lee Colvin, maintains a Web blog on early education coverage with daily commentary on media publications with associated links (Colvin 2007).

Pew provided a grant to the Education Writers Association to publish a series of reform briefs on early childhood education and to conduct a survey of preschool reporters across the country to assess preschool media coverage. One of the aims of the report was to inform development of the training seminars provided with Pew funding. Among the many findings of the 2006 report, 20 percent of survey respondents had attended a training seminar, most of which were provided by Hechinger Institute (Education Writers Association 2006).

*Strategic Partner: Law Enforcement and the Courts*

Pew partnered with law enforcement through its grantee, Fight Crime: Invest in Kids (FCIK). FCIK began advocating for early childhood investment in 1999, and has published studies of twenty-three states (Fight Crime: Invest in Kids 2007). In 2002, Pew provided FCIK with $600,000 to "build a cadre of their members who will help educate state and federal policymakers on the importance of high-quality preschool education and its strong link to reducing criminal behavior in juveniles and adults" (Pew Charitable Trusts 2005b). Pew also funds reports targeted to advance universal preschool in specific states. For example, Pew provided a grant to FCIK to publish a report and create outreach that FCIK used to combat proposed cuts to New York's universal preschool program by the Pataki administration. Based on the Perry Preschool program data, Fight Crime made forceful statements about the link between early education and decreased crime (Fight Crime: Invest in Kids New York 2003).

In some states the courts are the most promising path for creating universal preschool. Pew provided a grant to the Education Law Center (ELC) in 2003 to assist legal teams in eight states to win early-education litigation (Pew Charitable Trusts 2005c). With Pew funding, the Education Law Center created "Starting at 3" to promote and support legal advocacy to include preschool in school finance litigation and state legislation. According to the ELC's Web site, "The project collects and disseminates research, information and strategies and provides direct technical assistance to attorneys and advocates involved in litigation and policy initiatives to create and expand state prekindergarten programs" (Education Law Center 2007b).

### Strategic Partner: National Advocacy

While Pre-K Now funds state advocates for preschool, Pew funded the national advocacy group, Voices for America's Children. Voices is a non-profit membership organization with the broad mission to improve the well-being of children (Voices for Children 2007). Pew funds, which ended in 2005, were used to disseminate information about preschool to state children's advocacy organizations to encourage them to make preschool a priority issue (Council of Chief State School Officers 2007a). Voices has state affiliates, many of whom receive Pew funding to support state advocacy for universal preschool. Thus, Voices provided a mechanism for Pew to direct resources and information to state preschool advocates.

### Strategic Partners: Education

An important strategic partner for Pew is the Council of Chief State School Officers (CCSSO). Pew provided funding, which ended in 2006, for CCSSO to "educate and serve its membership to build support among the chiefs for expansion of quality, universal preschool opportunities for 3 and 4 year olds" (Council of Chief State School Officers 2007b). Pew funded the development of CCSSO's "Cadre of Champions" for preschool. This group of member superintendents and commissioners provides oversight and advises the project, and also serves as national, regional, and state spokespersons for preschool. The Pew funding was used to hold regional meetings to develop state preschool action plans, to hold sessions on preschool at all CCSSO membership meetings, and to design a communication strategy including media interviews, editorials, letters to the editor, and the dissemination of evidence-based reports, research, and resources on early education (Council of Chief State School Officers 2007b).[14]

In all of the CCSSO meetings, the list of speakers draws from well known preschool advocates, many of whom receive Pew funds. In 2003, CCSSO's Cadre of Champions sponsored a Governor's Forum on Quality Preschool in which ten state school officers addressed four governors. Among the speakers, Sandy Garrett, State Superintendent of Oklahoma, presented the results of the Gormley et al. evaluation of the Tulsa pre-school program (Council of Chief State School Officers 2003). In 2004, CCSSO hosted a Pew-sponsored forum, Advancing Quality Preschool for All, in conjunction with the 2004 CCSSO Annual Legislative Conference (Washington 2004). Presenters included other Pew strategic partners such as NIEER's W. Steve Barnett (Lee 2004). Also in 2004, CCSSO began a series of three regional meetings "to engage the [state] teams in strategic planning to advance quality and access to preschool in their states" (Martella 2004, 2). At the meetings, funded by Pew, the teams developed strategies that would serve as the focal points for state action plans. Each state had to report on the actions it would take in the next three months (Runfola 2004).

In 2006, a meeting was held in Montana to encourage states without preschool programs to invest. The meeting brought together representatives from states without preschool programs including: Idaho, Indiana, Mississippi, Montana, North Dakota, South Dakota, Utah, and Wyoming. The presenters consisted of a cross section of preschool supporters, including elected officials, state agency representatives, advocates, and researchers. Representatives from states with universal preschool were brought in to tell of their experiences (e.g., Ramona Paul from Oklahoma, Karen Schimke from New York). Presenters from states moving in the universal preschool direction were highlighted (Arkansas, Tennessee, and Illinois). The program included Pre-K Now, NIEER, Fight Crime: Invest in Kids, and the National Conference of State Legislatures (Council of Chief State School Officers 2007c). The meeting provided an opportunity for states without preschool programs to gain exposure to successful programs and resources available if they chose to pursue development of a preschool program.

To address the needs of rural children, Pew funded the Frederick D. Patterson Research Institute of the United Negro College Fund to create the Pew Rural Early Education Initiative. The aim of this project is to research the challenges of rural education with the aim of improving educational outcomes, particularly for African-American children (Council of Chief State School Officers 2007a).

### Strategic Partnership: Elected Leadership

To build support for universal preschool among elected leadership, Pew created strategic partnerships with the National League of Cities and the National Conference of State Legislatures. The National League of Cities partnership aimed to determine the level of mayoral knowledge and interest in preschool. The grant, which is now closed, provided funds to identify local leaders with the potential to champion universal preschool in their home states (Council of Chief State School Officers 2007a).

The National Conference of State Legislatures (NCSL) receives Pew funding to provide nonpartisan information and support to all state policy-makers on high-quality preschool. NCSL is building a network of interested legislators, hosting annual policy institutes, developing written materials, and providing intensive support in "selected states" (Council of Chief State School Officers 2007a, 2-2). NCSL had already been a champion for early childhood investment since the research on the importance of early brain development emerged. In 1998, a state legislative report issued by NCSL documented the state policy responses (Groginsky, Christian, and McConnell 1998). The Pew funding placed more emphasis on preschool but NCSL's focus remains more broadly constructed and includes: child care subsidy programs, birth-to-five (funded by the Buffet Early Childhood Fund), as well as preschool (funded by Pew). With funding from Pew and public agencies, NCSL held a Prekindergarten Leadership Institute in June 2006 titled, "Designing Early Childhood Assessment and Accountability Systems" (National Conference of State Legislatures Prekindergarten Leadership Institute 2007). Presenters included representatives from Pre-K Now and NIEER, state preschool program officials and elected leadership from several states. The Institute presenters reviewed research and provided examples of successful states to inform policy making. It also served to publicize the work of the National Early Childhood Accountability Task Force, discussed below.

### Strategic Creation: Task Force

In 2005, Pew launched the National Early Childhood Accountability Task Force, together with the Foundation for Child Development and the Joyce

Foundation to assess the performance of preschool programs. The Task Force is chaired by renowned early childhood researcher Dr. Sharon Lynn Kagan of Columbia University's Teachers College, and includes Dr. W. Steve Barnett of NIEER and other experts in child development, early education, and state policy. The goal of the Task Force is to help states develop measurement tools to set standards, assess programs, and use the results to help policy makers assess the performance of state preschool systems (Pew Charitable Trusts 2007d). The NCSL Prekindergarten Leadership Institute held in June 2006 was led by Dr. Thomas Schultz, Pew's former Project Director of Early Education Accountability, and National Early Childhood Accountability Task Force Vice-Chairperson Dr. Eugene Garcia (National Conference of State Legislatures Prekindergarten Leadership Institute 2007). The Task Force published a report in October 2007, to provide "guidance to help states set and review standards for early childhood programs, select appropriate measures and assessment tools and report and use accountability data (Pew Charitable Trusts 2007).

**Conclusion**

The Web of Pew-funded organizations provides a complex network of mutually reinforcing Web sites. Links are provided on Pew-funded organization Web sites to other Pew-funded organization Web sites and they post each other's research, publications, events, and so forth. For example, research by NIEER is publicized on strategic partner Web sites and mentioned in Hechinger Institute Director Richard Lee Colvin's Web blog. The Web sites create a tight, interconnected network of mutual publicity as well as links to every imaginable source of information on early childhood education. It is a brilliantly comprehensive strategy for building momentum for policy change.

To understand the impact of Pew funding on states, the following chapter examines Pew and Pew-funded actors' investments in the pioneer states and the states of Tennessee and Illinois. Tennessee passed preschool legislation in 2005, and Illinois is the most recent state, passing legislation in 2006.

# 5

# Pew Investments in States

Pew's strategy is to invest strategically in advocacy organizations in states that are likely to create or expand access to preschool. Pre-K Now explicitly selects states for investment that demonstrate (1) political leadership and (2) an existing advocacy network. For the last three years, Pre-K Now has released a report titled "Leadership Matters: Governors' Pre-K Proposals." The report assesses governors' budgetary proposals and State of the State addresses for their commitment to preschool. In fiscal year 2006, twenty governors recommended increased spending for preschool, three recommended decreased spending, and nine states did not have a preschool program (Scott 2005). In fiscal year 2007, twenty-four governors proposed funding increases, two states proposed decreased, and the same nine states had no preschool program (Doctors 2006). For fiscal year 2008, twenty-nine governors proposed spending increases and no governors recommended decreased spending. In addition, South Dakota proposed creating a state preschool program, thereby reducing the number of states without state preschool to eight (Doctors 2007). While Pre-K Now funding cannot be directly linked to the decisions of all those governors, it is fair to say that it has raised the profile of the issue substantially. Pre-K Now directly funds advocates in fifteen states but monitors all fifty states and the District of Columbia (Rubin, Stephanie, telephone communication, June 28, 2006).

This chapter explores three states: New York, Tennessee, and Illinois. While pioneer states passed legislation prior to the Pew universal preschool giving program, they experienced differing levels of success in achieving political and budgetary stability for their preschool programs. Both New York and West Virginia faced challenges in building stable political and budgetary support for their preschool programs, but two organizations in New York received Pre-K Now funding that contributed to winning increased funding for the universal preschool program.

In the last few years, three states passed legislation that would allow for the creation of universal preschool: Florida, Tennessee, and Illinois. Organizations in all three of these states received funding from Pew either directly or through Pre-K Now. In Florida, the Early Childhood Initiative received a $260,000 grant from Pew in June 2002. In the grant announcement Pew states, "As a state that demonstrates the possibility of moving towards universal high-quality early education, Florida is a prime candidate for intensive support from the Trusts" (Pew Charitable Trusts 2005a, 1). The Early Childhood Initiative chose to use the grant to fund a media campaign, an economic study of preschool costs, and a public opinion poll to gauge Floridians' willingness to pay for early education. With the efforts of longtime Florida advocate David Lawrence, voters passed an initiative in November 2002 to change the state constitution to allow for the creation of universal preschool, eventually culminating in the passage of legislation in 2005 to create universal preschool in Florida. However, Florida has turned out to be a disappointment in that the legislature did not fund the program at a level to deliver quality preschool (Doctors 2006, 2007).[1] But both Tennessee and Illinois are success stories in that they passed legislation in 2005 and 2006, respectively, and have won continued increases in funding. Neither has achieved universality but both have legislation that would allow for it if the political will and budgetary support were to develop.

## Pew Investments in Pioneer States

As discussed in the previous chapters, the pioneer states created their programs with very weak advocacy environments. With the exception of New York, early childhood advocates were not pushing for adoption of universal preschool. And even in New York, advocates were caught by surprise when Assembly Speaker Silver chose to push for universal preschool as part of the LADDER legislation. However, since the passage of preschool legislation in pioneer states, Pew has invested when needed to solidify support for the preschool programs. Pew has not invested substantially in Oklahoma or Georgia, mainly because its investment was not needed because both of these states have achieved stable policy monopolies for their universal preschool programs. Georgia participated in Pew-funded advocacy activities (e.g., educating journalists through Hechinger Institute seminars, serving on the National Early Childhood Accountability Task Force, presenting at NCSL conferences) and has received technical assistance from Pre-K Now but has not needed Pew funds to protect funding or to generate political support for the preschool program. The only issue that Pew funding could address is the need for independent evaluation of the preschool program but Georgia's leaders at this point are not inclined to allow NIEER to conduct an evaluation.

In 2002, the Trust for Early Education, the precursor to Pre-K Now, provided funds to the Oklahoma Institute for Child Advocacy when the controversy over the Smart Start legislation occurred, but Oklahoma's preschool program was never threatened. The biggest impact Pew funding has had is due to its partial funding of the evaluation of the Tulsa preschool program and the subsequent publicity of the study findings. Oklahoma has also benefited from the positive publicity surrounding NIEER's Annual State Report. Oklahoma's top ranking for access was heralded by the *Oklahoman* and undoubtedly raised the profile of the program among other states. Pre-K Now also raised the profile of Oklahoma through publicizing the Tulsa study and the NIEER ranking, and inviting preschool advocates such as Dr. Ramona Paul and State Superintendent Dr. Sandy Garrett of the Oklahoma State Department of Education to speak to other states about Oklahoma's preschool program.

The other two pioneer states struggled to achieve stability but only one, New York, is home to organizations that have been the recipient of significant investment by Pew-funded actors. West Virginia's small population and underdeveloped advocacy environment did not fit the criteria for Pre-K Now investment. It was included in a NIEER five-state evaluation of preschool programs (Barnett, Lamy, and Jung 2005) but the findings did not result in much publicity. Dr. Cathy Jones of the West Virginia Department of Education received funding from Pew to present at conferences, such as the 2006 NCSL Prekindergarten Leadership Institute, but by and large, West Virginia has not been the beneficiary of the Pew giving program beyond technical assistance from Pre-K Now. That may change as the deadline for achieving universality by 2012 approaches. According to Pre-K Now, they are in contact with advocates and they are prepared to invest, if needed, so that the state can achieve universality by the legislated deadline (Doggett, Libby, personal communication, Washington, DC, June 20, 2006).

In contrast, advocacy organizations in New York were brought together, after some initial division among advocates focused on child care, by TEE's and later Pre-K Now's grants to both the Schuyler Center for Analysis and Advocacy and Child Care Incorporated to support public education and advocacy. With a large population and supportive political leadership by the Speaker of the Assembly, Pre-K Now's investments were aimed at strengthening the advocacy environment in order to create political pressure to fully fund the preschool program. These funds allowed advocates to hire a top-of-the-line marketing firm to design their advocacy campaign. New York also benefited from the e-communications package provided by Pre-K Now. This allowed advocates to effectively rally support at critical political junctures. According to Nancy Kolben, Executive Director of Child Care Inc., "Pre-K Now funds were critical in advocates' ability to position, leverage, and bring in other groups, such as Fight Crime: Invest in Kids, to advocate for the UPK program. We were able to do things in a sophisticated way that got responses from across the state and press coverage. Without those funds, we would not have been able to mount a coordinated campaign (telephone communication, July 12, 2007).

One of the strengths of the New York program is the collaborative arrangements between public schools, child care, and Head Start. Pre-K Now funds were used to bring attention to New York's preschool program by publishing a 2006 report that held New York's collaboration up as a model for the rest of the country (Holcomb 2006).

Pre-K Now funds were also used to rally reluctant supporters, such as the business community. Calling the lack of business support in New York "puzzling," a Pre-K Now 2005 report highlighted that "the nation's most influential business community, including more *Fortune 500* companies than any other state, [to] let another year pass without state-level action to promote new funding" for preschool (Pre-K Now 2005b, 6). To try and increase business support of public preschool investment throughout the country, in 2006 a conference was held to persuade the business community that public investment in preschool was in business's best interest (Watson, Sara, e-mail communication, January 3, 2008). The conference was held in New York by the Committee for Economic Development, the Pew Charitable Trusts, and the PNC Financial Services Group (Pre-K Now 2005b, 6).

Pew also drew on its strategic partnerships to create alliances at the state level. It funded Fight Crime: Invest in Kids New York to produce a report linking preschool investment to decreased crime. The expansion of preschool advocates to include law enforcement was part of a concerted effort to combat proposed cuts to New York's universal preschool program by the Pataki administration. The report, based on the Perry Preschool program data, made forceful statements about the link between early education and decreased crime (Fight Crime: Invest in Kids New York 2003, 1–5).

All of the investment in New York paid off in 2006, when $50 million in new funding was appropriated for universal preschool. In the buildup to the budget negotiations, Pre-K Now sent out an action alert to all subscribers urging them to send letters to Governor Pataki to approve the $50 million increase for preschool (Doggett 2006). The Schuyler Center's electronic advocacy was fully activated sending alerts to subscribers asking them to call and write to legislators and the governor to express their support. Pre-K Now and New York state advocates hope to keep the momentum moving forward. Pataki's successor, Democrat Governor Spitzer, publicly announced his support for additional preschool investment. In 2007, the UPK budget was increased 50 percent and distributed through a foundation formula, separate but parallel to K–12 funding (Schimke, Karen, e-mail communication January 18, 2008). If Governor Paterson maintains support for UPK, then New York may finally be in reach of achieving universality.

## Pew Investment in Recent States

The ascendance of preschool across the country has been aided by the Pew Charitable Trusts and the actions of its strategic partners. Pre-K Now monitors activity in all fifty states and has provided funds, technical assistance, or facilitated networking among policy actors and advocates in nearly every state. Pew-funded grantees helped to create political momentum with state actors who share the same goal: expanding access to public preschool. Two victories have been particularly sweet. Tennessee passed preschool legislation in 2005, and Illinois, in 2006, became the first state to pass legislation to create universal preschool for three and four year olds. In each of these states, Pew's grantees provided support at critical junctures that contributed to successful passage of the legislation.

### Tennessee

Tennessee passed legislation in 2005 with the potential to create universal preschool but the investment in preschool began a decade earlier with a pilot program for children who qualified for free or reduced lunch. The program was created in 1996 under the leadership of Republican Governor Don Sundquist (1995–2003) who in 2001 advocated for expansion to universal access in his State of the State address (Cass 2001). However, several sources interviewed noted that it was an idea whose time had not yet come. Governor Sundquist ended his term as an unpopular governor because of his support for creating a state income tax. In addition, the universal preschool proposal was part of a much larger reading initiative and therefore did not receive much attention. But the pilot program was successfully created and received $3 million in state funds to open thirty classes in 1998 and serve 600 children. The same amount was allocated the following year. The funding was doubled in 2000 to $6 million with an additional $9 million funding from the federal Temporary Assistance to Needy Families allocation added to the preschool program in January 2001. The additional funds allowed the pilot program to expand to 150 classes serving 3,000 children (Tennessee Department of Education 2006). Governor Sundquist advocated for increased funding, stressing the "invest now, or pay later" theme in which investments in early education pay off with decreased incarceration rates in the future (Cheek 2002, 6B); but when he left office, support for expanding preschool was less than certain.

The political environment for preschool began to change with the creation of a Tennessee State Lottery and the election of Democratic Governor Phil Bredesen in 2002, who would make universal preschool a top agenda item in his administration. In 2002, after nearly 20 years of debate, Tennessee followed Georgia's example when it created a lottery to fund education. Tennessee's constitutional amendment states that lottery revenues will be allocated to college scholarships, but Tennessee did not place preschool on equal footing with college scholarships. Lottery funding for preschool would only be available if there were "excess" revenues after funding college scholarships. The challenge for preschool advocates was to secure preschool's claim on lottery revenues by incorporating preschool language into the lottery enabling legislation.

Including preschool legislation became even more important with the 2003 announcement that $9 million in TANF funds would be discontinued. Without the TANF funds, preschool programs faced closure around the state. The *Tennessean*, the newspaper of record, ran articles supportive of preschool with heart-tugging stories of preschool children and included a quote from NIEER's Steve Barnett stating that Tennessee was not taking preschool seriously (Riley 2003a, 3B).

But since the passage of the constitutional amendment creating the lottery, advocates had been hard at work to include funding for the preschool program in the lottery enabling legislation. If successful, the lottery legislation could replace the lost TANF funds and provide additional resources to expand the preschool program. But success did not come easily. The State Board of Education as well as key leaders in the state government supported inclusion of preschool in the lottery legislation. The State Board of Education Executive Director Douglas Wood was appointed to the Lottery Commission, the body responsible for advising the General Assembly on designing the enabling language for the lottery. While he and one other representative from K–12 education advocated for inclusion of preschool, the majority of the commission members favored initially limiting lottery revenues for college scholarships. Funding for preschool was not opposed but rather priority was given to college scholarships and the Commission's recommendations to the General Assembly excluded language for preschool (Cass 2003, 1A). In response, Dr. Wood gathered his staff and leaders in the Department of Education to draft legislative language for preschool and then literally traversed the state to "sell" the idea to community groups. Dr. Wood's now famous Powerpoint presentation drew on the research on "the preschool payoff" and extolled the benefits of preschool investment. A particularly powerful slide included a comparison of per capita state budget outlays for incarceration versus education for five year olds. According to Wood (2007, telephone communication, May 31, 2007), these data were critical for winning the hearts and minds from business organizations such as the Rotary club to community organizations in church basements. With its potential for decreasing future social service expenditures, preschool appealed to conservative and more liberal interests all over the state.

Initially there was opposition from Head Start because the preschool language required all preschool programs to comply with state board standards, including a requirement that each classroom have a certified teacher. Federal Head Start requirements do not require teacher certification, and there was a fear that preschool program expansion would negatively impact Head Start enrollments because without certified teachers Head Start programs would not be able to participate in the state preschool program. Meetings between the State Board of Education and Head Start representatives led to an agreement that both would work toward assuring that Head Start teachers would have the ability to earn their certification.

With Head Start on board and grassroots support across the state, the time arrived to present the case for preschool to the K–12 Subcommittee of the House Education Committee. According to Wood (telephone communication, May 31, 2007), the grassroots supporters of preschool turned out in great numbers for the committee meeting. There were representatives from across the state and each one of the committee members' districts was represented. An article in the *Tennessean* by reporter Claudette Riley covered the meeting and closed with a quote from a subcommittee member stating, "I find it sort of unbelievable that there would be any thought of not funding this initiative with lottery dollars. It's inconceivable. This is a great opportunity for us to do some good" (Riley 2003b, 5B). A few days later, she published another article advocating for preschool teacher training and pointing out the unmet demand for state preschool (Riley 2003c, 4B).

Ultimately the preschool language was included in the lottery enabling legislation; however, the definition of excess funds for preschool was not included in the legislation. In January 2004, before the lottery had even begun operating, the governor and Senator Steve Cohen (sponsor of the lottery legislation) agreed to split the estimated $70 million excess lottery funds with 80 percent targeted for preschool and 20 percent for after-school programs (de la Cruz, 2004, 1A). In the first six months, the lottery generated net revenues of more than $123 million with $88 million directed to scholarships and potentially $35 million in "excess" funds that could be allocated to preschool and after-school programs (Cheek 2004, 1B). While the estimate was half what was expected in January, the Bredesen administration was cautious about committing even that much to preschool because of concerns about the stability of lottery revenues.

With hopes of lottery funding for preschool dashed, the Tennessee chapter of Stand for Children, along with other advocates, held an early childhood forum in October 2004 to expand support for preschool. Director Francie Hunt stated, "About 120 state and local officials, business leaders and early childhood experts have been invited" (Riley 2004a, 2B). The State Board of Education included preschool funding as part of its master plan for schools and even with the resignation of Douglas Wood, the support was maintained by his successor, Gary Nixon (Riley 2004b, 1B).

But while advocates were united behind preschool, finding the funding for expanded preschool was no easy task for Governor Bredesen. In 2004, he tried to tackle the thorny issue of Tennessee's health insurance program for the poor and uninsured, TennCare, and redirect savings to fund universal preschool. The governor stated, "Half the $650 million in projected cost increases in TennCare next year could fund a free education program for every four-year-old in the state" (Wadhwani 2004, 2A). This proved particularly challenging and by the end of the year, Bredesen had shifted to advocating that lottery funding should be allocated to preschool program expansion (Riley 2005a). But despite challenges from TennCare, the governor's support of preschool remained strong.

When Governor Bredesen announced his support of preschool, the Tennessee Association for the Education of Young Children's (TAEYC) Public Policy Co-Chair Dr. Diane Neighbors, jumped at the opportunity to increase investment in early childhood (personal communication, Nashville, April 16, 2007). Neighbors, described as an "idea leader" in the state, pulled together a group of advocates including the Tennessee Commission of Children and Youth, the League of Women Voters, the Nashville Chamber of Commerce, and others to brainstorm. TAEYC is an all-volunteer organization mostly representing nonprofit child care centers that has historically focused on quality issues. Without any paid staff, TAEYC had serious administrative capacity issues. The Tennessee Chapter of Stand for Children had three staff with limited ability to focus scarce resources on preschool. In late 2004, advocates entered into discussions with Pre-K Now and Drew Kim in Governor Bredesen's office to set up an alliance between McNeely, Pigott and Fox (a private, public relations firm), Stand for Children, and the Tennessee Association for the Education of Young Children. What emerged was the Tennessee Alliance for Early Education. With TAEYC's Diane Neighbors as chair and Stand for Children's Francie Hunt as vice chair, the membership organization brought together a wide range of interests to advocate for preschool. With Pre-K Now funds, the Alliance was able to fund an annual conference, hire a staff member at Stand for Children to focus specifically on preschool advocacy, and pay for a professional media/education campaign. According to Dr. Libby Doggett of Pre-K Now, Governor Bredesen had a good idea for preschool with good staff and a strong advocacy environment (personal communication, Washington, DC, June 20, 2006). This is exactly the type of policy environment ripe for Pre-K Now investment.

In late 2004, NIEER's annual report rated Tennessee high for quality but low for access. On the front page of the *Tennessean,* reporter Claudette Riley quoted NIEER's Steve Barnett as stating, "It's a pretty good model. Tennessee could clearly vault to the top in providing a universal preschool program with these kinds of standards" (Riley 2004c, 1A).

The media coverage and advocacy work culminated in Governor Bredesen calling for preschool expansion in his 2005 State of the State address. The plan was to earmark $25 million of lottery funds for the preschool program (Riley 2005b, 7A). He followed up the budget proposal with preschool legislation sponsored by Democratic House and Senate members (Riley 2005c, 6B). Bredesen framed the preschool legislation as providing a better foundation in children's early years that would then provide a better chance at successful education (Seibert 2005, 3B).

Advocates sprang into action to support passage of the legislation. With Pre-K Now funding, the Alliance held a legislative breakfast in early 2005 to increase support for the voluntary preschool legislation. Even though support for expanding state preschool was increasing, it also met with some resistance. One legislator remained bitter from the passage of legislation that mandated kindergarten participation in 2002 and blamed it for juvenile delinquency. He took the mug the Alliance had given him, crossed out pre-K and wrote "parents" and used it in a press conference advocating against the preschool program and in favor of home schooling (Neighbors, Diane, personal communication, Nashville, April 16, 2007).

Opposing voices also came from the Tennessee Center for Policy Research (TCPR), a free-market think tank opposed to government expansion. During the legislative debate, TCPR published a report coauthored by its President Drew Johnson and Goldwater Institute's Darcy

Olsen arguing that investments in early education do "little to improve children's education outcomes." The report criticized Georgia's preschool program for failing to raise standardized test scores and also criticized the Head Start program. The authors did support funding preschool for poor children but opposed funding for a universal preschool program (Olsen and Johnson 2005, 1–33).

In every other state researched for this study, an association of child care providers existed and was involved to varying degrees in the universal preschool policy process. But in Tennessee, there was no contact information available for a similar organization and no membership for Tennessee in the National Child Care Association. There was a Tennessee Family Child Care Alliance that represented family child care homes, but this type of provider typically operates from the owner's home and provides care for ten or fewer children ranging in age from infants to preschool. The president of the Tennessee Family Child Care Alliance declined to participate in the study. Without a functional membership association representing the for-profit child care centers, they were not an effective voice within the political realm in Tennessee. Without a website or reference in any media account, for-profit child care center owners appear to have been in disarray. The child care industry's advocacy voice came from TAEYC, which has been instrumental in the advocacy supporting universal preschool.

The preschool legislation (HB 2333 and SB2317) had broad bipartisan support in the legislature and passed the ninety-nine-member (53D-46R) Democratic majority House in April 2005 with only twenty-one votes against. In the thirty-three-member Senate, it passed 27–2 (there were four nonvoting senators). But while the legislation passed, opposition continued from some Republican legislators who challenged the framing of preschool as an important public investment for improved educational outcomes. Some legislators viewed early childhood as babysitting, favored home environments for young children, or they only supported a targeted program. Senate Majority Leader Ron Ramsey (R-Blountville), although ultimately voting in favor, supported a preschool program for at-risk children but opposed creating a "thirteenth grade." He also voiced concerns about the impact of universal preschool on the private child care industry (Seibert 2005, 3B). Republican Senator David Fowler questioned the educational benefits of preschool, stating, "How much is there you can teach a four-year-old?" but, in the end, he too voted in favor (Riley 2005d, 1A). The two opposing votes came from two senators who had not voiced opposition during the debate over the preschool legislation (Riley 2005d, 1A).

The preschool legislation created a new office within the Department of Education, the Office of Early Learning, to administer the preschool program and earmarked $25 million in lottery funds for the program. The "voluntary pre-K program" runs in parallel with the prior "pilot pre-K" program but the program rules are similar.[2] All pre-K programs offer a minimum of five and one-half hours of instruction per day without charge to parents. The Office of Early Learning was charged with developing the administrative process for providers to participate in the pre-K program, training staff, and monitoring use of pre-K funds (Casha, Connie, personal communication, Nashville, April 17, 2007). The pre-K funds are available for at-risk children who qualify for free or reduced school lunch. But if there are additional slots available, they may be allocated to special needs children, children in state custody, children who speak English as a second language, and children who are victims of abuse and neglect. Beyond these priorities, school districts, in conjunction with the pre-K advisory councils, are able to set at-risk criteria that are based on local conditions (e.g., children of deployed soldiers, children being raised by grandparents, etc.) (Lussier, Bobbi, telephone communication, June 12, 2007).

The legislation does not mandate collaboration with Head Start or private providers but there is a strong emphasis on collaboration from the Office of Early Learning. Private providers and Head Start are encouraged to "come to the table" and participate in the pre-K program through events hosted by the Alliance and the Office of Early Learning, through their local community pre-K advisory councils, or through participation on the state-level pre-K advisory council (Lussier, Bobbi, telephone communication, June 12, 2007). In order to apply for pre-K funds, each school district has to create an advisory council representing parents, teachers, school board, business, Head Start, for-profit and nonprofit child care providers, and city or council commissioners. There is an awareness both within the Office of Early Learning and the state legislature of the importance of including, rather than displacing, existing providers. However, there is also an awareness of the importance of the quality of providers participating in pre-K. In order to participate, providers must have a "three-star" quality designation (star rating determined through child care licensing in the Department of Human Services). In this way, the legislation encourages participation of private providers but limits participation to those willing to invest in quality (Casha, Connie, personal communication, Nashville, April 17, 2007; Lussier, Bobbi, telephone communication, June 12, 2007). In the 2006–07 school year, of the 529 voluntary pre-K classrooms, 148 were in collaborative settings (there were an additional 146 pilot pre-K classrooms) (Lussier, Bobbi, telephone communication, June 12, 2007).

In 2005, 106 of the 136 school systems applied for pre-K lottery funds despite the requirement of a local match and the requirement to create a community advisory council. All of the 106 that applied were awarded at least one pre-K classroom for a total of 300 new classrooms (Riley 2005e, 1B). Depending on the Basic Education Program share required, a school district had to provide a 2 percent to 53 percent match (Casha, Connie, personal communication, Nashville, April 17, 2007). In addition, $10 million in general revenue funds continued to support 146 pilot pre-K classrooms. The challenge for Governor Bredesen was to con-vince the legislature to allocate additional funds each year to expand the voluntary pre-K program to universal access. But there are two main impediments to expanding the voluntary pre-K program to universal access: funding and political opposition.

To institutionalize funding for pre-K, Governor Bredesen advocated for including pre-K funding in the Basic Education Program, the state funding program for K–12 education (Associated Press State and Local Wire 2005, 1–2). The *Tennessean* published an editorial supporting the idea stating, "As promising as pre-K programs are now, the state cannot truly rely on them until they have the stability that would come with being part of the automatic funding to keep them vibrant. Educators, legislators and taxpayers should all recognize the value of this step. No one is obli-gated to participate, but everyone should recognize the advantages of a pre-K plan in the life of a child" (*Tennessean* 2005, 12A). In his 2006 budget, Governor Bredesen called for a 5 percent increase in the education budget that included $20 million to pay for 250 new pre-K classrooms. He also included $25 million in lottery funds to maintain the 300 class-rooms created in 2005 (Riley 2006, 8A). Although Bredesen was success-ful in funding pre-K expansion in 2006, local school districts still have to fund the local match in order for pre-K to expand. To assist local school districts, the governor asked the United Way to raise funds to support forty new pre-K classrooms (Prager 2006, 1B).

At the 2006 annual meeting of the United Way, Rob Grunewald of the Federal Reserve Bank in Minneapolis, a strong supporter of preschool investment, gave a keynote address linking early childhood investment to improved economic development. This is an important shift in the pre-school framing: instead of preschool as wise public investment to improve educational outcomes, the causal story shifted to investment in preschool to improve future economic development. The end result was that the United Way raised enough funds to support forty-seven classrooms (Lussier, Bobbi, telephone communication June 12, 2007).

But while the shift in framing was effective in winning United Way support, the political support for making the pre-K program universal has not yet taken hold in the political realm. There is sufficient unity for a tar-geted pre-K program for children at-risk of academic failure, but not for universal access. Unlike pioneer states in which evaluation has not been a priority, legislators from both sides of the aisle in Tennessee are calling for an independent evaluation to prove that the public investment in pre-K is worth it. House Speaker Jimmy Naifeh (Naifeh 2006, 14A) and the Democratic majority agree with Governor Bredesen's support for expanding pre-K, but many legislators want proof that the investment will pay off in improved educational outcomes. The *Tennessean* fired back an editorial stating that "It shouldn't take a lot of statistical data to make the case for the value of pre-kindergarten programs" but also pointed out that the evidence already exists from the pilot pre-K program. Participants in the pilot program, tracked since 1998, had higher reading and math scores than children who did not attend pre-K (*Tennessean* 2006a, 18A). After the legislature approved the governor's request for an additional $20 million for pre-K, the *Tennessean* ran another editorial stating, "The value of pre-K education cannot be overstated" and connected pre-K to reducing dropout rates and improving test scores (2006b, 8A). But the Tennessee legislation requires evaluation by the Offices of Educational Accountability Research (OEAR) in the Comptroller of the Treasury Office. In 2007, OEAR contracted with a private firm to undertake the evaluation.

Advocates report that by 2010 they expect to be serving all at-risk four-year-olds but there are considerable obstacles to expansion to universal access. Despite the continued financial support from Pre-K Now, support from the advocacy community, and leadership by a popular governor in his second term, expansion of pre-K beyond poor children is not assured.

One of the contrasts between Tennessee and the pioneering states is the media attention directed specifically to preschool. Oklahoma was able to make incremental changes that eventually led to universal preschool and did so without any coverage by the *Oklahoman*. In West Virginia, the legislation passed without any media coverage at all. In Tennessee, preschool was a high-profile agenda item and had nearly daily media coverage in the spring of 2005. The attention from the *Tennessean* came primarily from one journalist, Claudette Riley, who had participated in the Pew-funded Hechinger Institute training on preschool. She regularly utilized information provided by NIEER and Pre-K Now in her articles. For example, as the Senate and House were working out differences in their preschool bills, Riley wrote a supportive article on preschool touting the benefits of preschool and quoting Steve Barnett of NIEER as saying, "If Tennessee does this program, this will pay dividends for years to come.... You're going to close that achievement gap right from the beginning. It also positions Tennessee to be a leader in education" (Riley 2005f, 1A). Riley's consistent, informative coverage kept preschool in the news.

Not only had reporter Claudette Riley participated in the Hechinger Institute training, State Board of Education Executive Director Douglas Wood had actively encouraged Riley's access to the decision-making process for including preschool in the lottery enabling legislation (Wood, Douglas, telephone communication May 31, 2007). But the tone and depth of knowledge of the coverage shifted when Riley left the *Tennessean*. Starting in 2007, the coverage of preschool gave more space to opponents regardless of their credibility and the headlines were more likely to be negative. The new reporters had not participated in the Hechinger Institute training and did not possess Riley's depth of knowledge. The difference was noticeable. Whereas Riley appended basic information explaining the preschool program with most of her articles, the new reporters did not. The new reporters would quote Steve Barnett from NIEER but also gave equal footing to the Tennessee Center for Policy Research, an organization without a history of well-respected research on the topic (Mielczarek 2007, 1A).

With the loss of Riley's expertise, advocates had to allocate additional resources to soliciting letters of support for preschool. Four days after a front-page article with the headline "Governor's pre-K passion not universal" appeared in the *Tennessean*, an opinion piece by Sister Sandra Smithson, cofounder of a charter school and executive director of an anti poverty children's advocacy nonprofit organization, was published titled "Those who discredit pre-K ignore how much it transforms children" (Smithson 2007, 13A).

In the Tennessee case, Doggett states that the outcome may have been different had Pre-K Now not gone into Tennessee (Doggett, Libby, personal communication, Washington, DC. June 20, 2006). According to advocates, Pre-K Now brought Stand for Children and the Tennessee Association for the Education of Young Children along with the League of Women Voters, National Association of Social Workers, Tennessee School Board Association, Tennessee Voices for Children, and others together, which gave them a unified voice to champion preschool. According to the advocates, the Pre-K Now funding was critical because without it they did not have the administrative capacity or the expertise for implementing a state of the art, professional media campaign. Tennessee Association for the Education of Young Children is an all volunteer organization. Stand for Children is a membership association advocating for a range of early education issues with three professional and one administrative staff member. The Pre-K Now funding enabled the creation of the Tennessee Alliance for Early Education so as to have the resources to sustain attention on preschool.

With Pre-K Now funds, the Alliance was able to hire the public relations firm, McNeely, Pigott and Fox, to produce packages of information to educate legislators about preschool. Pre-K Now provided funds to organize "a day on the hill" event; however, changes in ethics laws in Tennessee preclude repeating that event (Neighbors, Diane, telephone communication, May 29, 2007). In 2006 and 2007, Pre-K Now funds, combined with other funding sources, enabled the Tennessee Alliance for Early Education, along with the Tennessee Office of Early learning and Head Start Collaboration Office, to host an Early Childhood Summit. In 2006, Dr. Libby Doggett of Pre-K Now gave the keynote address, and in 2007 NIEER's Dr. Steve Barnett gave the keynote address (Neighbors, Diane, personal communication 2007b). Bobbi Lussier, Executive Director of the Office of Early Learning states that Steve Barnett and Libby Doggett were invaluable influences in Tennessee for basing the advocacy on solid research and providing the funds to advocates to build support for preschool investment (telephone communication, June 12, 2007).

The building blocks for universal preschool in Tennessee are in place. The incremental expansion of the program will likely continue through 2010 when Governor Bredesen's second term ends. However, whether the program will actually achieve universal access remains to be seen. Without the financial support of Pre-K Now, advocates will not be able to sustain the media campaign, which is critical for building the momentum toward a unified policy image for preschool for all. In time, the political environment in Tennessee may or may not coalesce around universal access. But while future legislatures may reduce funding, it is unlikely that the program would ever be eliminated.

*Illinois*

The 2006 passage of Preschool for All in Illinois was a sweet victory for all supporters of preschool because Illinois was the first state in the country to include three and four year olds in its legislation. The victory was particularly sweet for all the advocates and their funders who had been building support for early education investment for decades. Voices for Illinois Children, Ounce of Prevention Fund, and Illinois Action for Children are the "big three" statewide advocacy organizations in Illinois that have been instrumental in the successful passage of universal preschool legislation. But in Illinois the statewide advocacy is built on a grassroots organization structure of child care providers, community organizations, and parents. The Illinois example of universal preschool presents the most developed advocacy structure of the six states in this study. Because Illinois has a well-developed, well-funded advocacy structure, the role of Pew funding in the state was quite different than in either New York or Tennessee.

To begin to understand how universal preschool legislation was passed in Illinois, a likely place to start is with the big three advocacy organizations and their history of involvement. Voices for Illinois Children was started in the 1980s after University of Chicago studies showed that the trend data for child indicators were getting worse (Stermer, Jerry, telephone communication, June 7, 2007). Voices' mission is to mobilize action to change policies in order to improve the lives of children. Currently Voices advocates for changes to Illinois budget and tax policy so that they better support families and services for children. It advocates for a full spectrum of children's issues, including health, mental health, early childhood education, education reform, foster care, and policies to support parental involvement and working families (Voices for Illinois Children 2007a). Voices advocates for children of all ages but there has been a focus on preschool from the outset. Every year since its founding, Voices has taken a preschool proposal to the legislature along with proposals to increase the subsidy rate for child care and to make child care more available to working families (Stermer, Jerry, telephone communication, June 7, 2007).

In 1982, longtime child advocacy philanthropist Irving B. Harris[3] helped found the Ounce of Prevention Fund. Through a combination of private foundation funds and state funds, the organization was formed to focus attention on early childhood, with emphasis on birth to three. Ounce is an advocacy organization but it also provides direct services for early education (Head Start, Early Head Start, Educare) and home-visiting programs aimed at educating parents to improve early childhood experiences and health outcomes. The Ounce of Prevention Fund leverages change for at-risk children from birth to age five through direct services to children and families, training for early childhood professionals, research on what works, with a major focus on advocacy for young children and families (Shier, Nancy, telephone communication, June 15, 2007).

Action for Children is a nearly forty-year-old membership organization representing child care providers with three main foci: public policy and advocacy, program services, and program development. It began in 1970 as a grassroots volunteer movement led by Sylvia Cotton to advocate for child care services to support women entering the workforce. Called the Day Care Crisis Council of Chicago, then Day Care Action Council, and now Action for Children, it has been a vocal advocate for quality early education. Advocacy is the soul of the organization but over the last twenty years it began delivering services to low-income families across the state. Its president, Maria Whelan, states that Action's main goal is to generate broad-based, impassioned organizing that gives power to parents to enable them to give the best care for their children (Whelan, Maria, telephone communication, June 13, 2007). Its membership consists mostly of child care providers through which Action reaches parents both for service delivery and calls for action.

In the 1980s, when the deep social-spending cuts of the Reagan administration were beginning to impact service delivery, leadership at the three Illinois child advocacy organizations realized that they should work together. They decided to focus on quality as a proxy for moving the experiences of children into a more complete developmental picture. A fundamental issue was the commitment that any early childhood policy should include the four domains of child development (social, emotional, physical, and cognitive). They called themselves the "Quality Alliance for Early Childhood Settings" and met regularly to discuss policy advocacy for children ages birth-to-five.[4] The Alliance is not an incorporated nonprofit organization but rather a metaphorical table that everyone agreed to sit around to discuss strategies for advancing early childhood issues. The advocates met regularly, whether at an office, coffee shop or on the phone to carefully discuss their "core values" (term used by advocates). They agreed that the values were most important and that they would walk away from funding if it did not support a birth-to-five policy focus, a commitment to quality services, and a commitment to a diverse delivery system that builds on the full range of child care providers. All interviewed were quick to clarify that while there were disagreements about smaller issues, the group never wavered from its commitment to the core values.

In addition to the big three, other organizations such as Chicago Metropolis 2020, a membership organization of business and civic leaders addressing the regional needs of the seven county area around Chicago, and Fight Crime: Invest in Kids Illinois have been involved in advocating for preschool investment. In 1999 Governor Ryan convened the Early Care and Education Assembly. Metropolis 2020 received funding from the McCormick Tribune Foundation to provide staff support for the Assembly. This group of eighty people from around the state came together to summarize and prioritize recommendations; they listed voluntary universal preschool for three and four year olds as their number one policy recommendation.

Subsequently in 2001, the Task Force on Universal Access to Preschool was created and charged with developing a blueprint for implementing preschool for all. The Task Force released its report in February 2002, outlining cost estimates and a ten-year implementation plan. To elevate their plan on the state policy agenda, Metropolis engaged business and civic leaders in early childhood public policy issues through a 2003 breakfast meeting with the Committee for Economic Development, which had recently released its *Preschool for All Report*.

In 1999, Fight Crime: Invest in Kids Illinois began publicly calling for increased investment to make quality preschool education available to all Illinois children (State Journal-Register 1999, 6). The involvement of Fight Crime in Illinois predates Pew investment and is in line with the creation of a broad group of organizations advocating for early childhood investment. With frequent letters to the editor and opinion pieces, Fight Crime made the case that investment in early childhood would reduce expenditures on juvenile delinquents in the future. According to advocates, Fight Crime was an important ally because it was outside of the "usual suspects" in early education. The fact that law enforcement endorsed greater investment in early education as a preventative strategy against juvenile delinquency and future correctional budget outlays strengthened the case for universal preschool (Shier, Nancy, telephone communication, June 15, 2007).

In addition to the statewide groups, each region of the state had advocates working for change. The Chicago Coalition of Site-Administered Child Care Programs, Metropolitan Association for the Education of Young Children, and numerous other regional and local advocates all worked to advance the universal preschool cause.

An absolutely critical factor in the ability of the Alliance to sustain the push for early childhood investment is the long-term committed funding by foundations. The late Irving B. Harris's approach to philanthropy was "to invest in people and trust them to do their best work" (Frances Stott, Vice President and Dean of Academic Affairs at the Erikson Institute, quoted in Erikson Institute 2004, 6). He was an early catalyst for raising awareness about the importance of the early years, in particular the infant and toddler years, and used his wealth to establish many institutions such as the Ounce of Prevention Fund, ZERO TO THREE, and the Yale Child Study Center, among others (Erikson Institute 2004, 1–18). Phyllis Glink, executive director of the Irving Harris Foundation states, "Irving had a vast circle of business associates, policymakers, practitioners, academics, friends, and family, and he would talk to anyone and everyone about the findings of child development research and the opportunities of the early years" (Quoted in Shore 2006a, 10–11).

In 1993, the McCormick Tribune Foundation began funding early childhood and the shift in focus was the result, according to many involved, of a meeting between the foundation's board and Irving Harris at which he passionately described the research on the importance of early brain development and encouraged the board to investment in early education in order to improve outcomes for children. He was persuasive, as he was in convincing people around the country, and subsequently McCormick Tribune focused its Education Program on "creating a statewide system that provides access to quality early care and education for all children ages birth-to-five and improves the quality of programs serving those young children in low-income communities in the Chicago region" (McCormick Tribune Foundation 2007a). From 1993 to 2006 the Education Program awarded a total of more than $74 million to early care and education in Illinois (McCormick Tribune Foundation 2007b). The strategy was to invest resources in three areas: public policy, quality assurance, and public awareness. To effect public policy change, the foundation decided to invest in three main organizations: Action for Children, Ounce of Prevention, and Voices for Children.[5] The foundation chose to invest, much like Irving B. Harris, by taking a chance on the leadership at the three organizations and deciding to provide operating funds to build their capacity for achieving their missions. For over ten years, these organizations have been able to rely on a steady stream of funding from McCormick Tribune. For example, in 2005–2006 each of the three advocacy organizations received between $350,000 to $400,000 (McCormick Tribune Foundation 2007b). Maria Whelan, president of Illinois Action for Children, describes McCormick Tribune's decision as "visionary for realizing that the time frame for effecting change would take longer than the standard three-years of foundation funding." Whelan continues, "At the end of the day, we can focus on objectives rather than worrying how to keep the lights on" (telephone communication, June 13, 2007). All three organizations agree that the impact of McCormick Tribune funding on their ability to achieve objectives cannot be overstated.

A key aspect of the McCormick Tribune funding is that it did not require that the three organizations form an alliance. The advocacy organizations *chose* to participate in the Quality Alliance for Early Childhood Settings, but McCormick Tribune resisted the impulse to formalize or institutionalize collaboration. The provision of operating funds allowed the leadership at the organizations to choose to sit down at the table for cooperative discussions. McCormick Tribune did not staff the Quality Alliance or set benchmarks for accomplishment. Stermer states, "They got out of the way—and let it thrive" (Jerry Stermer quoted in Shore 2006a, 10).

With the successful passage of the Preschool for All legislation in 2006, the McCormick Tribune Foundation could have decided to shift focus, but, according to Education Program Director Sara Slaughter, the board ultimately decided to stay the course and continue funding early education and care on the policy, quality, and public awareness dimensions (Slaughter, Sara, telephone communication, June 12, 2007). At a minimum it will take another three years to work toward fully funding the Preschool for All program and McCormick Tribune wants to fund efforts to assure that the infrastructure to support quality is in place. But as they have from the beginning in 1993, McCormick Tribune has a broad vision of early care and education that includes but is not limited to universal preschool.

Unlike Pew's intensive focus on results-driven philanthropy, McCormick Tribune is focused on capacity building to achieve systems change. Pew's universal preschool giving program was originally conceived to last for seven to ten years, although it may be extended. McCormick Tribune has an even longer-term investment strategy and maintains its commitment during times of success as well as challenge. Slaughter reports that the board is fully supportive of the giving strategy and realizes that systems change requires a longer-term investment. Because McCormick Tribune directs its funding to Illinois rather than a national focus like Pew, it interacts with its grantees in many capacities. According to Slaughter, they are often at the same meetings and events and because of their frequent contact, McCormick Tribune is kept abreast of grantees activities and does not have to rely primarily on formal reports (telephone communication, June 12, 2007).

In addition to the Harris Foundation and the McCormick Tribune Foundation, more recently the Joyce Foundation began funding early childhood education in Illinois and elsewhere.[6] In Illinois, Joyce has funded Voices for Children (2004, 2-year grant for $200,000; 2006, 2-year $150,000), Ounce of Prevention (2004, 2-year grant for $250,000; 2006, 2-year $150,000), Action for Children (2004, 2-year grant for $700,000), and Metropolis 2020 (2006, 1-year $60,000), among others. In addition, Joyce has supported the national Fight Crime: Invest in Kids (2004, 2-year $250,000). It has also partnered with grantees of the Pew Charitable Trusts. First, in 2003 Joyce made a $215,000 grant to the Education Trusts' Trust for Early Education to support early childhood workforce development, followed by a grant to Pew's strategic partner NIEER (2004, 1-year $200,000). Finally, it made a grant directly to Pew for the National Early Childhood Accountability Task Force (2005, 2-year $100,000) (Joyce Foundation 2007).

The history of foundation support in Illinois has created the capacity of nonprofit organizations to fund multiple staff who advocate in the state capital of Springfield, support statewide planning processes through the Early Learning Council (discussed below), conduct policy research and analysis, form relations with the media, organize parents and providers, educate legislators, and reach out to opinion leaders (Shore 2006a, 12–13). There is a depth of expertise in Illinois that is unrivaled among the states with universal preschool policies. The leaders of the big three advocates Jerry Stermer, Maria Whelan, and Harriet Meyer have been working on these issues for decades. In addition, there is local and regional leadership that has been actively working for change over the same time period. There is strength in activism at the local, regional and state level that, combined, creates a formidable advocacy structure.

The unity in the advocacy community mirrors the unity within the state bureaucracy. Kay Henderson, administrator for the Division of Early Childhood, at the Illinois State Board of Education (ISBE), has been at ISBE for sixteen years and Division Administrator for four. Linda Satersfield, State Child Care Administrator at the Illinois Department of Human Services (ILDHS) has been at IDHS for most of her career and Child Care Administrator for nine. These two women have worked to build a strong professional relationship based on mutual respect. Similar to the advocates, the state agencies, together with Head Start (the Head Start Collaboration Office is located within IDHS), meet regularly to discuss collaboration issues, specific local issues, and the need for policy changes. Their metaphorical table is called "Good Start Growth Smart" and was initially created when the U.S. Department of Health and Human Services funded two annual meetings in which ISBE, IDHS, and Head Start focused on strategic planning. After the federal funding ended, the group continued to meet (Henderson, Kay, telephone communication, June 18, 2007).

The history leading up to the passage of Preschool for All spans several decades. There were calls for state preschool as far back as 1979 (Leff and Kirp 2006, 12). After years of advocacy, in 1985 the state created the Pre-Kindergarten Program for Children At-Risk of Academic Failure (O'Connor 1995a, 11; 1995b, 6). The program for three and four year olds was created under Republican Governor James R. Thompson (1977–1991) as part of broader education reform legislation. The pre-K program was framed as an education program, rather than a child care program (Henderson, Kay, telephone communication, June 18, 2007). The education emphasis is evident from the evaluation reports required to be submitted to the legislature every three years. The focus of the reports is on school readiness and academic performance of pre-K participants in later grades (Illinois State Board of Education 2001, 1–53; Illinois State Board of Education 2004, 1–53). ISBE administered the program through a competitive grant system that was available only to public schools.[7] Each school district was able to define "at-risk" criteria for program participation that includes diagnostic screenings for developmental delays and criteria tailored to the local conditions (e.g., parental education level, English as a second language, referral from another state agency, parental incarceration, homeless family, parental illness, etc.) (Illinois State Board of Education 2001, 1–53). In 1987, the first full year of the program, approximately 7,000 three- and four-year-old children participated in the program in 202 (of 893) school districts. During the 1990s Republican Governor James R. Edgar (1991–1999) supported increased funding for early childhood education, and enrollment grew in spurts to serve nearly 50,000 children in 607 school districts in 1999 (Illinois State Board of Education 2007, table 1).

But while support for pre-K was strong, advocates wanted to protect a birth-to-five focus for early childhood funding. The advocates pushed to combine the pre-K program and two birth-to-three programs (the Parental Training program and the Prevention Initiative program) into one funding stream. In the late 1990s advocates successfully lobbied for the creation of the Early Childhood Block Grant (ECBG). As Jerry Stermer, Executive Director of Voices for Illinois Children, explains, they used the term "block grant" as a way to piggyback on the success of Chicago Mayor Richard M. Daley in persuading the state legislature to separate state funding for the Chicago Public Schools into a block grant that then allowed the city greater freedom in directing education funds (Stermer, Jerry, telephone communication, June 7, 2007). The use of "block grant" for early childhood programs does not provide the flexibility in spending that is typically associated with a block grant; rather the ECBG combines the pre-K and birth-to-three program funding with the stipulation that 8 percent (now 11 percent) of the total ECBG amount will be allocated to birth-to-three programs (Henderson, Kay, telephone communication, June 18, 2007). The ECBG was not aimed at increasing flexibility in spending for early childhood funds but rather protecting individual programs by combining vulnerable line item programs into one fund and setting aside a portion for birth to three programs. This change, regardless of the accuracy of the title, proved to be critical for keeping faith with the advocates' birth-to-five core value when the push for Preschool for All began in 2003.

Advocates hoped that when Republican Governor George H. Ryan took office in 1999 he would increase early education funding and that did occur in his first two years in office (Illinois State Board of Education 2007, table 1). But the state experienced serious budget crises in the wake of the September 11th terrorist attacks, and by the last year of Ryan's term in 2002 he was calling for budget cuts (*State Journal-Register* 2002, 3). He tried to eliminate twenty-two separate grant programs, including the ECBG, to shift $400 million into general revenues (State Journal-Register 2002, 3). But advocates successfully fought his proposal, and funding for pre-K remained constant during FY 2002 and 2003, allowing nearly 56,000 children to participate in 642 (641 in 2002) school districts (Illinois State Board of Education 2007, table 1).

The tides turned in the advocates' favor when Democrat Rod Blagojevich, who campaigned on a platform of creating universal pre-school, was elected and proceeded to include universal preschool in his first State of the State address (Blagojevich 2003b, 15). Governor Blagojevich became committed to early education through a confluence of factors including exposure to the research on the important of early brain development, a visit to an Educare (model preschool program run by Ounce of Prevention Fund), and his own daughter's experience in a Montessori preschool. According to several people interviewed for this study, the governor felt strongly that if his daughter benefited from pre-school then all children should have that opportunity. Despite inheriting what the press referred to as "the worst fiscal situation in Illinois' history" (Finke 2003, 1), the new governor remained committed to universal pre-school. Governor Blagojevich called for new spending of $25 million to begin to create universal preschool for all three and four year olds. Even though the media questioned his priorities and some advocates were even willing to reduce the amount for preschool, Governor Blagojevich plowed forward and ended up winning $30 million for early childhood and prom-ised to match the increase in 2004 and 2005 (Blagojevich 2004; State Journal-Register 2003, 6).

The election of Governor Blagojevich captured the attention of Pre-K Now. Because of the history and funding support of advocates in Illinois, the arrival of Pre-K Now funding was welcomed, but advocates were not desperate for funds. Unlike Tennessee, in which the advocates had little capacity for advocacy (TAEYC was an all volunteer organization and Stand for Children had a staff of three), the McCormick Tribune's long-term funding allowed the advocacy organizations to build capacity over the past decade. However, advocates are quick to point out that the Pre-K Now funds came at exactly the time needed to build support for passing the Preschool for All legislation. Pre-K Now provided funds to each of the big three advocacy organizations to jointly create the Early Learning Illinois (ELI) campaign. The ELI is described as a "big empty tent" that was filled with supporters. By 2006, when the legislation passed, more than 200 individuals and organizations had come into the ELI tent. On the ELI Web site, individuals and organizations can sign on to support Preschool for All and get quick access to NIEER and Pre-K Now reports and Illinois-specific reports and news items (Early Learning Illinois 2007). Funds were also used for a media campaign. Pre-K Now funds were used to create radio ads supporting early childhood investments and opposing budget cuts to child care (Voices for Illinois Children 2007b).

While Governor Blagojevich's increased funding for the pre-K pro-gram enabled the state to serve approximately 12,000 additional at-risk preschool children, new legislation would be necessary in order for the program to expand to universal access. The state legislature passed Senate Bill 565 to create the Illinois Early Learning Council (IELC) to "develop a high quality early learning system that will be available to children age five and younger throughout the state" (Blagojevich 2003a, 1). The IELC was charged with developing a proposal for the universal pre-K program. The forty-six council members are appointed primarily by the governor with the House and Senate leadership each able to name one appointment. Governor Blagojevich appointed Harriet Meyer, President of the Ounce of Prevention Fund, and Brenda Holmes, Deputy Chief of Staff for Education, from the Governor's Office to cochair the Council. Harriet Meyer was well positioned to lead the Council after having cochaired the Early Childhood Committee for the Blagojevich transition team and, in 2002, cochaired the Finance Committee of the Illinois Task Force on Universal Preschool (2003a, 1–2). Brenda Holmes was appointed to the State Board of Education and in September 2004 Elliot Regenstein, who had recently joined the governor's administration as the director of Education Reform, became the cochair of IELC. A lawyer by training, Regenstein soon found himself completely absorbed in the process of creating Preschool for All.[8]

When the IELC was formed ISBE and IDHS worked very closely with the Council, as did representatives from some local and regional agencies. Each agency had representatives on committees with IDHS focusing on delivery of pre-K in community-based settings and ISBE working with the Council to assure recommendations complied with ISBE regulations and identifying what supports would be necessary to maintain a quality pre-K program.

The IELC worked intensively for over a year through a committee structure that involved approximately 200 people from all over the state to develop recommendations for universal preschool legislation. When their report was presented to the governor and discussed in the legislature, the Council did not have to work hard to educate lawmakers about the importance of universal preschool. With six lobbyists working on early education (for six different organizations) the legislators were already well informed (Shore 2006a; Regenstein and Meyer 2005). The Council's report was used as the basis for writing the Preschool for All legislation (Shore 2006b).[9]

ISBE Early Childhood Division Administrator Kay Henderson notes that the Early Learning Council's recommendations were complete and based on the shared understanding of a wide range of interested participants. The independence and legitimacy of the recommendations were increased, in her opinion, because the state did not provide any funds to support the Council's work. The Ounce of Prevention Fund provided extensive staff support for the Council and the more than 200 participants each paid his or her own travel expenses, as well as donating the staff time to attend committee meetings to advance the work of the Council.

With the recommendations well received and with support in the General Assembly, the Preschool for All legislation was passed in May 2006, with strong bipartisan support. The legislation passed unanimously in the House and by a vote of 47 to 10 in the Senate (Lightford, Flynn Currie, et al. 2006, chapter 122, par. 14-7.03). The opposing votes were cast by Republicans who opposed the governor's budget. The 94th General Assembly had a 65-53 Democratic majority in the House and a 31-27-1 Democratic majority in the Senate. The majority in the Senate expanded in the 2006 election.

Preschool for All, like its predecessor, is a grant program administered through the Early Childhood Block Grant by the Illinois State Board of Education (ISBE). All preschool providers (outside of the Chicago Public School District) must apply to ISBE for pre-K funds and funds are granted based on three levels of priority. The first level is for children at-risk of academic failure. Once at-risk children are served, pre-K is available to children whose family income is less than four times the federal poverty level ($82,600 for a family of four in 2007) (U.S. Government 2007, 3147–3148). The third tier of funding is available to all children, regardless of family income. The Preschool for All Program is voluntary and provides two and one-half hours of preschool education by a teacher certified in early childhood through a diverse delivery system. The legislation requires ISBE to annually report on the number of children served by priority funding category and to develop evaluation tools to be used by pre-K grantees to evaluate school readiness. ISBE is required to report on the results and progress of students every three years (Lightford, Flynn Currie, and et al. 2006, chapter 122, par. 14-7.03).

The legislation reflects the core values of the advocates: maintains a birth-to-five focus (because any increase in ECBG also increases funds for birth-to-three), sets standards for a quality program, and is delivered through a diverse array of preschool providers (Koch 2007, 1–9). But an important part of the Preschool for All story in Illinois is that passing the legislation was never the end goal. Preschool was the "public" issue but it was always tied to the larger policy focus of birth-to-five and encompassed far more than preschool education. Passing the legislation was one step on the road to improved early childhood policy in Illinois. In the words of Jerry Stermer, they decided "to ride the universal preschool horse because it had legs" but they never lost sight of the broader focus (telephone communication, June 7, 2007). In the same year Preschool for All was created, the legislature also passed increased funding for children's mental health and early intervention, increased reimbursement rates for child care providers, raised the cost-of-living adjustment for voluntary home-visiting programs for at-risk families, and removed barriers for early education practitioners to pursue teacher certification (Shore 2006a).

Advocates, the Illinois Early Learning Council, IDHS, and ISBE are intensely focused on the challenges of expanding the pre-K program while at the same time assuring high quality of services through a diverse array of providers. According to Henderson, the completeness of the recommendations from IELC has been helpful to her Division during the implementation phase (Henderson, Kay, telephone communication, June 18, 2007). From her perspective, IELC has been able to champion early childhood in ways that complement the work of ISBE. The IELC raised the Preschool for All legislation on the state agenda and will keep Preschool for All implementation on legislators' minds.

A curious aspect of the Illinois case is the relatively low-level of print media attention to the process of winning support for universal preschool. Back in 1994 *Chicago Tribune* reporter Ron Kotulak was awarded the Pulitzer Prize for Explanatory Journalism for his series of articles on the scientific advances in early brain development (Shore 2006a). But since that time there has been little focus on how the brain research has resulted in policy change. There have been many letters from advocates published in newspapers and occasional editorials in support but there was not the sustained, informed coverage that occurred in Tennessee.

In the states of Oklahoma and West Virginia, there was no media coverage of universal preschool but there was also no grassroots movement to create the program. Many interviewed for this book explained the low-level coverage as a negative byproduct of the advocates' successful presentation of a united front. Because of their agreement on core values, the advocates consistently projected a unified position. It was a very successful legislative strategy but without controversy there was little interest from newspaper reporters. It is not that the papers opposed investment in early education; they just did not cover it very often.

The strength of the internal structure of advocacy for early childhood education in Illinois creates an environment in which Illinoisans look inward for the answers. In other states, the NIEER annual pre-K ranking and Pre-K Now reports were important tools in directing attention toward universal preschool. In New York and Tennessee, the reports were used in essence to say, "Look at us, we're getting national attention. Increase our funding/pass our legislation so that we can be a national leader." But in Illinois, there was no similar media coverage of either Pre-K Now reports or NIEER's annual pre-K rankings.

In response to passage of the Preschool for All legislation, the *Chicago Tribune* ran a now famous editorial titled "Preschool for Some," in which it criticized Governor Blagojevich for advocating to include access to state-funded preschool for families "whose parents strap the kid into the car seat of their Mercedes E500 sedan" (*Chicago Tribune* 2006, 26). But in the same editorial the *Tribune* admitted that "Preschool is tremendously valuable." The *Tribune* did support investment in pre-K, it just did not support making the program universal. The *Tribune* is a conservative newspaper and did not support Governor Blagojevich's candidacy and continues to disagree with the governor's policy agenda.

But lack of media coverage has not affected the ability of advocates to build a solid foundation of support. Action for Children President Maria Whelan credits their strong history of activism. If a new legislator is elected, her members are out there inviting him or her to their centers, informing the legislator about their concerns, and in general making themselves heard. Ounce of Prevention Fund has an influential board that it can mobilize to contact legislators as well as a database of 4,000 people to whom it sends e-mail action alerts. The reality is that effective advocacy requires significant investments of time and time translates into salaries. The statewide, regional, and local advocates are everywhere, active, and vocal. There are six organizations with lobbyists for early childhood issues whose associated leadership personally donate six figure sums to political campaigns (Shore 2006a).

It also helped that there was no lasting opposition to early education funding. In 1995 a "ready to learn" bill died in the House due to behind-the-scenes maneuvering by conservative religious interests. The bill would have provided a grant program for education and parental counseling to improve education in child care settings and, according to activists, there were enough votes to pass the bill (Stermer, Jerry, telephone communication, June 7, 2007). But religious interests opposed the bill because they viewed it as government infringing on the domain of families and threatened to run conservative candidates against Republicans if the bill was passed (Bush 1995, 7). But by 2006, the religious opposition to state investment in early education had dissipated. Some in the legislature had concerns about financing universal preschool but not about the value of early education.

There was also no opposition from the child care industry. There was initial pushback when the pre-K program recommendations required certified teachers in all pre-K classrooms. To retain staff, child care centers would have to pay market rates to certified pre-K teachers and this would create a wage gap with the other child care center staff. The ISBE Early Childhood Division and advocates worked to counter the opposition by helping child care industry workers realize that "they have worked hard for certification and deserve to be paid more" (Henderson, Kay, telephone communication, June 18, 2007). Another pushback occurred when ISBE implemented early learning standards that required centers to focus on learning outcomes. But ISBE provided funding for technical assistance to help centers adjust. The child care industry has had to adapt but in the end a "mind shift" occurred that led them to support not only Preschool for All but also the components for quality pre-K (Henderson, Kay telephone communication, June 18, 2007). Another factor that led the child care industry to support Preschool for All was the strong commitment from all actors to a diverse delivery system. When the pre-K program was created in 1985, initially it was only available to school districts but after 2003 private organizations were allowed to submit proposals to ISBE to start pre-K programs. All child care centers knew that they could participate in the delivery of Preschool for All if their children met the criteria.

Part of the success has to do with long-term advocacy to raise awareness about the importance of the early years. But the framing took years to develop. According to advocates, child care still faces challenges in framing, with some holding on to the "babysitting" perpective and others viewing it as a private domain. But, since 1985, the pre-K program has been framed as an educational program, which is established as distinct from child care. Preschool-age children have clearly emerged as a dependent target group worthy of public investment (Schneider and Ingram 1997, 241). With the strength of the advocacy community behind them, it has become politically advantageous for politicians to support increasing benefits for preschool children.

The challenges ahead for Preschool for All are to increase funding for universal access and to assure that pre-K is a quality program. All interviewed were optimistic about Governor Blagojevich's commitment to increase funds through his second term (ending in 2011).[10] It is likely that the program will be made available for the first two tiers, which means it will be available to all children in families with incomes less than four times the federal poverty level. Even though Illinois has a challenging fiscal environment with many competing causes, advocates point out that even when the budget was in crisis in 2003, the governor managed to increase funding for pre-K. This is one of Governor Blagojevich's most important priorities and those involved agree that he will successfully fund the preschool program. After Blagojevich leaves office the new governor may have other priorities but in Illinois the pre-K program, and early childhood more broadly, was built during both Republican and Democratic administrations. In the 2006 gubernatorial election, Blagojevich's Republican opponent supported a $30 million increase each year for preschool (*State Journal-Register* 2006, 49), as opposed to Blagojevich's pledge of $60 million (Blagojevich 2006, 58). There is high confidence that whichever party ascends to the governor's mansion next, support for the Preschool for All program will continue.

## Analysis

In New York, Tennessee, and Illinois, the investment in advocacy organizations by Pew and Pew-funded actors helped to pass or increase funding for universal preschool, but the impact of the funding varied among the states. While Illinois advocates will vehemently state that "all money is important," in the Illinois case the impact of Pew funding is not as obvious as in New York or Tennessee. In contrast to the Tennessee and New York cases in which Pew grants were the catalyst for unifying advocates, in Illinois the advocates were already unified. Illinois advocates had been meeting together for over a decade before Pew funded the Early Learning Illinois Alliance for advancing universal preschool. But Pre-K Now State Policy Director Stephanie Rubin (telephone communication, June 28, 2006) explains that this is part of the strategy. Pre-K Now invests in advancing preschool where it is most likely to succeed, but the use of funds varies depending on the needs of the states. In all three states, the investment of Pew and Pew-funded actors in state advocacy organizations succeeded in moving the states toward universal preschool

In both New York and Tennessee, the advocates absolutely needed funding and technical assistance to effectively push for change. In both states, Pre-K Now funds were used to hire public relations or marketing firms. This was especially important in Tennessee because of the limited administrative capacity of TAEYC and Stand for Children. The public relations/marketing firms brought the capacity and expertise to develop marketing materials and provided administrative support for the campaign to pass or win increased funding for preschool.

But the Pew funding, while positive for the creation and funding of universal preschool, can create divisions among advocates. In New York, the Pre-K Now funding was critical in building the support to win preschool funding, but it initially created resentment among advocates for two reasons. First, it created a split in advocacy for early childhood that had not previously existed. With preschool separated from the other early years and receiving all the investment, advocates for younger years resented the relative wealth of the preschool advocates. The advocates unified only after Governor Pataki threatened to eliminate funding for the universal preschool program. In Illinois, Pew's focus on preschool conflicted with the birth-to-five focus that had existed among the state advocates for decades. But because the Illinois Early Childhood Block Grant automatically increased funding for birth-to-three when preschool funding increased, advocates did not face a conflict in their core values. Pre-K Now funding enabled advocates in Illinois to win additional resources for Preschool, which in the end benefited all children from birth-to-five.

Alaska presents an example of the type of bind that state early childhood advocates face when they need the funds but are not willing to champion universal preschool. In that state, advocates considered universal preschool because of the lure of Pre-K Now funds but concluded that the challenges of remote locations with small populations made home-based solutions that address a range of issues more appropriate (Hensley 2006). Pre-K Now did not invest in Alaska because advocates were not willing to advocate for universal preschool (and because of insufficient political leadership). Advocates are struggling to implement a strategic plan but have few resources to achieve it.

But it is important to note that Pew is not the first to advocate for investing in preschool. Pew's strategic partners are all organizations that are committed to early childhood and collaborating with Pew allows them to jointly advance their objectives. Fight Crime: Invest in Kids was championing early childhood investment before Pew started its giving program. It has published reports, many with Pew funds, in California, Utah, Rhode Island, Oregon, Minnesota, Maine, Colorado, Pennsylvania, Ohio, New York, Illinois, Iowa, Tennessee, New Mexico, Florida, Arkansas, Michigan, Washington, Wyoming, Nebraska, South Carolina, and North Dakota (*Fight Crime: Invest in Kids* 2007, 3). NIEER was working, under a different name, to provide research support for preschool investment. The funds from Pew expanded its focus and capacity for research but NIEER continues to receive funds from multiple sources for early childhood research. Pew also participates in the Early Childhood Funders' Collaborative, a group of foundations and public charities who all fund early education, some of whom have specifically funded preschool. In this way, Pew leverages its own funds with others to effect change, which has been a part of its strategy but especially so after it became a public charity in 2004. For example, Pew funded Pre-K Now at IEL, which receives funding from multiple sources, although approximately 90 percent of its budget comes from Pew (Doggett, Libby, personal communication, Washington, D.C., June 20, 2006).

Pew chose preschool because of the potential that "measurable progress can be made toward the long-term goal in three to five years"; however, the giving program is intended to last from seven to ten years, and perhaps longer. Rather than take on the entire pie of early childhood education and care, Pew's strategy was to focus concentrated attention on one slice at a time. Managing Director of the State Policy Initiatives at Pew, Dr. Susan Urahn, continues, "our philosophy is to target issues where there is a unique window of opportunity to advance change, and when that window begins to close, move to the next issue" (Urahn and Watson 2007, 5–8). Strategically selecting universal preschool does not mean that Pew does not recognize the importance of earlier years, but rather reflects a decision to focus narrowly with considerable depth to effect change.

The emphasis on strategic investment of funds to achieve a particular policy alternative contrasts sharply with the McCormick Tribune Foundation's strategy of long-term investments in people and organizations to achieve improved outcomes for children ages birth-to-five. Both of the giving strategies are rooted in the brain research and both foundations want to improve child outcomes by investing in the early years. But they have chosen very different strategies for achieving this result.

# Conclusion

Prior to the state universal preschool programs analyzed in this study, public provision of preschool has been limited to children from poor families and special needs children. The impetus for this study was to understand why some U.S. states are creating publicly funded preschool programs for all children, regardless of family income. What emerges from the study of Georgia, New York, Oklahoma, West Virginia, Tennessee, and Illinois is the development of a widely shared causal story (Stone 1997) in which investment in early education will result in improved educational outcomes, which by extension provide societal benefits through decreased incarceration rates, better educated workforces, and ultimately improved economic development. The policy entrepreneurs in these states successfully linked the problem of educational outcomes to the policy solution of publicly funded preschool.

The logical link was aided by the longitudinal studies of preschool programs that showed gains in a variety of measures of the life course of children benefiting from preschool. States were exposed to these findings through state organizations such as the National Governors' Association, the Conference of State Legislators, and regional organizations such as the Southern Region Education Board. Currently forty-one states and the District of Columbia provide state funding for preschool. Some states chose to focus on targeted programs and others allocated additional funds to Head Start, but the six states analyzed in this study chose to pass legislation to expand access to all children regardless of income.

The key to the successful creation of universal preschool programs in all of the cases has been the separation of policy for preschool-age children from policy for infants and toddlers. Prior to the state investment in universal preschool, all of these ages were lumped together under the rubric of child care policy. In order to successfully pass universal preschool, preschool had to be aligned with education and distanced from child care. Because of this split, policy entrepreneurs were able to reframe preschool education as a program worthy of public investment, thereby making it politically advantageous to confer benefits on preschool children. Politicians can now champion preschool investment as a wise public investment to improve educational outcomes, create a high-quality workforce, and ultimately improve economic development.

In all of the states analyzed here, the process of reframing preschool-age children as a separate target group took many years. Policy entrepreneurs had to overcome constructions of preschool as "babysitting" and individuals and groups who opposed public preschool as an infringement of government on the family's domain. But in all six states, eventually "preschool as a wise public investment" began to take hold and policy entrepreneurs were successful at crafting policy change.

Analysis of the six states and the arrival of the Pew Charitable Trusts provide insights for understanding policy change, the challenge to achieve stability for new programs, and the role of foundations and public charities in the policy process. This chapter draws the implications from the preceding analysis to inform each of these areas. The chapter concludes with a discussion about the future of preschool and directions for future research.

### Implications for Understanding Policy Change

In all six states, the push for universal preschool came from the elected officials, often without the participation of advocates. There were three governors, one senator, one representative, and one speaker of the assembly. Contrary to Kingdon's (1995) three streams framework, none of the states had a separate policy stream in which nonelected policy entrepreneurs were waiting for an opportunity to advance universal preschool. With the exception of Oklahoma in which one individual advocated for expanded (not universal) preschool, none of the states had advocates that were pushing the preschool alternative. That is because the advocates supported child care policies and had not separated preschool policy from policies for infants and toddlers. Once the elected officials announced their support for preschool, advocates rallied to the cause but there was no separate policy stream for universal preschool. Even in Illinois, the state with the most well developed advocacy structure, the focus was on birth-to-five, not preschool as a separate policy issue. In Georgia and West Virginia, the preschool advocacy came directly from the governor and senator, respectively, with very little advocacy structure in place to support or oppose. In New York and Tennessee, when the elected policy entrepreneur announced support of preschool, the advocates rallied. But this had not been the advocates' focus prior to the elected officials' announcements. In Oklahoma there were no advocacy organizations, only individual advocates. While the Oklahoma advocates wanted preschool expansion, they were not advocating for universal access, which ended up coming from an unexpected source (the chair of the House Education Committee who had not previously been a strong advocate for preschool investment). In each of these scenarios, the elected policy entrepreneurs identified the problem, chose the policy alternative, and raised it on the agenda.

As Mintrom (2000) conceptualized, the key to success is the ability of the policy entrepreneur to frame the issue and choose language that builds the support of others. In all six states the framing of preschool as a solution for improving educational outcomes was persuasive. All of the elected policy entrepreneurs were embedded in a milieu that each had the opportunity to shape. But that shaping came after years of softening up from previous policy entrepreneurs. In the six states, kindergarten legislation had already been passed either to make attendance mandatory or to provide full-day kindergarten or was on the agenda at the same time (e.g., New York's LADDER legislation included full-day kindergarten and universal preschool). Through the kindergarten policy processes, policy makers had the opportunity to debate the appropriate division between private and public responsibility for the education of young children. In some states, the debate brought on the ire of conservative, often religious advocacy interests. In some states, there was newspaper coverage of the policy debate that brought the issue into public consciousness.

Softening up also occurred through prior public expenditure on preschool. All of the states had some public provision of preschool that predated the universal preschool program. New York has the longest history of public provision of preschool dating back to state funding of a targeted program in the 1960s (and public school programs in the 1940s). Oklahoma and Illinois started targeted preschool programs in the 1980s and Tennessee started a targeted preschool program in the 1990s. In West Virginia and Georgia, some public schools provided preschool individually without state funds. In varying degrees, policy entrepreneurs were able to advance because of the softening up period for both kindergarten and targeted preschool.

The timing of preschool passage reflects the successful softening up period in each of the states. Baumgartner and Jones's (1993) concept of positive and negative feedback fits well for explaining previous failures and ultimate success. In several states, preschool had been introduced earlier but had failed. In the 1980s, New York's Governor Cuomo attempted to make the Early Pre-K program universal. In the 1990s, Tennessee's

Governor Sundquist and Illinois's Governor Edgar both tried to advance preschool. But in all three cases, the governors were unsuccessful. In the words of advocates, universal preschool was a policy whose time had not yet come. Utilizing Baumgartner and Jones's language, when the governors tried to advance preschool there was negative feedback that resulted in small marginal gains. But over the course of the next decade, the framing of preschool as a wise public investment had become more widespread and preschool moved up the S-shaped curve into the positive feedback region, where investments of resources yield increasingly larger marginal returns. In all cases, the elected officials' championing of preschool was embraced by advocates and majorities in the state legislature, resulting in successful legislative passage of universal preschool. But without the efforts of earlier policy entrepreneurs and the softening up that resulted in these prior years, the new construction of preschool as a wise public investment for improving educational outcomes would not have been widely shared.

Policy entrepreneurs identified correctly the opportunity to move up the S-shaped curve into the positive feedback region. Even in West Virginia where Senator Jackson inserted the preschool program on the last day of the legislative session, there was general consensus that the state was going to take some action related to early education. Unfortunately for the supporters of Educare, the universal preschool policy alternative supplanted their birth-to-five program. Even in Georgia, local school districts had begun offering preschool (without state aid) and since initially candidate Miller advocated for a targeted program, there was limited opposition to providing preschool to poor children.

In the states of Illinois and Tennessee, the arrival of the Pew Charitable Trusts and the impacts of its network of funded actors must also get some credit for moving the issue up the S-curve. Pew began funding Illinois advocates in 2002, and Tennessee was awarded its first grant from Pre-K Now in 2005. The intensity of the spotlight on these states is qualitatively different than the pioneer states. All of the actions of the network of Pew-funded actors were brought to bear on the policy change process. In addition to the grant funding to advocates, Pre-K Now sent out action alerts to its national database to draw attention to important developments in the state legislative processes, as well as its daily email digests of news coverage around the country related to preschool. For anyone attuned to early education issues, news of Illinois and Tennessee was everywhere. When key committee meetings, votes in the Senate or House, or final approval of the governor's budgets were occurring, subscribers to Pre-K Now's action alerts were directed to contact officials in Tennessee and Illinois to encourage them to support preschool. Advocates and politicians were exposed to the many opportunities to learn about early education through the National Conference of State Legislatures, National Governors' Association, and regional organizations, and could point to Oklahoma and Georgia as success stories. In both Tennessee and Illinois, the option to quietly pass legislation was no longer possible. Preschool was a high profile, new, publicly funded program with intense scrutiny and support by a range of Pew-funded actors. In both cases, the legislation passed with large majorities, which indicates that the time had finally come for preschool legislation in these two states. The framing of preschool children as a worthy public investment created a policy milieu in which the majority of politicians could support awarding benefits to a dependent group without fear of political repercussions.

Baumgartner and Jones hypothesize that if the policy is a new principle the policy making will be volatile but if it is a general principle then the policy making will be incremental. When a policy-making process is volatile, it creates challenges to maintaining stability for the new status quo. If the change is incremental then it is unlikely to experience challenges to its stability because the general principle is still in place. For all six states, expanding to universal access was a shift in the status quo that required policy actors to coalesce around a new policy image of preschool for everyone (the exception is Georgia for whom the governor advocated for a targeted program but later expanded it to universal to stabilize support for the program). Because it was a new principle, all of the policy-making processes should have been volatile.

The exception to volatility is Oklahoma. In that state, policy entrepreneurs made successive changes over a decade that eventually culminated in universal preschool but the expansion to universal was a new principle and should have been volatile. To avoid volatility the policy entrepreneurs purposely framed the changes as incremental. They were able to do this because they framed the preschool change very narrowly, rather than heralding it as a bold policy change. By not using the term "universal" but rather the phrase "let's make it available to all the kids" the legislation passed without waking the proverbial sleeping lion of conservative interests. Once the legislation came out of committee, the groundwork had been laid for unanimous passage in the House and majority passage in the Senate.

In two of the states, the preschool program was nested in larger policy issues. In New York, the universal preschool program was part of a suite of programs aimed at improving the education of children in preschool to third grade. Universal access to preschool was a new principle but the controversy was not over the merits of preschool but rather the volatility was due to opposition to the budgetary outlays necessary to implement the program. Similarly, in Georgia the volatility was due to the creation of the lottery, not preschool.

In West Virginia, the stealth passage of the preschool legislation led to intense volatility to maintain the new status quo. In both Tennessee and Illinois, each governor made universal preschool his signature issue, had the support of organized advocates funded by Pre-K Now, and in the case of Illinois other foundations, and eventually won overwhelming majorities in both houses.

In situations of volatile policy change, which includes all states except Oklahoma, Baumgartner and Jones state that waves of enthusiasm sweep through the political system as political actors become convinced of the value of some new policy, often in the absence of serious opposing voices. This is the case in all of the states. The legislation was able to sail through with very little opposition from advocacy groups. But the opposition that did occur came from several areas. Some opposition came from nested issues such as the lottery in Georgia or the budgetary battles in New York. In some states, Head Start initially had concerns about the preschool program but those issues were resolved sufficiently to prevent Head Start advocates from opposing the universal preschool program. Private child care providers could and, in some cases, should have opposed preschool on the basis that it would decrease their enrollments. But none of the state child care associations in the pioneer states were sufficiently mobilized to oppose preschool. In both Tennessee and Illinois, the child care provider associations were at the forefront of preschool advocacy. The Tennessee Association for the Education of Young Children is a membership organization for primarily nonprofit child care providers and its leader is the chair of the Pre-K Now funded Tennessee Alliance for Early Education, the key advocacy alliance supporting the preschool legislation. Illinois Action for Children is a membership organization for child care providers (as well as a service provider) and is one of the "big three" advocacy organizations, also funded by Pre-K Now, that has been critical to the successful passage of universal preschool.

Conservative interests who hold a construction that young children should be home with their mothers did exist in all states. But none were able to exert sufficient influence to defeat the legislation because the reframing of preschool as a wise public investment to improve educational outcomes had become dominant. The state legislation in these cases appears to have unfolded as Baumgartner and Jones predict: in the absence of serious opposing voices.

The role of the media in preschool policy change was not a major factor in agenda setting but once preschool was on the agenda, some newspapers of record for their states did vocally support preschool. In five of the states there were editorials addressing preschool, some supportive and some not. But eventually all of the newspapers researched for this book came to support public investments in early education and the preschool programs in their states. The frequency and content of the coverage was variable. Tennessee had consistent, educational, coverage that was supportive of preschool. The articles were written by a journalist who had attended the Pew-funded Hechinger seminar. In other states, the media coverage focused on controversies (e.g., New York State budget battles, Georgia's lottery controversy) with little emphasis on the merits of preschool. In Illinois, the *Chicago Tribune* only supported targeted preschool programs, not universal. In Oklahoma there was no coverage at all in the *Oklahoman* until years after the legislation was passed. The state newspaper coverage of preschool in the six states was of insufficient frequency for quantitative analysis,[1] but it does support Kingdon's finding at the federal level that media can help to shape alternatives depending on what angles they decide to cover but that they are not an important force in raising issues on the agenda (1995).

In all six states, policy entrepreneurs were successful in achieving policy change, but it was not due to stream convergence as Kingdon's (1995) multiple streams framework describes for federal policy-making. Rather, the problem, policy, and political streams were fused from the beginning. The elected policy entrepreneurs had raised the indicator of educational outcomes to a problem, connected it with the preschool policy alternative, and all of this was done within the political stream. In both Georgia and New York, the preschool policy solution was nested within larger policy issues, the lottery for education and LADDER legislation respectively, but in all the other states, preschool was its own policy issue. Only in Illinois was there a well-organized advocacy structure that resembles Kingdon's policy stream. But in Illinois the advocacy structure had a broader focus than preschool including a birth-to-five focus, quality programs, and a diverse delivery structure. When Illinois Governor Blagojevich decided to champion preschool, advocates were able to rally support for preschool because it did not require that they sacrifice their broader aims.

For the passage of preschool legislation, Baumgartner and Jones's (1993) punctuated equilibrium model has greater explanatory power. Because of the limited print media coverage of universal preschool, it was not possible to replicate their methodological approach used to analyze federal policy change, but the concepts of new versus general principles and positive and negative feedback were particularly useful for understanding why and how policy change occurred.

## Implications for Policy Stability

The successful policy change in all six states came as the result of shifting the education of preschool children from a private to a public responsibility. But the volatility of the policy change process created challenges in stabilizing universal preschool as the new status quo. The challenge for all states was to secure political, budgetary, and, in some cases, institutional stability to protect the new status quo. To maintain the new status quo, Baumgartner and Jones's model requires a policy monopoly with a (1) a definable institutional structure responsible for policy making that can effectively limit access to the policy process and (2) a powerful supporting idea associated with the institution generally connected to core political values, which can be communicated directly and simply through image and rhetoric (1993, 298). The pioneer states, with the exception of Oklahoma, faced challenges in creating stable policy monopolies. Oklahoma's preschool program was firmly ensconced in the very stable education monopoly. With an elected state superintendent who was herself a policy entrepreneur for universal preschool, and preschool funding incorporated in the K–12 budget, the program immediately achieved stability. Other states have not been as fortunate.

Georgia had budgetary stability due to the lottery funding but it faced institutional instability that threatened its successful implementation. Georgia has an elected state superintendent but, unlike Oklahoma's, she was opposed to the preschool program on the grounds that it was an expansion of the state into the private realm. The diverging policy images threatened the survival of the preschool program. To stabilize support for preschool in Georgia, the governor expanded the program to universal access and created a new state agency to administer the program. Only after taking these actions and actively "selling" preschool as an education program that would pay off in improved educational outcomes, did political support stabilize and a unified policy image take hold. Georgia's preschool program is now considered the "third rail" of politics in that no one wants to touch it for fear of getting zapped. In other words, it is politically risky to confer anything but benefits on the preschool target group.

In New York, the budget battles between the assembly and the governor made preschool funding unstable, even though there was widespread support for the preschool program. With the investment of Pew-funded actors, the advocates have been able to sustain pressure to increase funding, finally winning increases in 2006 and 2007. New York may finally be on the way to achieving stability.

In West Virginia, initially there was political instability due to opposition from one legislator. But after two years of trying to kill the preschool program, he left office. But that same year the preschool program's policy entrepreneur, the Chair of the Senate Education Committee, also left office. To date, preschool has been able to fly under the radar because West Virginia's declining K–12 enrollments have allowed the program to expand without additional state budget outlays for education. But with the universal access requirement approaching in 2012, the preschool program will become the focus of policy debate. West Virginia is a poor state with many competing demands for public funds. The preschool program lost its champion in the senate but his replacement, as Chair of the Senate Education Committee, is supportive of the preschool program. But whether the new Chair of the Senate Education Committee, will be able to build support for budget allocations to expand preschool to universal access is unclear. Pre-K Now is monitoring West Virginia and stands at the ready to invest. But the challenge for West Virginia is that the advocates do not share a unified policy image for universal preschool. Proponents of the eliminated Educare program retain their preference for a birth-to-five focus and have actively sought to reframe the early childhood policy image by linking public investment in birth-to-five to improved economic development. They are trying to engage the previously disinterested business community to expand the range of actors willing to support their policy image. There are also institutional challenges in the implementation of preschool. The initial goodwill between the Head Start, WVDHHR and WVDOE was seriously damaged when the WVDOE unilaterally revised the rules for the preschool program, which was repeated again in 2007. The preschool program is protected to the extent that it is part of state school funding formula and within the education monopoly. But the question is to what degree the political leadership will be able to build support for additional budget outlays.

In the more recent states of Tennessee and Illinois, both governors are committed to winning additional funding and they have the support of unified advocacy communities. However, in each state preschool advocates have to rally support for incremental increases in program funding. Both governors have been successful in winning annual additional funding for their preschool programs, but there may be a limit to this on the horizon. In both states, even though the legislation allows for all children to participate in preschool, there is priority for at-risk children. There is a unified policy image for preschool among legislators but it is for a targeted program, not universal. The governors in both states are pushing for universal access, but the status quo may stabilize for at-risk children. For Governor Miller of Georgia, expanding a targeted preschool program to universal access was necessary to save it from being constructed as a welfare program. But in both Illinois and Tennessee, the political support may not be forthcoming for all children to participate.

At this point, Georgia and Oklahoma have stable policy monopolies for their universal preschool programs and New York is well on its way. There is a unified policy image that every four-year-old should have access to the state preschool program and stable institutional structure for policy making. The other three states have stable political support for their preschool programs, but the budgetary support has not been sufficient to lead to universal access. The instability in the policy-making process is connected to the annual budget negotiations. In West Virginia, the legislation mandates universal coverage by 2012, but in Illinois and Tennessee, the policy image for preschool may unify around preschool for some, rather than preschool for all. Preschool investment to improve educational outcomes is the dominant framing, but the link to universal access is not sufficiently connected to it. In Illinois, a *Chicago Tribune* editorial that criticized universal access by using the image of a wealthy parent strapping her child into the Mercedes on the way to public preschool is emblematic of the image challenges for achieving universal access.

*Advocacy Coalitions*

Baumgartner and Jones's conceptualization of a policy monopoly includes the creation of a powerful supporting idea associated with the policy-making institution, but Sabatier and Jenkins-Smith's concept of an advocacy coalition places more emphasis on the degree to which the policy actors' internalized shared values creates a shared foundation for action. In the advocacy coalition framework, a group of actors share a particular belief system that includes a set of basic values, causal assumptions, and problem perceptions, and they coordinate activity over time.

While all of the states have policy actors committed to preschool, Illinois stands apart as the only state that has a mature advocacy coalition. The advocates in that state have a clearly articulated belief system and have coordinated their activity for over a decade. In interviews with advocates, they used the term "core values" to describe their commitment to policies that have a birth-to-five focus, provide quality services, and utilize a diverse delivery structure. The successful passage of preschool could not have occurred without the concerted efforts of the Illinois advocacy community, their relationships with elected and appointed officials, state agency personnel, and grassroots and grass-tops connections around the state. But in the other states, there was no advocacy coalition, mature or nascent.

**Role of Foundations and Public Charities in the Policy Process**

The policy-process literature does not address the role of foundations or public charities in the policy process. Historical accounts of foundations tend to be case specific or address subsets of foundations and do not attempt to provide a theory of foundations' role in the policy process. The only theoretical discussions of foundations and their relation to policy have been from the elite power theorists. As discussed in chapter Four, Dye (1979 and subsequent editions) models foundations as funding research at universities, providing grants to policy planning groups, and providing research reports and personnel to government commissions and councils. All of these activities were evident in the Pew strategy for advancing universal preschool policy change. But rather than one-way arrows from foundations to other entities, Pew has created a web of actors that is much more complex.

The main difference in the policy-change processes between three pioneer states and states with organizations receiving Pew funding is the role of advocacy organizations. In Georgia, Oklahoma, and West Virginia, there were no organized advocacy organizations involved in the policy change process. But in Tennessee and Illinois, with the aid of philanthropic funding, advocates were very involved in supporting policy change.

The starkest impact of philanthropic giving is on the creation of alliances for preschool. In all three states with organizations receiving Pre-K Now funding (New York, Tennessee, and Illinois), funding from Pre-K Now created alliances and funded the administrative support (via public relations firms) to launch effective issue campaigns. Without the Pre-K Now funding, the advocates would not have had the resources to hold legislative breakfasts or annual conferences, create professional marketing campaigns, or develop sophisticated e-advocacy technological capacity. Without Pew's strategic network of actors individually working to advance preschool, it would not have been possible for advocates to access materials supporting preschool investment, to utilize NIEER and Pre-K Now reports to draw attention to their states. In all three states, Pre-K Now funding enabled advocates to create and fund an alliance that built the capacity of advocates to sustain pressure for passing preschool legislation or funding preschool. All of the funded entities report that this funding was crucial to their success. Even in the Illinois case, in which there is a mature advocacy coalition, without Pew funding the advocates would not have been able to fund the staff time necessary to focus attention on preschool at the same level.

Pew and its grantees' comprehensive, expertly implemented strategy moved ahead in its first few years virtually without opposition. But the policy environment in recent years has changed with the entrance of opponents to universal preschool. Conservative think tanks, such as the Cato Institute, Arizona-based Goldwater Institute, and California's Reason Foundation, all oppose public investment in preschool. As Pew raised the profile of preschool, it drew the attention of advocacy groups against universal preschool including homeschool advocates (see www.universalpreschool.com) and national conservative issue advocacy groups such as Phyllis Schlafly's Eagle Forum. However, there is no foundation that is funding the opposition that can rival Pew's investment of approximately $10 million per year. But think tanks, particularly at the state level, are having an impact.

In 2006, an initiative to establish universal preschool in California met with strong opposition from the Reason Foundation. It charged, "Universal preschool will expand government provision of education, destroy the private market for preschool, and expand the power of teachers' unions. Taxpayers would be forced to subsidize not only the poor but also the middle class and wealthy" (Snell 2006, 1). The Reason Foundation also published a critical assessment of a RAND Corporation study that claimed California would realize a $2 to $4 dollar return on preschool investment (Cardiff and Stringham 2006). In addition to think tank opposition, television ads countered preschool investment with calls for greater K–12 investment. Public intellectuals such as University of California at Berkeley Professor Bruce Fuller exploited the public's fuzziness about the difference between pre-K and preschool to effectively argue for a targeted program by claiming that nearly two-thirds of California's children were already in preschool (Fuller 2006, E1). When the initiative failed, the loss was particularly bitter for Pre-K Now because it had tried to distinguish universal pre-K from the existing targeted state preschool program.

As opposition to preschool has emerged, a key part of the Pew-funded strategy is to keep the research and advocacy activities "on message." There are monthly phone calls between Pre-K Now, NIEER, and Pew to coordinate action. With the proliferation of negative information and misinformation on preschool, NIEER is spending more time on reactive responses (Barnett, Steven, telephone communication, September 6, 2006). The strategy is to counter opposition through the presentation of solid research on the benefits of universal preschool. Director Barnett reports that NIEER serves as a source for quick information retrieval that is increasingly necessary. Pew is also directly funding publications such as David Kirp's 2007 book, *The Sandbox Investment*, and a December 2007 special issue of the *American Prospect* titled, "Life Chances: The Case for Early Investment in Our Kids."

Pew's strategy is to select a policy alternative firmly based on research and fund a network of organizations that will advance policy change. But its strategy does raise larger issues beyond the creation of universal preschool. Is Pew bringing its considerable resources to bear on critical problems or is Pablo Eisenberg's (2003) characterization of Pew as a bully that tries to impose its priorities on other organizations more appropriate? Based on the research conducted in this study, the practices of Pew in its grant program for universal preschool does not warrant the bully label. The strategic partners such as Fight Crime: Invest in Kids and the Committee for Economic Development had already begun to champion early childhood education prior to Pew's giving program and each state had an elected policy entrepreneur who was already advocating for preschool.

A key issue is that the giving program was based on research that demonstrates benefits of high quality early childhood programs. Pew's funding of NIEER, the Tulsa study and others led to additional program evaluations that demonstrated positive cognitive gains from preschool. Pew did not start from scratch to impose an ideological preference on the rest of the country but it did choose a particular policy alternative and build a network of funded entities to achieve its goal. It funded national advocacy groups, law enforcement, business think tank, media training for journalists, media reports and videos, and professional associations of elected and appointed leaders (governors, state legislators, mayors, chief state school officers). But while the emphasis on preschool might have been a narrower focus, all of these entities had focused on young children previously. Pew was successful in raising the profile of preschool in profes- sional associations. At the state level, Pre-K Now invested in state advo- cates but these advocates were already organizing to support preschool.

What Pew and its grantees' strategy appears to be doing is moving the compass needle toward universal preschool. There have been notable set- backs in some states, particularly California, but the ubiquitous invest- ments by Pew through its network of funded actors are raising the profile of preschool investment as a strategy to improve educational outcomes. More recently Pew has shifted the framing to investment as a strategy to improve economic development. This was a conscious choice by Pew to expand the range of actors (Urahn and Watson 2007).

But while Pew is not accurately labeled a "bully," there are other important issues raised by their giving strategy. The big question for pre- school is: What will happen when Pew shifts its funding program else- where? There is no set date for ending the preschool giving program but the 2007 report conveyed that Pew is halfway into the giving program. Pew wants to claim victory, but the challenge will be in deciding how much victory is enough. Is it sufficient to have seven states (including Florida) with universal preschool programs (in theory, if not in practice)? Will victory be determined after a certain percentage of preschool-age children are served across the nation?

As is clear from the analysis of the pioneer states, passing the legislation is only one part of the challenge; creating stability for the program is another. Both Georgia and Oklahoma were able to secure budgetary and political support for preschool but New York is securing stability only after a decade of organizing and significant investment by Pew. In West Virginia there is a clear split between the preschool program and the advocates' focus on birth-to-five. With the deadline for universality approaching in 2012, it remains to be seen if the advocates will unify and if the political leadership will be able to rally support for investing the necessary resources. In both Tennessee and Illinois, the governors are committed to universal expansion but there is no unified policy image for universal access. There is stability for the existing targeted programs but expansion to universal access will require additional investment of resources and require political leadership and the continued pressure from advocates. The funding from Pre-K Now has been critical to the success in passing legislation in both of these states and it has an important role to play in funding the continued advocacy for universal access. When the Pew funding ends, advocacy for preschool will continue in Illinois because there is a mature advocacy coalition and advocates have alternative sources of funding. But in Tennessee, the advocates are heavily dependent on Pre-K Now funds. What Pew has been tremendously successful at is creating dialogue between and among state actors about preschool that builds a strong advocacy environment, supports political leadership, and creates and attracts media attention. But the lasting power of their giving power may be challenged due to the temporary capacity building of the advocacy communities.

The potential challenges to maintaining the new universal preschool status quo raises the question of whether a foundation or public charity should champion a particular policy alternative or invest in the broader issue areas such as early childhood but let the individual grantees develop the specific focus? There is solid research on the benefits of high-quality preschool for young children, and by extension society. But what about the relative importance of preschool to other policy concerns? Should a foundation or public charity have the power to privilege policy alternatives? In Sealander's (1997) study of foundation policy making from the Progressive Era to the New Deal, she found that when foundations were able to win approval for their policy alternatives, it often led to tangled outcomes. Could the same occur for universal preschool?

Tangled outcomes is precisely the concern raised in Bruce Fuller's *Standardized Childhood* (2007). He is concerned about the negative impacts that could occur as state governments take control of preschool education and respond to the pressure for improved educational outcomes. He asks whether more access to preschool will outweigh the costs of diminishing involvement of neighborhood organizations and parents and narrowing expectations for young children's development. The impact of state preschool programs on the "organizational pluralism" of the child care industry has not been studied. But it is important to note that Oklahoma is the only state that does not mandate collaboration with Head Start, private providers, or both. But even in that state, 40 percent of the school districts collaborate (Illgen and Garrett 2007). The larger issue is the degree to which universal preschool will narrow expectations for young children's development. The framing of universal preschool as a separate policy image was a successful strategy for decoupling early education from child care but Fuller is right on target in sounding the alarm for the potential of "pre-K" to narrow the focus to academic skills and away from the full-range of developmental needs of three and four year olds. Fuller states,

> What progressive reformers have been slow to learn is that, once government gains broad authority and invokes its regulatory habits, it's tempting for advocates, governors, and legislators to intensify their Weberian ways, simplifying and standardizing what children are to learn and how social relations are to be regimented inside classrooms. And when public funds are scarce or declining, even progressives will push for stronger accountability and ever more frequent testing of a narrowing range of skills. The mechanics of government structure come to dominate what, and through what social relations, children are to learn, regardless of how virtuous policymaker's aims may be. (2007, 27)

The six states analyzed in this study are at the vanguard of the preschool movement that now includes forty-one states and the District of Columbia. All of these states have public programs for preschool and some are moving in the direction of universal access and are home to organizations receiving investment from Pew, directly or indirectly. With Pew funding, the movement has a far more integrated network of associations and advocacy groups attempting to shift the framing of preschool-age children state-by-state. If the movement takes hold, publicly funded, universal preschool may become the new status quo across the country. Many advocates for increased investment in preschool, most notably NIEER, passionately make the case that the programs have to be of high

quality. But if the goal of the program is to improve educational outcomes, then the obvious measures of program success are the cognitive
gains. The pressure for public schools to make adequate yearly progress
as required by the No Child Left Behind Act intensifies the downward
pressure to improve cognitive gains. The accountability movement, which
originated in the South, is precisely why it was a brilliant strategy to
frame preschool as *the* policy solution for improving educational outcomes. The cognitive gains are what please politicians and make the
headlines. But will states intensify their Weberian ways to the point that
cognitive gains are all that matter? Therein lies the paradox: reframing
preschool as improving educational outcomes was a successful strategy in
the six states studied in this book but will demonstrating educational outcomes dominate the state programs to the exclusion of a developmentally
appropriate education?

Universal preschool was an issue whose time had come and Pew created a brilliantly comprehensive giving strategy that is having the intended
result of increasing access to preschool for more and more three and four
year olds. But it is an open question whether state programs will be high
quality and developmentally appropriate. If the dream can match reality,
then the universal preschool movement has great potential to improve
children's early childhood experiences and beyond.

# Notes

## Chapter 1

1. The term "child care" refers to the care and education of children under five. Preschool is restricted to children ages three and four years old (and five year olds not ready for kindergarten).

2. In 1981, Title XX was amended to create the Social Services Block Grant program.

3. Kingdon defines "political" colloquially to mean electoral, partisan, or pressure group factors, and not a broader definition typically used in political science that includes any activity related to the authoritative allocation of values.

4. Florida voters passed an initiative to change the state constitution in order to create universal preschool. The legislature did ultimately pass the enabling language to create the program and Pew invested resources into the policy process. The Florida case is omitted from this study because the initiative process is a different venue than the six other states with universal preschool legislation.

## Chapter 2

1. The push for pari-mutuel betting has a history going back to the 1950s when Georgia's House passed pari-mutuel betting on horse races with a voice vote but then reversed the vote during roll call. Over the next thirty years supporters continued to face legislators who would privately support betting but, due to opposition from constituents, would not publicly vote in favor of it (Hopkins 1985).

2. In 1998 a second constitutional amendment was passed to further specify the categories for which lottery money could be appropriated. The categories included: (1) tuition grants, scholarship, or loans to citizens of Georgia to attend College (colloquially known as the Hope Scholarship), (2) voluntary pre-kindergarten, (3) financial reserves not less than 10 percent of the net lottery proceeds

for the preceding year, (4) funds for K–12 and higher education to purchase technology and train teachers, and (5) funds for building educational facilities (Georgia Constitution Art. 1, § 2, ¶ 8). A subsequent constitutional amendment has been introduced to remove appropriations for uses 4 and 5 until all persons eligible for Hope Scholarships and Pre-K have received funding. Most recently Governor Perdue announced plans for another constitutional amendment to limit lottery revenues to only HOPE and pre-K.

3. The pre-K program in Georgia was made universal in 1995. The process of that change is discussed in chapter 3.

4. Preliminary analysis of media coverage presented at the 2007 Annual Meeting of the American Political Science Association by Doug Imig and David S. Meyer indicate that *Tulsa World* did cover the preschool policy change; however, sources in Oklahoma report that there is considerable competition between the two regions and coverage by *Tulsa World* would not necessarily reach the ears of legislators in Oklahoma City. The newspaper for the capital region is the *Oklahoman*.

5. Professor Edward F. Zigler was one the main architects of the federal Head Start preschool program and founder of the School of the Twenty-first Century, a community school model that incorporates child care and family support services into schools. See http://www.yale.edu/21c/history.html for a full description.

6. In West Virginia, all school districts are county-level governments.

7. Soon after the passage of preschool legislation, the leadership of the Governor's Cabinet for Children and Families resigned in protest. When WVDHHR, WVDOE, and Head Start developed the preschool program, they chose not to include the Governor's Cabinet. The Cabinet still exists and is chaired by First Lady Manchin, but as of July 2005 it lost its remaining staff support and is considered defunct.

8. Information taken from National Governors Association Web site http://www.nga.org on March 1, 2007.

## Chapter 3

1. The study authors state, "Pre-K participation was associated with more positive outcomes than other preschool experiences on eleven of sixteen measures, but the differences were not statistically significant during the first grade (Henry et al. 2005, vii)

2. The quality of public school preschool classrooms will be evaluated using the Early Childhood Environmental Rating Scale (Harms, Clifford, and Cryer 1998, 60). ECERS is a well-known evaluative instrument that requires trained evaluators to assess quality through classroom observation. The main contention is that according to the revised rules, the evaluation can be done by county staff without training in ECERS. Many of the people interviewed for this study

expressed concern that the evaluations will not result in accurate assessments of classroom quality. However, while many would prefer that trained ECERS evaluators be involved, one person involved with preschool stated that "Even though ECERS will be done internally by untrained people, the impact of doing it at all will be tremendous." From the public education perspective, there are areas where the public school standards are higher than WVDHHR standards. For public schools, all teachers must be certified or "permitted" in early childhood. For those programs licensed by WVDHHR teachers need only an associate's degree. Critics point out that because of the "permitted" loophole, public schools can place a teacher into a pre-K classroom with no training in early education provided the teacher is actively pursuing early childhood certification. Early childhood advocates fear that as public schools lose enrollments and try to protect teacher's jobs, teachers unqualified in ECE will be placed in pre-K classrooms. In short, their concern is that decisions will be made on what is best for the teachers rather than what is best for the children.

## Chapter 4

1. The Pew Charitable Trusts was a foundation when the universal preschool giving program began but it became a public charity in 2004.

2. Sealander studied vocational education, parent education, mothers' pensions, "child-helping" and the juvenile court, antiprostitution and sex research, and public moral health.

3. In fact, the debate over pluralism versus elite power theory was itself funded through Ford Foundation grants to scholars (Colwell, Mary Anna Culleton 1993, 276).

4. More recently, Jarol Manheim updated Dye's schematic to represent the "out-of-power elite model" with a pluralist addition. This model explicitly addresses the resurgence of liberal elites after the election of Ronald Reagan.

5. John D. Rockefeller III initiated the Commission on Foundation and Private Philanthropy in 1968 to secure an independent appraisal of American philanthropy and to assess the long-range role of philanthropy and foundations in American life. The Commission, referred to as the Peterson Commission, had members representing business, university, union, law, and former government officials. Their report provides a biased yet insightful assessment of the relationship between the federal government and foundations in the 1950 and 1960s.

6. Nielsen provides a lengthy footnote on the degree to which IRS oversight was abused by the Nixon administration to harass activist organizations in opposition to Nixon's policies.

7. While Pew will no longer be legally required to pay out a minimum of 5 percent of its endowment, Pew is committed to paying out at least that much.

8. The Education Law Center filed the famous *Abbott v. Burke* case in 1981 on behalf of all children attending poor and urban schools in New Jersey. Seven

years later after many delays, the judge ruled in the plaintiffs' favor. In 1990, the Supreme Court affirmed the decision and ordered the state to provide the urban school districts with funding at "parity" with suburban schools and other supplemental programs to address special needs. The Supreme Court then had to issue six more decisions—in 1994, 1997, 1998, 2000, and two in 2001—to assure state compliance with its ruling. According to the Education Law Center, with these decisions, New Jersey's urban schoolchildren now have the most comprehensive set of educational rights anywhere in the nation (Education Law Center 2007a, 1).

9. The states without pre-K programs in 2004–05 were Alaska, Florida, Idaho, Indiana, Mississippi, Montana, New Hampshire, North Dakota, Rhode Island, South Dakota, Utah, and Wyoming. Since the 2006 publication, Florida created a state funded pre-K program.

10. The study was also published in the *Journal of Policy Analysis and Management* in 2008 (vol. 27, no. 1).

11. The evaluation of the Tulsa program was funded by NIEER, Pew, and the Foundation for Child Development.

12. The states included: Texas, Ohio, Pennsylvania, Illinois, California, Florida, New York, and North Carolina.

13. In 2006, Pre-K Now funded the e-advocacy package for New York, Massachusetts, New Jersey, California, Florida, Vermont, Texas, Oregon, and Kentucky (Rubin, Stephanie, state policy director 2006).

14. According to the CCSSO Web site, there have been two Op-ed publications by the Cadre of Champions and eight "spotlight articles" written by Council staff (Council of Chief State School Officers 2007b, 2-2).

# Chapter 5

1. The Florida case was omitted from in-depth analysis in this study because the initiative process places it in a category separate from states that created universal preschool through legislation drafted by and passed in state legislatures. In Florida, the initiative was a constitutional amendment that forced the hand of the legislature.

2. There are two main differences between the pilot programs and the voluntary pre-K programs. First, pilot programs can serve three year olds but the voluntary pre-K program is limited to serving children who turn four by September 30. Second, pilot programs are created through a grant process directly with the state, but voluntary pre-K program funds are allocated to school districts. Therefore, if pre-K in the voluntary pre-K program is delivered through collaboration with Head Start or private child care centers, it must be negotiated with the school district.

3. Irving B. Harris has been fundamental to raising awareness about the importance of the early years in the United States by funding research, programs,

scholarships for students, endowed positions at universities, and many other venues. For a tribute, see (Erikson Institute 2004, 1–18). For Harris's book, *In His Own Words*, see www.ounceofprevention.org.

4. The Chicago Metropolitan Association for the Education of Young Children also participated in the formation. In later years many other organization participated such as Fight Crime: Invest in Kids Illinois, Chicago Metropolis 2020, Illinois Association for the Education of Young Children, Illinois Head Start Association, and many others (Shore 2006, 1–32).

5. The organizations also received project-specific funding. For example, Voices for Illinois Children received a $2.5 million grant from McCormick Tribune to develop commercials aired in January 2000 and May 2001, to support increased professional development funding for child care workers (Stermer, Jerry, personal communication 2007; Voices for Illinois Children 2007b).

6. Additional early childhood funding was provided from: W. Clement and Jessie V. Stone Foundation, the Woods Fund of Chicago, the Chicago Community Trust, the John D. and Catherine T. MacArthur Foundation, the Michael Reese Health Trust, the Illinois Children's Healthcare Foundation, Northern Trust, Prince Charitable Trusts, the Pritzker Cousins Foundation, Chase, and a number of dedicated family foundations (Shore 2006, 1–32). In the last year, the Chicago Mercantile Exchange Trust began to fund early education (Slaughter, Sara, Telephone communication, June 12, 2007). In addition the Early Childhood Funders' Collaborative, comprised of foundations with early childhood giving programs, funds the multistate Build Initiative. The focus is on developing systems delivery for early childhood programs. In Illinois, the Build Initiative funds the Birth to Five project administered by the Ounce of Prevention Fund (Build Initiative 2007).

7. The preschool program was delivered in public schools but schools were encouraged to collaborate with private providers to offer full-day care. In Chicago, preschool was delivered in community-based settings, but the option for private providers in other parts of the state was allowed in 2003 after Governor Blagojevich was elected.

8. When Elliot Regenstein joined the governor's administration he first worked on the reorganization of the Illinois State Board of Education. In Governor Blagojevich's 2004 State of the State address, the governor announced plans to abolish the State Board of Education and replace it with a Department of Education that would have leadership appointed by the governor (Blagojevich 2004). The end result was that the governor won the power to appoint the nine-member board, as opposed to having staggered terms with appointees from the previous governor. In the initial transition, the governor appointed seven of the nine members (the remaining two completed their six-year terms). Regenstein worked on the transition, which provided him with the opportunity to develop working relationships with the incoming Board members and ISBE civil servants. Mr. Regenstein found that he was the only education staff member in the governor's office after the governor appointed Deputy Chief of Staff for Education

Brenda Holmes to ISBE. With her departure, and, because of all his work on the ISBE transition, he was well positioned in the Governor's Office and ISBE to cochair the Early Learning Council.

9. The report was made public, with Pew funding, in Spring 2006.

10. Governor Blagojevich was arrested on federal corruption charges on December 9, 2008 and it is unlikely that he will complete his term.

## Conclusion

1. Newspaper archives were searched for reference to pre-K, prekindergarten, preschool, and early childhood education from 1985 for the following papers: the *Atlanta Journal and Constitution*, the *New York Times*, the *Times Union*, the *Oklahoman*, the *Charleston Gazette*, the *Tennessean*, the *Chicago Tribune*, and the *Journal-Register*. These were chosen because they are the newspapers of record for their states or because they cover the capital region.

# References

70 Oklahoma Statute Annotated § 18-201.1. 2004. *Weighted membership for calculation of foundation aid—1997-98 and thereafter.*

70 Oklahoma Statutes Annotated § 1-114, vol. 70. 2004. *Free attendance—admission to early childhood programs—enrollment in kindergarten and first grade—nonresident tuition fee.*

Akerman, Robert. 1992. "Lottery-for-education sales pitch is a well-polished one." *Atlanta Journal and Constitution*, September 24, sec. A16.

Archibold, Randal C. 2001. "As Albany quarrels, schools race to cut budgets." *New York Times*, September 3, sec. A1 Late-Final. http://web.lexis-nexis.com/universe/ (accessed September 8, 2006).

Associated Press State and Local Wire. 2005. "Bredesen says he wants permanent funding plan for pre-K." *Tennessean*, October 13, 2005, sec. State and Regional. LexisNexis by Credit Card (accessed April 4, 2007).

*Atlanta Journal and Constitution*. 1986. "Legislative briefs: House decides to reject plan to let charities hold lotteries." *Atlanta Journal and Constitution*, February 6, 1986, sec. A1.

———. 1990a. "The lottery and other trivia." The *Atlanta Journal and Constitution*, February 1, sec. Editorial A14.

———. 1990b. "Lottery plan becoming goofy." *Atlanta Journal and Constitution*, October 24, sec. Editorial, A14.

———. 1991a. "Heavy demands on a lean budget; a look at the major issues facing the 1991 Georgia Legislature; lottery; don't bet on quick vote." *Atlanta Journal and Constitution*, January 13, sec. G3.

———. 1991b. "VERBATIM; lottery doesn't do anything in long run." *Atlanta Journal and Constitution*, January 23, sec. B3.

———. 1991c. "The house vote on lottery bill." *Atlanta Journal and Constitution*, February 1, sec. E3.

————. 1991d. "Lottery gets thumbs-up; other education bills, nursing home measures are approved by Miller." *Atlanta Journal and Constitution*, April 18, sec. D2.

————. 1991e. "A realistic education plan." *Atlanta Journal and Constitution*, December 17, sec. A24.

————. 1991f. "Governor Miller has wise plans for investing in education." *Atlanta Journal and Constitution*, December 17, sec. A24.

————. 1995. "An agency for Georgia's youngest." *Atlanta Journal and Constitution*, December 25, sec. Editorial, A16.

Barnett, W. Steven. 1996. *Lives in the balance: Age-27 benefit-cost analysis of the High/Scope Perry preschool program.* Ypsilanti, MI: High/Scope Press.

Barnett, W. Steven, Jason T. Hustedt, Kenneth B. Robin, and Karen L. Schulman. 2004. *The state of preschool: 2004 state preschool yearbook.* Newark, NJ: National Institute of Early Education Research. http://nieer.org/yearbook2004/ (accessed October 13, 2006).

————. 2008. *The state of preschool 2007 state preschool yearbook.* Newark, NJ: National Institute for Early Education Research, http://nieer.org/yearbook/pdf/yearbook.pdf (accessed October 9, 2008).

Barnett, W. Steven, Cynthia Lamy, and Kwanghee Jung. 2005. *The effects of state pre-kindergarten programs on young children's school readiness in five states.* Newark, NJ: National Institute for Early Education Research.

Baumgartner, Frank R., and Bryan D. Jones. 1993. *Agendas and instability in American politics.* Chicago: University of Chicago Press.

————. 2002. *Policy dynamics.* Chicago: University of Chicago Press.

Baxter, Tom. 1991. "Politics; lottery deck holds a few wild cards." *Atlanta Journal and Constitution*, January 28, sec. D2.

Belfield, Clive. 2004. *Research briefing: the pre-k payback.* Albany, NY: Center for Early Care and Education.

Blackmon, Douglas. 1990. "Bad budget news hits southeast with full force." *Atlanta Journal and Constitution*, November 30, sec. A1.

Blagojevich, Rod. 2003a. *Blagojevich revisits Chicago childcare center to fulfill promise to enhance early childhood development.* Springfield, IL: Office of the Governor, July 24.

————. 2003b. "State of the state address." State of Illinois (database online). Springfield, IL, 2003 (cited June 15, 2007). Available from http://www.illinois.gov/Gov/pdfdocs/2003sosspeech.pdf (accessed June 15, 2007).

————. 2004. "State of the state address." State of Illinois (database online). Springfield, IL, 2004 (cited June 15, 2007). Available from http://www.illinois.gov/Gov/pdfdocs/2004soseducationplan.pdf.

―――. 2006. "Helping kids learn." In Governor's Office (database online). Springfield, IL, 2006 (cited June 28 2007). Available from http://www.illinois.gov/includes/GOV_education_reform_ plan. ppt (accessed June 28, 2007).

Bratcher, Michael. 2002. "National educators praise early childhood program." *Oklahoman*, November 16, 2. http://olive.newsok.com/ Repository/ml.asp (accessed June 27, 2006).

―――. 2004. "Groups' report praises Oklahoma for access to preschool programs." *Oklahoman*, November 22, sec. State. 6. http://olive. newsok.com/Repository/ml.asp (accessed June 27, 2006).

Bright from the Start Georgia Department of Early Care and Learning. 2006. "Guidelines and appendix." http://www.decal.state.ga.us/Pre-K/PrekServices.aspx?Header=2&SubHeader=9&Position=2&HeaderName=Project%20Directors (accessed January 23, 2007).

Brown, E. Richard. 1979. *Rockefeller medicine men: medicine and capitalism in the progressive era.* Berkeley: University of California Press.

Build Initiative. Illinois build, in Build Initiative (database online). Denver, CO, 2007 (cited June 19, 2007). Available from http:// www.build initiative.org/state_il.html (accessed June 19, 2007).

Bush, Bill. 1995. "'Voices' of state's children to be heard; group to advocate early start program for preschoolers." *State Journal-Register*, December 14, 1995, sec. Local (accessed January 25, 2007).

Campbell, Frances A., and Craig T. Ramey. 1994. "Effects of early intervention on intellectual and academic achievement: A follow-up study of children from low-income families." *Child Development* 65, 684–698.

Campbell, Frances A., and Craig T. Ramey. 1995. "Cognitive and school outcomes for high-risk African-American students at middle adolescence: Positive effects of early intervention." *American Educational Research Journal* 32, 743–772.

Cardiff, Christopher F., and Edward Stringham. 2006. *Is universal preschool beneficial? An assessment of RAND Corporation's analysis and proposals for California.* Los Angeles, CA: Reason Foundation, Policy Study 345.

Carnegie Corporation of New York. 1994. *Starting points: meeting the needs of our youngest children.* Waldorf, MD: Carnegie Corporation of New York.

―――. 1996. *Years of promise: a comprehensive learning strategy for America's children. The report of the Carnegie Task Force on Learning in the Primary Grades.* Waldorf, MD: Carnegie Corporation of New York. http://www.carnegie.org (accessed December 20, 2006).

Cass, Michael. 2003. "Advisory unit wants to focus on scholarships in first year." *Tennessean*, February 7, 2003, sec. Main News. LexisNexis by Credit Card (accessed April 4, 2007).

Casteel, Chris. 1989. "State lacks teachers for Lewis' proposal." *Oklahoman*, August 20, 1.

Center for Early Care and Learning. 2004. *New York's action plan for young children and families.* Albany, NY: Center for Early Care and Learning.

Charleston Gazette. 2005. "Preschool good for business." *Charleston Gazette*, October 9, sec. Commentary E2.

———. 2006a. "Preschool: promising national rank." *Charleston Gazette*, May 18, sec. Commentary. http://lexis-nexis.com.silk. library.umass.edu:2048/universe/. (accessed October 22, 2006).

———. 2006b. "Preschool: all day for tots." *Charleston Gazette*, August 25, sec. Commentary. http://web.lexis-nexis.com.silk.library.umass. edu:2048/universe. (accessed October 22, 2006).

Cheek, Duren. 2004. "Lottery funds might not go to pre-K." *Tennessean*, July 27, 2004, sec. Local. LexisNexis by Credit Card (accessed April 4, 2007).

———. 2002. "Reading new life into preschool program." *Tennessean*, February 15, 2002, sec. Local. LexisNexis by Credit Card (accessed April 4, 2007).

Chicago Tribune. 2006. "Preschool for some." *Chicago Tribune*, February 16, 2006, sec. Editorial. LexisNexis by Credit Card (accessed June 11, 2007).

Cohen, Sally S. 2001. *Championing child care.* New York, NY: Columbia University Press.

Colvin, Richard L. "Early stories weblog," Hechinger Institute (database online). New York, NY, 2007. Available from http://www.early edcoverage.org/ (accessed February 8, 2007).

Colwell, Mary Anna Culleton. 1993. *Private foundations and public policy.* New York, NY: Garland Publishing.

Commission on Foundations and Private Philanthropy. 1970. *Foundations, private giving, and public policy: Report and recommendations of the commission on foundations and private philanthropy.* Chicago, IL: The University of Chicago Press.

Committee for Economic Development. 2006. *The economic promise of investing in high-quality preschool: Using early education to improve economic growth and the fiscal sustainability of states and the nation.* Washington, DC: Committee for Economic Development, http://www.ced.org/docs/report/report_prek_econpromise. pdf (accessed July 6, 2006).

―――. "Message from CED's president and chairman." Committee for Economic Development (database online). Washington, DC, 2007 (cited February 23, 2007). Available from http://www.ced.org/about/chairman.shtml (accessed February 23, 2007).

Cook, Rhonda, and Charles Walston. 1991. "Murphy seeks quick vote on lottery." *Atlanta Journal and Constitution*, January 22, sec. C1.

Council of Chief State School Officers. 2003. "Ten chiefs convene with governors during preschool forum." *Chiefline Newsletter*, www.ccsso.ord/Whats_New/newsletters/chiefline/3650.cfm (accessed February 22, 2007).

―――. 2007a. "Pew partners." Council of Chief State School Officers (database online). Washington, DC (cited February 22, 2007). Available from http://www.ccsso.org/Projects/early_childhood_and_family-education/projects/2974.cfm (accessed February 22, 2007).

―――. 2007b. "Building a cadre of champions." Council of Chief State School Officers (database online). Washington, DC, 2007 (cited February 22, 2007). Available from http://www.ccsso.org/Projects/early_childhood_and_family-education/projects/2973.cfm (accessed February 22, 2007).

―――. 2007c. "Education leadership: advancing quality pre-kindergarten for all—regional meetings." Council of Chief State School Officers (database online). Washington, DC, 2007 (cited February 22, 2007). Available from http://www.ccsso.org/Projects/early_childhood_and_family-education/projects/5353.cfm (accessed February 22, 2007).

Council for School Performance. 1998. *Report on the expenditure of lottery funds fiscal year 1997*. Atlanta, GA: Georgia State University.

Cribb, Bryan. 1996. *Georgia Christian Coalition opposes governor's proposed education plan*. Atlanta, GA: Christian Coalition of Georgia.

Cummings, Jeanne. 1991a. "Miller programs lack support in house, survey finds." *Atlanta Journal and Constitution*, January 13, sec. A1.

―――. 1991b. "Cannons, country music for Miller." *Atlanta Journal and Constitution*, January 15, sec. F.

―――. 1991c. "Winning ways; governor mends a few fences and gains house support." *Atlanta Journal and Constitution*, March 17, sec. D1.

―――. 1991d. "Miller wants to phase out prisoner early releases; education changes also pledged." *Atlanta Journal and Constitution*, January 16, sec. A1.

Dao, James. 1997. "Legislators in Albany face hurdles on school bond act." *New York Times*, July 16, sec. Metropolitan. B7. http://web.lexix-nexis.com/universe (accessed August 28, 2006).

de la Cruz, Bonna. 2004. "Lottery may net $70M in excess funds." *Tennessean*, January 10, 2004, sec. Main news. LexisNexis by Credit Card (accessed April 4, 2007).

Dedrick, Charles, and Terrance Brewer. 2004. "Consistent assistance to districts." *Times Union*, April 25.

Denton, David R. 2001. *Improving children's readiness for school: preschool programs make a difference, but quality counts!* Atlanta, GA: Southern Regional Education Board. www.sreb.org (accessed January 3, 2007.)

DeSiato, Donna J. 2003. *Research briefing: The full-day advantage.* Albany, NY: Center for Early Care and Education.

Dickerson, Jeff. 1996. "Georgia's first state pre-k program and investment in the future." *Atlanta Journal and Constitution*, March 13, sec. A18. http://web.lexis-nexis.com/universe (accessed January 17, 2007).

———. 1988. "4-year-olds head to class." *Atlanta Journal and Constitution*, February 5, sec. A14.DiLorenzo, Louis T. 1969. *Prekindergarten programs for educationally disadvantaged children.* Albany, NY: New York State Education Department, Office of Research and Evaluation.

Doctors, Jennifer V. 2006. *Leadership matters: Governors' pre-K proposals fiscal year 2007.* Washington, DC: Pre-K Now, May.

———. 2007. *Leadership matters: Governors' pre-K proposals fiscal year 2008.* Washington, DC: Pre-K Now, April.

Doggett, Libby. 2006. Give a boost to NY's pre-K, children. Pre-K Now, Washington, DC (accessed April 7, 2006).

Domhoff, G. William. 1998. *Who rules America? Power and politics in the year 2000, 3rd ed.* Mountain View, CA: Mayfield Publishing Company.

Dowie, Mark. 2001. *American foundations; an investigative history.* Cambridge, MA: The MIT Press.

Dutcher, Brandon. 2001. "Early childhood ed: personnel is policy," *Oklahoman*, May 25, sec. Opinion.

Dwyer, DeSylvia W. 2006. *Interview by author*, October 11, Albany, NY. New York State Education Department, NY.

Dye, Thomas R. 1979. *Who's running America? The Carter years*, 2nd ed. Englewood Cliffs, NJ: Prentice-Hall.

———. 1986. *Who's running America? The conservative years*, 4th ed. Englewood Cliffs, NJ: Prentice-Hall.

———. 1990. *Who's running America? The Bush era*, 5th ed. Englewood Cliffs, NJ: Prentice Hall.

———. 2001. *Top down policymaking.* New York, NY: Chatham House Publishers of Seven Bridges Press, LLC.

Early Learning Illinois. "Learn more about early learning." Early Learning Illinois (database online). Chicago, IL, 2007 (cited June 19, 2007). Available from http://www.earlylearningillinois.org/resources.htm.

Education Law Center. "History of education law center." Education Law Center (database online). Newark, NJ, February 18, 2007 (cited February 18, 2007). Available from http://www.edlawcenter.org/ELCPublic/AboutELC/History.htm (accessed February 18, 2007).

———. 2007. "Starting at 3." Newark, NJ. Available from http://www.startingat3.org/index.html (accessed February 7, 2007).

Education Reporter. 2002. "Drumbeat grows for universal preschool." eagleforum.org/educate/2002/ar02/pre-school.shtml (accessed June 26, 2006).

Education Writers Association. 2006. *The pre-k beat; a national survey of pre-k education media.* Washington, DC: Education Writers Association, April, http://www.ewa.org/files/docs/preksurvey.pdf (accessed February 21, 2007).

Eisenberg, Pablo. 2003. "Pew's shift to charity status goes against what is best for the public." *Chronicle of Philanthropy* 16, (5) (11 December): 38–38, http://weblinks3.epnet.com (accessed October 19, 2005).

Erikson Institute. 2004. *2004 annual report.* Chicago, IL: Erikson Institute, http://www.erikson.edu/files/nonimages/harristribute.pdf (accessed June 18, 2007).

Ezzard, Martha. 1995. "Universal pre-kindergarten is not as easy as ABC." *Atlanta Journal and Constitution*, October 23, sec. A10.

Family Concerns, Inc. 1996. *Think again before placing your child in the free state four year old pre-kindergarten program.* Atlanta, GA: Family Concerns, Inc.

Ferris, James M. 2003. *Foundations and public policy: Leveraging philanthropic dollars, knowledge, and networks.* Los Angeles, CA: The Center on Philanthropy and Public Policy.

Ferris, James M., Guilbert C. Hentschke, Hilary A. Joy. 2006. "Philanthropic strategies for school reform: An analysis of foundation choices in education policy." Research paper 25 (February). Los Angeles: The Center on Philanthropy and Public Policy.

Fight Crime: Invest in Kids New York. 2003. *Cutting pre-kindergarten with increase crime in New York.* Washington, DC: Fight Crime Invest in Kids.

Fight Crime: Invest in Kids. 2007. "Early education." In Fight Crime: Invest in Kids (database online). Washington, DC, 2007 (cited June 21, 2007). Available from http://www.fightcrime.org/issue_earlyed.php (accessed June 21, 2007).

Finke, Doug. 2003. "Blagojevich 'dreams big': Outlines proposals on slim budget." *State Journal-Register*, March 13, 2003, sec. News. LexisNexis by Credit Card (accessed January 28, 2007).

Finn, Scott. 2005. "West Virginia leads and lags in early childhood education." *Charleston Gazette*, October 10, sec. C3.

Fleishman, Joel L. *The Foundation: A great American secret: How private wealth is changing the world.* Cambridge, MA: Perseus Books Group.

Frumkin, Peter. 2006. *Strategic giving: The art and science of philanthropy.* Chicago: The University of Chicago Press.

Fuller, Bruce. 2006. "No toddler left behind?" *Sacramento Bee*, May 7, sec. Forum. http://web.lexis-nexis.com/universe/ (accessed February 23, 2007).

Galinsky, Ellen. 2006. *The economic benefits of high-quality early childhood programs: what makes the difference?* Washington, DC: The Committee for Economic Development. http://www.ced.org/docs/report/report_prek_galinsky.pdf (accessed December 4, 2006).

Gallagher, Jay. 2001. "In Albany, the buck stops nowhere." *Times Union*, July 22, sec. B5 Three Star edition. http://timesunion.com/archives/ (accessed November 23, 2006).

Garcia, Eugene W., and Danielle M. Gonzales. 2006. *Pre-K and Latinos: the foundation of America's future.* Pre-K Now Research Series ed. Washington, DC: Pre-K Now.

Gardner, Joel R., and Sue Rardin. 2001. *Sustaining the legacy: A history of the Pew Charitable Trusts.* Philadelphia, PA: The Pew Charitable Trusts.

Gatenio, Shirley. 2002. *Taking a giant step: a case study of New York City's effort to implement universal pre-kindergarten services.* New York: Foundation for Child Development.

Georgia Finance and Public Utilities Committee. 1991. *Minutes.* February 5, 1991 meeting. Atlanta, GA: Georgia State Senate, RG 037-08-063, Georgia Archives.

Georgia Industry Committee. 1991. *Minutes.* January 29 meeting. Georgia House of Representatives. Atlanta, GA: RG 037-08-064, Georgia Archives.

Ginsberg, Jennifer. 2005. "Early childhood education pays big dividends, study says." *Charleston Gazette*, October 9. http://web.lexis-nexis.com (accessed October 22, 2006).

Gormley, Michael. 2001. "Pataki's plan to reform state school aid faces scrutiny." *Times Union*, January 7, sec. D10 Three Star edition. http://timesunion.com/archives/ (accessed November 23, 2006).

Gormley, Willian T., Jr. 2002. "Differential reimbursement policies and child care accreditation." Unpublished manuscript. Washington, DC, Georgetown University, October 19, 2002.

Gormley, William T., Ted Gayer, Deborah Phillips, and Brittany Dawson. 2004. "The effects of Oklahoma's universal pre-K program on school readiness: An executive summary." Georgetown University Center for Research on Children in the U.S. http://www.crocus.georgetown.edu/reports/executive_summary_11_04.pdf (accessed January 7, 2008).

Gormley, William T., Deborah Phillips, and Brittany Dawson. 2005. "The effects of universal pre-k on cognitive development." *Developmental Psychology* 41 (6): 13.

Government Innovators Network. 2006. "Voluntary pre-kindergarten program." http://www.innovations.harvard.edu/awards.html?id=3755 (accessed January 17, 2007).

Greiner, John. 1989. "State senators OK education improvement bill." *Oklahoman*, February 28, 12.

Groginsky, Scott, Steve Christian, and Laurie McConnell. 1998. "Early childhood initiatives in the states: Translating research into policy." *State Legislative Report* 23, (14) (June): 1–15, http://www.ncsl.org/programs/cyf/ccslr.htm (accessed February 22, 2007).

Hansen, Jane O. 1985. "Mandatory kindergarten stirs strong emotions." *Atlanta Journal and Constitution*, January 24, sec. A1.

———. 1987. "South learning education is crucial to economic growth." *Atlanta Journal and Constitution*, February 8, sec. S1.

———. 1988. "Day care solution seems elementary as public schools get into the business." *Atlanta Journal and Constitution*, August 14, 1988, sec. A1.

Harms, Thelma, Richard M. Clifford, and Debby Cryer. 1998. *Early childhood environment rating scale*, rev. ed. New York: Teachers College Press.

Hechinger Institute on Education and the Media. Available from http://hechinger.tc.columbia.edu/ (accessed February 8, 1007).

Heclo, Hugh. 1978. "Issue networks in the executive establishment." In *The New American Political System*, ed. A. King. Washington, DC: American Enterprise Institute.

Henry, Gary T., Craig S. Gordon, Laura W. Henderson, and Bentley Ponder. 2002. *Georgia pre-k longitudinal study: final report 1996–2001*. Atlanta, GA: Georgia State University Andrew Young School of Policy Studies.

Henry, Gary T., Dana K. Rickman, with Bentley D. Ponder, Laura W. Henderson, Andrew Mashburn, and Craig S. Gordon. 2005. *The Georgia early childhood study 2001–04 final report*. Atlanta, GA: Georgia State University Andrew Young School of Policy Studies.

Hensley, Abbe. 2006. "Ready to Read, Ready to Learn." Alaska Humanities Forum, Anchorage, AK (accessed December 18, 2007).

Hernandez, Raymond. 2000. "Albany's leaders reach agreement on spending plan." *New York Times*, April 5, sec. A1, Late Edition Final. http://web.lexis-nexis.com. (accessed September 8, 2006).

Herszenhorn, David M. 2003. "Who's afraid of deep preschool cuts? Scrambling parents." *New York Times*, March 13, sec. B1, Late Edition.

Holcomb, Betty. 2006. *A diverse system delivers for pre-k: lessons learned in New York state.* Washington, DC: Pre-K Now, July.

Hopkins, Sam. 1985a. "Macon OKs lobby effort for lottery; council cites '86 loss of revenue." *Atlanta Journal and Constitution*, September 19, sec. A29.

———. 1985b. "Don't bet on OK for lottery, horse racing; despite victory at polls, legislators are skeptical." *Atlanta Journal and Constitution*, October 10, sec. B12.

———. 1985c. "The push for pari-mutuel betting in Georgia in starting gate again." *Atlanta Journal and Constitution*, October 23, sec. A1.

Hustedt, Jason T., W. Steven Barnett, Kwanghee Jung, and Jessica Thomas. 2007. *The effects of the Arkansas better change program on young children's school readiness.* Newark, NJ: National Institute for Early Education Research, http://nieer.org/resources/research/ArkansasYear1.pdf (accessed February 19, 2007).

Hyatt, Richard. 1997. *Zell: the governor who gave Georgia hope.* Macon, GA: Mercer University Press.

Illgen, Susan, and Sandy Garrett. 2007. "Early childhood programs." Powerpoint presentation for the State Superintendent's Annual Leadership conference. Oklahoma City, July 10–12, 2007, http://www.sde.state.ok.us/pro/conference/Leadership/Presentations/concurrent/ECPrograms.ppt (accessed January 11, 2008).

Illgen, Susan, Paul Ramona, and Sandy Garrett. 2006. *Oklahoma's universal pre-kindergarten.* Oklahoma City, OK: Oklahoma State Department of Education.

Illinois State Board of Education. 2007. "Illinois PreKindergarten program 1990–2005." Illinois State Board of Education (database online). Springfield, IL, 2007 (cited June 18, 2007). Available from http://www.isbe.state.il.us/research/pdfs/prek_history_table.pdf (accessed June 18, 2007).

———. 2004. *Illinois preskindergarten program for children at-risk of academic failure FY 2003 evaluation report.* Springfield, IL: Illinois State Board of Education, July, http://www.isbe.state.il.us/research/pdfs/prek_evaluation.pdf (accessed June 18, 2007).

————. 2001. *Illinois PreKindergarten program for children at risk of academic failure FY 2000 evaluation report*. Springfield, IL: Illinois State Board of Education Research Division, June, http://www. isbe.net/research/pdfs/atrisk.pdf (accessed June 18, 2007).

Imig, Doug, and David S. Meyer. 2007. "The Politics of Universal Pre-Kindergarten." Paper presented at the annual meeting of the American Political Science Association. Chicago IL. August 31, 2007.

Jakes, Laura. 1999. "New numbers for new set of voters, observers day," *Times Union*, January 28, sec. Main A4, Three Star Edition. http://timesunion.com/archives/ (accessed August 29, 2006).

Jensen, Laura. 2003. *Patriots, settlers, and the origins of American social policy*. New York, NY: Cambridge University Press.

Jochnowitz, Jay. 2000. "Silver set to return as assembly speaker." *Times Union*, December 5, sec. A1, Three Star edition. http://timesunion. com/archives/ (accessed November 22, 2006).

————. 2001. "Economic slowdown likely to delay state budget." *Times Union*, January 3, sec. S3, Three Star edition. http://timesunion. com/archives/ (accessed November 23, 2006).

Joyce Foundation. "Grants list." DeepBlue.com (database online). Chicago, IL, 2007 (cited June 18, 2007). Available from http://www. joycefdn.org/Programs/Education/GrantList.aspx (accessed June 18, 2007).

Judd, Dennis R., and Todd Swanstrom. 2006, 5th ed. *City politics: The political economy of urban America*. New York: Pearson Longman.

Karlin, Rick. 1997. "Regents encouraged to expand pre-kindergartens." *Times Union*, March 12, sec. Capital Region B2. http://timesunion. com/archives/ (accessed October 1, 2006).

Killackey, Jim. 1984. "State educators eye mandatory kindergarten." *Oklahoman*, November 16, 1–2.

Kingdon, John W. 1995. *Agendas, alternatives, and public policies*, 2nd ed. New York: Longman.

Kirp, David. 2007. *The sandbox investment: the preschool movement and kids-first politics*. Cambridge: Harvard University Press.

Koch, Christopher A. 2007. *Request for proposals (RFP): preschool for all children ages 3 to 5 years: 08*, vol. February. Springfield, IL: Illinois State Board of Education.

Kolbert, Elizabeth. 1997. "Metro matters: it's her party, too, she'll cry if she wants." *New York Times*, March 17, 1997, sec. Metropolitan B1. http://web.lexis-nexis.com (accessed August 28, 2006).

Laccetti, Susan. 1988. "Early education a nationwide trend; programs aim to serve ambitions of affluent, needs of disadvantaged." *Atlanta Journal and Constitution*, April 24, sec. B1.

Lagemann, Ellen Condliffe. 1989. *The politics of knowledge; the Carnegie Corporation, philanthropy, and public policy*. Middletown, CT: Wesleyan University Press.

Lee, Jinhee. 2004. "Nation's chiefs unite around early childhood education." *Press Releases*. March 16, http://www.ccsso.org/Whats_New/press-releases/4331.cfm (accessed February 22, 2007).

Lindsey, Gail. 1998. "Brain research and implications for early childhood education." *Childhood Education 75*.2 (Winter): 97–101.

Leff, Donna, and David L. Kirp. 2006. "Sandbox cum laude; A new state law promises free preschool to all kids. but can we really bring it off?" *Chicago Tribune*, July 16, 2006, sec. Magazine. Lexis Nexis by Credit Card (accessed June 11, 2007).

Lightford, Kimberly A., Barbara Flynn Currie, et al. 2006. *School child development-special education reimbursement*. Deletes reference to: 105 ILCS 5/14-7.03; adds reference to 105 ILCS 5/2-3.71 from ch. 122, par. 2-3.71. Trans. Illinois General Assembly, vol. SB1497. Springfield, IL. http://www.ilga.gov/legislation/votehistory.asp?DocNum=1497&DocTypeID=SB&LegID=19547&GAID=8&SessionID=50&GA=94&SpecSess= (accessed June 19, 2007).

Lindsey, Gail. 1998. "Brain research and implications for early childhood education." *Childhood Education 75*, (2): 97–4 (accessed December 4, 2006).

Loupe, Diane. 1995. "Miller optimistic about future of pre-k program: low-income kids won't be left out, governor says." *Atlanta Journal and Constitution*, July 9, sec. A2.

Martella, Jana. 2004. "Drilling deeper on quality universal preschool." *Chiefline Newsletter*. www.ccsso.ord/Whats_New/newsletters/chiefline/4700.cfm (accessed February 22, 2007).

May, A. L. 1990a. "Murphy stalled lottery bill, Miller says." *Atlanta Journal and Constitution*, January 9, sec. C3.

———. 1990b. "Loud and clear: it's Zell." *Atlanta Journal and Constitution*, August 8, sec. A1.

McAdams, Katherine C., Tamara Henry, Carol Guensburg, and Research Associates of Journalism 770. 2004. *An analysis of U.S. newspaper coverage of early childhood education*. Article ed. College Park, MD: Philip Merrill College of Journalism, University of Maryland.

McCormick Tribune Foundation. Education program mission. in McCormick Tribune Foundation (database online). Chicago, IL,

2007a (cited June 18, 2007). Available from http://www. mccormicktribune.org/education/education.aspx (accessed June 18, 2007).

———. "McCormick Tribune Foundation grants list." McCormick Tribune (database online). Chicago, IL, 2007b (cited June 18, 2007). Available from http://www.mccormicktribune.org/education/educationgrantlist.aspx (accessed June 18, 2007).

McDonnell, Brandy. 2004. "Early lessons important classes help prepare children for kindergarten." *Oklahoman*, November 29, sec. Families 23. http://olive.newsok.com/Repository/ml.asp. (accessed June 27, 2006).

Mielczarek, Natalia. 2007. "Governor's pre-K passion not universal." *Tennessean*, February 5, 2007, sec Main. LexisNexis by Credit Card (accessed April 4, 2007).

Miller, Dawn. 2005. "Preschool: so far, yet so close." *Charleston Gazette*, May 29, sec. A4.

———. 2005. "Good news for future adults." *Charleston Gazette*, August 20, sec. P4A. http://web.lexis-nexis.com. (accessed February 14, 2007).

———. 2005. "Preschool enters big-boy world." *Charleston Gazette*, October 15, sec. A4.

Mintrom, Michael. 2000. *Policy entrepreneurs and school choice.* Washington DC: Georgetown University Press.

Mitchell, Anne. 2004. *The state of two pre-kindergarten programs: a look at pre-kindergarten Education in New York State (1928–2003).* National Institute for Early Education Research.

Monastra, Pamela. 1992. "Lottery foes won't sit on their hands." *Atlanta Journal and Constitution*, November 5, 1992, sec. J. http://web.lexis-nexis.com/universe/ (accessed March 14, 2007).

Nagourney, Adam. 1998. "New democrat enters race for governor." *New York Times*, March 20, sec. B1.

Naifeh, Jimmy. 2006. "What should state priorities be? Pre-K classes show focus on education." *Tennessean*, December 20, 2006, sec. Main. LexisNexis by Credit Card (accessed April 4, 2007).

National Association for the Education of Young Children. 2006. *History of the national association for the education of young children.* http://www.naeyc.org/about/history.asp (accessed December 19, 2006).

National Conference of State Legislatures Pre-kindergarten Leadership Institute. "Designing early childhood assessment and accountability systems." National Conference of State Legislatures (database online). Washington, DC, 2007 (cited February 23, 2007). Available from http://www.ncsl.org/programs/cyf/shultz.com (accessed February 23, 2007).

Neal, Ken. 2000. "LaFortune's question." *Tulsa World*, February 19, sec. 5A.

New York State Assembly. 2006. "New York State Assembly-members." http://assembly.state.ny.us/mem/?ad=064&sh=bio (accessed December 20, 2006).

New York State Education Department. 1999. *New York, The State of Learning: A report to the governor and the legislature on the educational status of the state's schools.* Albany, NY.

———. 2000. *New York, the state of learning: a report to the governor and the legislature on the educational status of the state's schools.* Albany, NY.

———. 2001. *New York, the state of learning: a report to the governor and the legislature on the educational status of the state's schools.* Albany, NY.

———. 2002. *New York, the state of learning: a report to the governor and the legislature on the educational status of the state's schools.* Albany, NY.

*70 New York State Education Statutes.* 1997. § 3602-e .

Nielsen, Waldemar A. 1972. *The big foundations.* New York, NY: Columbia University Press.

———. 1985. *The golden donors.* New York, NY: Truman Talley Book E. P. Dutton.

O'Brien, Tim. 1998. "Albany $518 Million increase would go toward pre-kindergarten, charter schools, summer classes." The *Times Union*, January 18, sec. Main 7, Three Star edition. http://timesunion.com/archives/ (accessed August 28, 2006).

O'Connor, John. 1995a. "School layoffs looming; state, federal changes blamed for expected reductions in force." *State Journal-Register*, March 31, 1995, sec. Local. LexisNexis by Credit Card (accessed January 28, 2007).

———. 1995b. School jump-start; program helps children catch up with classmates. *State Journal-Register*, 30 May, 1995, sec. Local. LexisNexis by Credit Card (accessed January 25, 2007).

Odato, James M. 1999. "At long last, a done deal legislature approves final bills." *Times Union*, August 4, sec. Main 1, Three Star edition. http://timesunion.com/archives/ (accessed November 29, 2006).

———. 2000. "A confident governor offers a plan for 50,000 new teachers." *Times Union*, January 6, sec. Main 1, Three Star edition. http://timesunion.com/archives/ (accessed November 29, 2006).

————. 2002. "'Fallout' shapes $88B plan; Pataki cites challenges after attacks." *Times Union*, January 23, sec. A1. http://timesunion. com/archives/ (accessed January 22, 2007).

Office of Governor Brad Henry. 2003. *Early childhood development focus of state board that includes First Lady Kim Henry, 27 others.* Office of Governor Brad Henry. http://www.ok.gove/governor/display_ article.php?article_id=116&article_type=1&print=true. (accessed September 9, 2005).

Office of School Readiness. State of Georgia. 2000. *Georgia pre-kindergarten program record of accomplishment.* www.osr.state.ga.us/ Recordofaccomp.htm (accessed October 19, 2005).

————. 2004. *A new name...new responsibilities...a new look.* http://www.osr.state.ga.us/ (accessed January 23, 2007).

Oklahoma Academy for State Goals. 2003. "Success by 4 pre-k programs a hit in Oklahoma." *Oklahoman*, July 6, sec. Editorial 6. http:// olive.newsok.com/ Repository/ (accessed June 27, 2006).

————. 2005. *Our report card 20 years of progress: "approaching our centennial."* http://www.okacademy. org/1985_2005.pdf (accessed June 29, 2006).

Olsen, Darcy Ann. 2001. *Blueprint for a nanny state.* Oklahoma City: Oklahoma Council of Public Affairs. http://www.ocpathink.org/ ViewPolicyStory.asp?ID=350 (accessed September 9, 2005).

Olsen, Darcy, and Drew Johnson. 2005. *Hard lessons learned: Applying 40 years of government pre-K to benefit Tennessee's children today.* Nashville, TN: Tennessee Center for Policy Research, 05-01, http://www.tennesseepolicy.org/main/article.php?article_id=265&cat =8 (accessed June 4, 2007).

Palmer, Prentice. 1988. "Legislator pushing legalized gambling—and enforcement." *Atlanta Journal and Constitution*, August 23, sec. B4.

Pendered, David. 1990. "Gwinnett PTA opposes 'education lottery.'" *Atlanta Journal and Constitution*, October 10, sec. D5.

Perez-Pena, Richard. 1997. "Spending plan gives priority to education." *New York Times*, July 30, sec. Metropolitan A1. http://web.lexis-nexis.com (accessed August 28, 2006).

————. 1998. "Government by increment: Pataki speech takes few chances." *New York Times*, January 8, sec. B6, Late Edition—Final. http://web.lexis-nexis.com (accessed August 28, 2006).

————. 1999a. "Constraints over budget put Pataki in a bind." *New York Times*, January 25, sec. B1, Late Edition - Final. http://web. lexis-nexis.com (accessed August 29, 2006).

————. 1999b. "Agreement at last in Albany on $73 billion budget plan." *New York Times*, 17 July 1999, sec. B, Late Edition—Final. http://web.lexis-nexis.com (accessed September 8, 2006).

————. 1999c. "Pataki presents a tight budget, despite surplus." *New York Times*, January 28, sec. A1, Late Edition—Final. http://web.lexis-nexis.com (accessed August 29, 2006).

————. 1999d. "Budget freeze spreads a chill past Albany." *New York Times*, July 4, sec. A17, Late Edition—Final. http://web.lexis-nexis.com (accessed September 8, 2006).

Pew Charitable Trusts. 2001. "Education grant highlight December 2001." http://www.pewtrusts.org/ideas/ (accessed November 9, 2005).

————. 2003. "Education grant highlight: Trust for Early Education." http://www.pewtrusts.org/ideas/ (accessed November 9, 2005).

————. 2005a. "Education grant highlight: 2001." http://www.pewtrusts.org/ideas/ (accessed November 9, 2005).

————. 2005b. "Education grant highlight: action against crime and violence education fund." http://www.pewtrusts.org/ideas/ (accessed November 9, 2005).

————. 2005c. "Education grant highlight—Education Law Center." http://www.pewtrusts.org/ideas/ (accessed November 9, 2005).

————. 2005d. "Programs at a glance: the National Early Childhood Accountability Task Force." Pew Charitable Trusts (database online). Philadelphia, PA. Available from http://pewtrusts.org/ideas/ (accessed November 9, 2005).

————. 2007. *Pew prospectus*. Philadelphia, PA: The Pew Charitable Trusts.

Planning and Evaluation Department. 2001. *Returning results: planning and evaluation at the Pew Charitable Trusts*. Philadelphia, PA: Pew Charitable Trusts.

Pomerantz, Gary. 1991. "From the outside looking in; House's historic vote on lottery is long on wind, short on drama." *Atlanta Journal and Constitution*, February 3, 1991, sec. E3.

Prager, Jason. 2006. "Governor asks United Way to help fund pre-K." *Tennessean*, February 23, 2006, sec. Local. LexisNexis by Credit Card (accessed April 4, 2007).

Pratt, Julie. 2002. "Derailing Educare; funding for early education programs should be restored." *Charleston Gazette*, April 19, sec. Editorial. P5A.

Pre-K Now. 2005a. *Pre-K Now to lead national movement for pre-kinder-garten.* http://www.preknowinforcenter.org/preknow/launch_press_release.html (accessed June 8, 2005).

————. 2005b. *Pre-K and politics 2005.* Washington, DC: Pre-K Now.

Presley, Jennifer B., Brenda K. Klosterman, and Bradford R. White. 2006. *Pipelines and pools: meeting the demand for early childhood teachers in Illinois.* Edwardsville, IL: Illinois Education Research Council, IERC 2006-3, http://nieer.org/pdf/pipelinespools.pdf (accessed February 19, 2007).

Raden, Anthony. 1999. *Universal pre-kindergarten in Georgia: a case study of Georgia's lottery-funded pre-k program.* Foundation for Child Development. http://www.fcd-us.org/uploaddocs/columbia%20upk%20georgia.pdf (accessed June 16, 2006).

Ramey, Craig T., and Frances A. Campbell. 1984. "Preventive education for high-risk children: cognitive consequences of the Carolina Abecedarian Project." *American Journal of Mental Deficiency* 88, 515–523.

Ramey, Craig T., and Frances A. Campbell. 1991. "Poverty, early childhood education, and academic competence: The Abecedarian experiment." In A. Huston (Ed.), *Children reared in poverty*, pp. 190–221.

Rapaport, Robin. 2003. "Legislature can give public education a boost." *Times Union*, February 20, sec. A12, Three Star edition. http://timesunion.com/archives/ (accessed September 23, 2006).

Regenstein, Elliot, and Harriet Meyer. 2005. *Illinois Early Learning Council 2004–2005 annual report.* Chicago, IL: Illinois Early Learning Council.

Research and Policy Committee, Committee for Economic Development. 2002. *Preschool for all: investing in a productive and just society.* New York, NY: Committee for Economic Development.

Reynolds, Arthur J., and Judy A. Temple. 2006. "Economic returns of investments in preschool education." In *A vision for universal preschool education*, ed. Edward F. Zigler, Walter S. Gilliam, and Stephanie M. Jones, 1st ed., 37–68. New York, NY: Cambridge University Press.

Reynolds, Arthur J., and Judy A. Temple. 1995. "Quasi-experimental estimates of the effects of a preschool intervention: Psychometric and econometric comparisons." *Evaluation Review* 19, 347–379.

Reynolds, Arthur J. et al. 1993. *Schools, families, and children: sixth year results from the Longitudinal Study of Children at Risk.* Chicago: Chicago Public Schools, Department of Research, Evaluation and Planning.

Rich, Andrew. 2004. *Think tanks, public policy, and the politics of expertise.* New York, NY: Cambridge University Press.

Richardson, Lynda. 1996. "State education chief: a zealot for higher standards for all." *New York Times,* April 28, sec. Metropolitan 33. http://web.lexis-nexis.com (accessed August 28, 2006).

Riley, Claudette. 2003a. "Lack of money could jeopardize preschool classes." *Tennessean,* February 18, sec. Local. LexisNexis by Credit Card (accessed April 4, 2007).

———. 2003b. "Advocates push plan for preschool funding." *Tennessean,* March 5, 2003, 2003, sec. Local. LexisNexis by Credit Card (accessed April 4, 2007).

———. 2003c. "Action commission officials push for more training for preschool teachers." *Tennessean,* March 8, 2003, 2003, sec. Local. LexisNexis by Credit Card (accessed April 4, 2007).

———. 2004a. "Forum seeks more pre-K programs." *Tennessean,* October 29, 2004, sec. Local. LexisNexis by Credit Card (accessed April 4, 2007).

———. 2004b. "Experience gives new education chief big ideas." *Tennessean,* November 3, 2004, sec. Local. Lexis Nexis by Credit Card (accessed April 4, 2007).

———. 2004c. "Public preschools first-rate, but more needed, study says." *Tennessean,* November 22, 2004, sec. Main. LexisNexis by Credit Card (accessed April 4, 2007).

———. 2005a. "Educators thankful for money, wish for more." *Tennessean,* January 27, 2005. LexisNexis by Credit Card (accessed April 4, 2007).

———. 2005b. "Even more pre-K money coming later, governor says." *Tennessean,* February 1, 2005b, sec. Main. LexisNexis by Credit Card (accessed April 4, 2007).

———. 2005c. "Governor seeks support for pre-K proposal." *Tennessean,* February 23, 2005c, sec. Local. LexisNexis by Credit Card (accessed April 4, 2007).

———. 2005d. "Expanded pre-K program on way; Senate OKs $25M." *Tennessean,* May 13, 2005d, sec. Main. LexisNexis by Credit Card (accessed April 4, 2007).

———. 2005e. "State to add 300 pre-K classes." *Tennessean,* August 5, 2005f, sec. Local.

———. 2005f. "State's pre-K plan: Start small and learn." *Tennessean,* May 22, 2005, sec. Main. LexisNexis by Credit Card (accessed April 4, 2007).

———. 2006. "Bredesen looks to give pre-K another significant boost." *Tennessean*, February 8, 2006, sec. Main. LexisNexis by Credit Card (accessed April 4, 2007).

Ross, Betsy M. 1997. "View from a teacher's desk: the students aren't studying: early start helps." *New York Times*, June 16, sec. A14. http://web.lexis-nexis.com (accessed August 28, 2006).

Runfola, Tracy. 2004. "Chiefs meet in Ann Arbor to discuss universal pre-K." *Chiefline Newsletter.* www.ccsso.ord/Whats_New/newsletters/chiefline/4546.cfm (accessed February 22, 2007).

Sabatier, Paul A. 1999. *Theories of the policy process.* Boulder, CO: Westview Press.

Sabatier, Paul, and Hank Jenkins-Smith. 1993. *Policy change and learning: an advocacy coalition approach.* Boulder, CO: Westview Press.

Sack, Kevin. 1995. "Albany's budget: the overview; Pataki and state legislators say they have agreed on a budget." *New York Times*, June 3, sec. Metropolitan 1. http://web.lexis-nexis.com (accessed August 28, 2006).

Schuster, Lynn. 1998. *Steps to universal pre-kindergarten guidebook: a resource for superintendents, school boards, pre-kindergarten advisory boards, teachers, early childhood professionals, policymakers, parents and citizens.* Albany, NY: State Communities Aid Association.

Schuyler Center for Analysis and Advocacy. 2004. *Universal pre-kindergarten in New York state: 1997—January 2004 chronology.* Albany, NY: Schuyler Center for Analysis and Advocacy.

Schneider, Anne Larason, and Helen Ingram. 1997. *Policy design for democracy.* Studies in government and public policy. Lawrence, KS: University Press of Kansas.

———, eds. 2005. *Deserving and entitled; social constructions and public policy.* SUNY Series in Public Policy., eds. Anne Larason Schneider, Helen Ingram. Albany, NY: State University of New York Press.

Schweinhart, L. J., J. Montie, Z. Xiang, W. S. Barnett, C. R. Belfield, and M. Nores. 2005. *Lifetime effects: the High/Scope Perry preschool study through age 40.* Ypsilanti, MI: High/Scope Press.

Scott, L. Carol. 2005. *Leadership matters: governors' pre-K proposals fiscal year 2006.* Washington, DC: Pre-K Now, April.

Scrogging, Deborah. 1989. "Miller proposes public preschool, easier certification for teachers." *Atlanta Journal and Constitution*, December 28, sec. D6.

———. 1990. "The 1990 legislative session." *Atlanta Journal and Constitution*, March 9, sec. B3.

Sealander, Judith. 1997. *Private wealth and public life; foundation philanthropy and the reshaping of American social policy from the Progressive Era to the New Deal*. Baltimore, MD: The Johns Hopkins University Press.

Secrest, David. 1989. "Debate over state lottery to mix politics, religion." *Atlanta Journal and Constitution*, January 23, sec. A9.

Secrest, David, and A. L. May. 1989. "Miller calls for state lottery, ensuring fight with Harris." *Atlanta Journal and Constitution*, January 13, sec. A1.

Seibert, Trent. 2005. "Proposal to boost pre-K spending advances in Senate." *Tennessean*, May 11, 2005, sec Local. LexisNexis by Credit Card (accessed April 4, 2007).

Sherman, Mark. 1991. "Miller reveals lottery plans for education; he anticipates easy referendum passage." *Atlanta Journal and Constitution*, November 14, sec. A1.

Shonkoff, Jack P., and Deborah A. Phillips, eds. 2000. *From neurons to neighborhoods: the science of early development*. Washington, DC: National Academy Press.

Shore, Rima. 1997. *Rethinking the brain: new insights into early development*. New York, NY: Families and Work Institute.

Shore, Rima. 2006a. *Raising young children to the top of the policy agenda: lessons from Illinois*. Chicago, IL: Ounce of Prevention Fund, December, http://www.ounceofprevention.org/downloads/publications/Raising%20Young%20Children%20to%20the%20Top%20of%20the%20Policy%20Agenda%20-%20Lessons%20from%20Illinois%20Final%20PDF.pdf (accessed June 12, 2007).

———. 2006b. *Preschool for all; high-quality early education for all of Illinois' children*. Illinois Early Learning Council, Spring, http://www.illinois.gov/gov/elc/reports/Preschool-for-All_051006.pdf (accessed June 10, 2007).

Smith, Vicki. 2000. "Subsidized child care expanded; changes in eligibility will mean more families qualify." *Charleston Gazette*, September 1, sec. News. P1C. http://web.lexis-nexis.com (accessed October 22, 2006).

Smithson, Sandra. 2007. "Those who discredit pre-K ignore how much it transforms children." *Tennessean*, February 9, 2007, sec. Main. LexisNexis by Credit Card (accessed April 4, 2007).

Snell, Lisa. 2006. *The case against universal preschool in California*. February ed. http://www.reason.org/education/index.shtml (accessed February 6, 2007).

Southern Regional Education Board. 2003. *State-supported pre-kindergarten in the SREB region*. Atlanta, GA: Southern Regional Education Boards.

Spitzer 2006. *Let it shine.* http://www.youtube.com/watch?v=7YtdxY_woS8 (accessed January 23, 2007).

State Journal-Register. 1999. "Try new approach to crime prevention." *State Journal-Register*, May 6, 1999, sec. Editorial.

———. 2002. "Gov. Ryan budget cut proposals at a glance." *State Journal-Register*, June 11, 2002, sec. News. LexisNexis by Credit Card (accessed January 28, 2007).

———. 2003. "Vision first; details later." *State Journal-Register*, March 13, 2003, sec. Editorial.

———. 2006. "Good luck sorting out claims, counterclaims in ads." *State Journal-Register*, 10 September, 2006, sec. Editorial. LexisNexis by Credit Card (accessed January 28, 2007).

Stevens, Jean C. 2006. *Implementation plan for the regents policy on early education for student achievement in a global community.* Albany, NY: The State Education Department. http://www.regents.nysed.gov/2006Meetings/March2006/0306brd2.htm (accessed January 23, 2007).

Stone, Deborah. 1997. *Policy paradox: the art of political decision making.* New York: Norton.

Teepen, Tom. 1990. "Murphy-Miller duel on the lottery issue is making losers of all of us." *Atlanta Journal and Constitution*, February 1, sec. A15.

Tennessee Department of Education. 2006. *Pre-K in Tennessee.* Nashville, TN: Tennessee Department of Education, Presentation to the Senate Education Committee.

*Tennessean.* 2005. "Good signs in pre-K plan." *Tennessean*, October 19, 2005, sec. Main. LexisNexis by Credit Card (accessed April 4, 2007).

———. 2006a. "State knows pre-K works." *Tennessean*, April 12, 2006, sec. Editorial. LexisNexis by Credit Card (accessed April 4, 2007).

———. 2006b. "Progress in the pre-K plan." *Tennessean*, July 31, 2006b, sec. Editorial. LexisNexis by Credit Card (accessed April 4, 2007).

*Times Union.* 1998. "He can claim credit for a share of successes, but he should temper his rush to spend the surplus." *Times Union*, January 8, sec. Main 10, Three Star edition. http://timesunion.com/archives/ (accessed August 28, 2006).

———. 1999. "Pre-k: make it work." The *Times Union*, December 3, sec. Main 18, Three Star edition.

Tomblin, Earl Ray, Vic Sprouse. 2002. Relating to education generally. Enrolled SB 247. Charleston, WV: West Virginia Legislature. http://www.legis.state.wv.us/ (accessed March 14, 2007).

Trust for Early Education. 2007a. "TEE state activities—projects and planning grants." Pew Charitable Trusts (database online). Washington,

DC, b2007. Available from http://www.trustforearlyed.org/ activities_state.aspx (accessed February 5, 2007).

———. 2007b. "TEE national activities." Pew Charitable Trusts (database online). Washington, DC, a2007. Available from http://www.trustforearlyed.org/activities_national.aspx (accessed February 5, 2007).

———. 2007c. "Amy Wilkins testimony to house subcommittee on education reform." Pew Charitable Trusts (database online). Washington, DC. Available from http://www.trustforearlyed.org/report.aspx?idCat=0&strCat=&strSearch=&id=6 (accessed February 5, 2007).

———. 2007d. "Amy Wilkins testimony to senate committee on education." Pew Charitable Trusts (database online). Washington, DC. Available from http://www.trustforearlyed.org/report.aspx?idCat=0&strCat=&strSearch=&id=7 (accessed February 5, 2007).

Tulsa Chamber of Commerce. 1990a. *A plan for early childhood education.* Tulsa, OK: Tulsa Chamber of Commerce.

———. 1990b. *Preliminary report on scoping feasibility plan for early childhood education in the Tulsa public schools.* Tulsa, OK: Tulsa Chamber of Commerce.

United States Bureau of the Census. 1981. *Statistical abstract of the United States.* Washington, DC: U.S. Department of Commerce, Economics and Statistics Administration, Bureau of the Census, Data User Service Division.

United States Department of Education. "Preschool grants for children with disabilities." U.S. Department of Education (database online). Washington, DC, 2007 (cited March 11, 2007). Available from http://www.ed.gov/programs/oseppsg/legislation.html (accessed March 11, 2007).

United States Government. 2007. *Federal register.* Washington, DC: U.S. Government Printing Office, vol. 72, no. 15, http://aspe.hhs.gov/poverty/07poverty.shtml (accessed June 18, 2007).

Urahn, Susan K., and Sara Watson. 2007. "The Pew Charitable Trusts advancing quality pre-K for all; five years later." *Preschool Matters 5,* (1) (December/January): 1–12, http://nieer.org/resources/printnewsletter/DecJan2007.pdf (accessed February 18, 2007).

Veto of the Economic Opportunity Amendments of 1971. 1972. In Public Papers of the Presidents of the United States: Richard Nixon, December 10, 1971. Washington, DC: Government Printing Office.

Voices for Children. 2007. "Mission." In Voices for Children (database online). Washington, DC, 2007 (cited February 23, 2007). Available from http://www.voicesforamericaschildren.org/Template.cfm? Section=Store (accessed February 23, 2007).

Voices for Illinois Children. 2007a. "Issues." Voices for Children (database online). Chicago, IL, 2007a (cited June 20, 2007). Available from http://www.voices4kids.org/issues/policyagenda.html (accessed June 20, 2007).

———. 2007b. "Radio and TV ads." Voices for Illinois Children (database online). Chicago, IL, 2007b (cited June 18, 2007). Available from http://www.voices4kids.org/library/tvandradioads.html (accessed June 18, 2007).

Voices for America's Children and the Child and Family Policy Center. 2005. *Early learning left out: closing the investment gap for America's youngest children.* Washington, DC: Voices for America's Children; Child and Family Policy Center, April, http://www. voicesforamericaschildren.org/Template.cfm?Section=Browse_by_Issue&C ONTENTID=5436&TEMPLATE=/ContentManagement/ContentDi splay.cfm (accessed March 11, 2007).

Wadhwani, Anita. 2004. "TennCare savings could help pre-K." *Tennessean,* November 16, 2004, sec. Main. LexisNexis by Credit Card (accessed April 4, 2007).

Walston, Charles. 1991a. "Miller gambles on lucky 7's with a pair of lottery bills; sales tax, DUI changes also offered; wave of new faces marks 1991 session." *Atlanta Journal and Constitution,* January 14, sec. A1.

———. 1991b. "'91 lottery bill likely to avoid an early death." *Atlanta Journal and Constitution,* January 16, sec. D3.

———. 1991c. "Panel's 16-7 OK sends lottery to full House; measure likely up for vote Thursday." The *Atlanta Journal and Constitution,* January 30, sec. B1.

———. 1991d. "Lottery a sure thing for some; contracts, commissions could total $58 million." *Atlanta Journal and Constitution,* January 27, sec. C1.

———. 1992. "Miller: preschool needs lottery; gambling foes say Florida failing in education funding." The *Atlanta Journal and Constitution,* September 9, sec. C1.

Walston, Charles, and Gayle White. 1991. "Lottery hearing posing a test of clergy's support." *Atlanta Journal and Constitution,* January 29, sec. A1.

Washington, Kadesha. 2004. "Advancing quality pre-school for all meeting notes available online." *Chiefline Newsletter.* http://www.ccsso.ord/ Whats_New/newsletters/chiefline/4546.cfm (accessed February 22, 2007).

Weaver, Warren. 1967. *U.S. Philanthropic foundations: Their history, structure, management, and record.* New York: Harper and Row.

West Virginia Child Care United. 2007. "Welcome to our new lobbyist, Jason Webb." http://www.wvea.org/about/default.asp (accessed January 15, 2007).

West Virginia Department of Education. http://wvde.state.wv.us/boe/ (accessed January 15, 2007).

West Virginia Development Office. 2006. "Governor approves West Virginia's Appalachian Regional Commission investment package." http://wvdo.org/news/previous/0111arc.cfm (accessed August 26, 2005).

White, Betsy. 1988. "Board sets 12 goals for southern schools to reach by 2000." *Atlanta Journal and Constitution,* October 13, sec. A1.

———. 1990. "Educators may oppose lottery; many doubt schools will benefit." *Atlanta Journal and Constitution,* June 29, sec. E1.

———. 1996. "Schrenko backs up on pre-k controversy; schools chief admits 'anti-bias' material never part of the preschoolers' program." *Atlanta Journal and Constitution,* February 8, sec. B1. http://web.lexis-nexis.com. (accessed January 17, 2007).

Wilhelm, Ian. 2005. "Foundations urged to end their timidity over advocacy." *Chronicle of Philanthropy* 17.15 (May 12): 13.

Winning Beginning NY. 2006. *The best in the nation: a plan for early care and education.* Albany, NY: Winning Beginning NY.

Wooten, Jim. 1991. "Miller smart to abandon lottery panel without a fight." *Atlanta Journal and Constitution,* January 16, sec. A1.

Zahariadis, Nikolaos. 2003. *Ambiguity and choice in public policy: political decision making in modern democracies.* American Governance and Public Policy series. Washington, DC: Georgetown University Press.

Zigler, Edward, Walter S. Gilliam, and Stephanie M. Jones, eds. 2006. *A vision for universal preschool education,* 1st ed. New York, NY: Cambridge University Press.

# Index